Nature and Love in the Late Middle Ages

The Minnesinger Kristan von Hamle. Manesse MS (1300-1330)

NATURE AND LOVE IN THE LATE MIDDLE AGES

 By Aldo D. Scaglione

University of California Press
Berkeley and Los Angeles, 1963

University of California Press, Berkeley and
Los Angeles, California — Cambridge
University Press, London, England

© 1963 BY THE REGENTS OF THE UNIVERSITY OF CALIFORNIA

Library of Congress Catalog Card Number: 63-18743
Designed by Marion Jackson Skinner
Printed in the United States of America

to Jeanne

Contents

Illustrations

Juno, and Pallas." From G. Bazin, *Primitifs Français* (Paris: A. Skira, 1948). By courtesy of the Bibliothèque Nationale.

Cimon and Ephigenia

Miniature in the French version of the *Decameron* by Laurent de Premierfait. British Museum, Rotschild Bequest MS XIII. From E. Hutton, *Giovanni Boccaccio* (London: John Lane The Bodley Head, New York: John Lane, 1910).

Master of the Story of Griselda, *The Story of Patient Griselda* (Siena?, ca. 1500).

Parts I, II, III. London, National Gallery. Cf. Martin Davies, *Earlier Italian Schools*, II (London: National Gallery, 1953), p. 283. By courtesy of the National Gallery.

First Page of the *Decameron*, 1492 edition.

(Gregorio de Gregorii, Venice.) From G. B., *Decameron*, ed. N. Sapegno (Turin: Utet, 1956), I, 288.

Frontispiece of Spanish translation of the *Decameron*, 1539 (Valladolid).

From E. Hutton, *cit.* By courtesy of Messrs. J. and J. Leighton.

Meister der Liebesgärten, *Garden of Love* (ca. 1450)

German Etching. From Frank Crisp, *Medieval Gardens*, I (London: John Lane The Bodley Head Ltd., 1924), Pl. 21.

Introduction

Cursed be the social wants that sin against the strength of
   youth!
Cursed be the social lies that warp us from the living truth!
Cursed be the sickly forms that err from honest Nature's rule!
   Lord Tennyson, *Locksley Hall*

Certain terms of literary parlance, such as Classic,
Gothic, Baroque, Romantic, draw their validity from a historical context. Their most legitimate use is and should remain
historical, that is, with reference to movements, forms or patterns more or less clearly delimited by time and space. Other
terms have both a philosophical and a historical denotation;
such are 'realistic' and 'naturalistic.' In literary history we
technically designate as realism, first, the novel of Balzac and
the movement it represented and, partly, originated. Similarly,
we call naturalism Zola's school and its ramifications throughout the Western world. But philosophically speaking, the term
"naturalism" has a broader, though vaguer, meaning. In this
study I am not concerned with Zola's brand of naturalism: I

shall apply the term to the interpretation of literary texts in a strictly philosophical sense.

For the sake of clarity, I wish to avoid any equivalence of naturalism and realism. From the viewpoint of the present inquiry, 'nature' is the concept of our original being, the genesis of our existence, the way we have been formed from our birth as part of a physical, timeless, and impersonal environment, in distinction from what the evolution of human history has caused us to become, as part of civilized society; whereas "realism" is a factual, objective approach to our concrete situation as part of a conditioned, historical becoming through time and space. Briefly, we are "realists" when we propose to face the end result of our peculiar status of natural beings in civilized state, as distinct from what we imagine ourselves to be, or would like to be. Nature is a being, reality a becoming. And even though being realistic can well be an 'ideal,' realism and idealism are dialectically, conceptually opposed. Naturalism, on the other hand, is mostly a reaction to historical, conventional, 'artificial' reality in the name of a return to the wholesome purity of a (more or less ideal) *beginning.* And since I shall investigate, in particular, literature of love, I also wish to avoid a confusion between the naturalistic view of love and erotic, or sensual, love. What will concern us here is not so much the result, but rather the conscious motivation of passion, not its real or imagined cause or end in biological, physiological, or psychological terms, but its rational justification in terms of certain principles and laws. True enough, the material we are about to analyze will often prove to be made of 'earthly love.' But we shall see how, in a more or less polemical vein, sex, sensuality, carnal pleasures, traditionally down-graded as *luxuria, incontinentia, concupiscentia,* became acknowledged with militant sympathy for their value as irreplaceable goods. It is chiefly the polemic aspect of this attitude that I consider 'naturalistic.'

The need for an appeal to 'nature' has been felt by every age in varying forms and degrees. It is a need that evolved through time, but did not develop in a progressive direction. In the period I have chosen to study I shall endeavor to place the various literary works in their proper cultural context (philosophical, theological, religious).

As to the precise object of the inquiry, I shall deal with a major theme: that of the relationship of Love to Nature. In the course of our survey, be it ever so incomplete and unilateral, of this complex idea, we shall find it to have been intimately allied with several subthemes which can be traced as cultural constants through the centuries: (1) A critique of Social Laws, that is, (a) institutions, such as marriage (the grave of love, hence a methodic misogamy in this literature), or the family (with its tyrannic right to interfere with the young people's free choice of their destiny and the development of their emotional potentialities); (b) conventions, such as the privileges and prejudices of economic status, but especially that of artificial nobility by birth and rank, against the natural, truer nobility founded on personal worth and sensitivity to sublime values; (2) an uneasiness with positive Moral Rules, which are felt to be traditionally invoked in the name of stale virtue and abstract wisdom; (3) a vindication of a province of life which cannot be assimilated to Reason, and may even clearly conflict with it. Briefly, love has been seen as an irresistible force of nature, irrational but good, intolerant of any moral or social objection.

The path followed by this ideological complex is long and wide. I have not presumed to be able to cover it all, at all epochs and areas in the West. I have, instead, chosen an exemplary case, that of Boccaccio's *Decameron*, and treated it in the context of literary works which I consider relevant to the understanding of the place and 'function' of this most significant masterpiece within the framework of the concept of 'naturalistic love.' The book and the theme chosen demand the use of sources chiefly from Italian and French literature. Scattered borrowings from other areas will simply tend to suggest possible ramifications and applications of this case. The following, then, will be chiefly an essay in the cultural context of the *Decameron*.

The reader will not need a general bibliography. The theme that concerns us has practically none. At least I know of no study where such a topic is treated extensively. In a more specific way, titles such as *Boccace, Moraliste de la Chair* by Pierre Poirier (Brussels, 1943), appear tempting. I know no book of this kind that is not disappointing. This one, particularly, is not even a book: just a collection of disorganic notes, mostly trivial, altogether unreadable. I can only hope to have done better.

The age of the naturalist novel was appropriate for such studies as Paul Lenoir's *Histoire du Réalisme et du Naturalisme dans la Pensée et dans l'Art depuis l'Antiquité jusqu'à nos jours* (Paris, 1889). Unfortunately, this is totally outdated in content and outmoded in treatment. And it has no room for Boccaccio! Similarly, A. David-Sauvageot's *Le Réalisme et le Naturalisme dans la Littérature et dans l'Art* (Paris, 1890) is only concerned with medieval France. Italian literature, in turn, is ably surveyed from the origins to the end of the fourteenth century in F. Caffo Santoro's *Il Naturalismo del Popolo nella Letteratura italiana del Dugento e del Trecento* (Siracusa: Tamburo, 1916), a typically positivistic study where naturalism is understood in a broad sense of little specific use for our more particular undertaking. Of limited usefulness is Maria Fiumanò's *Il sentimento della natura e dell'eroico in G. Boccaccio* (Reggio Calabria: Giammusso e Pompeo, 1929).

For specific aspects of our inquiry a vast bibliography is, indeed, available: a selected list of basic titles can be found, for instance, in the well-known book by Denis de Rougemont, *L'Amour et l'Occident* (Paris, 1939, 1956²), translated as *Love in the Western World* (New York, 1940) by M. Belgion.

As a general introduction to the various possible meanings of the basic terms, there is some usefulness in R. M. Hutchins, ed., *Great Books of the Western World* (Chicago, 1952), II and III, "The Great Ideas, A Syntopicon," *s. vv.* 'Love' and 'Nature.'

For a recent, authoritative focusing of the theoretical and historical implications of the term realism (as distinct from naturalism), see René Wellek, "The Concept of Realism in Literary Scholarship," *Neophilologus*, XLIV (1960), 1-20, beside such well-known studies as A. S. McDowall, *Realism, A Study in Art and Thought* (London, 1918), E. Auerbach, *Mimesis, The Representation of Reality in Western Literature*, trans. W. R. Trask (Princeton, 1953 and New York, 1957), and the issue III, 3 (1951) of the journal *Comparative Literature*, entirely dedicated to the critical and historical questions of literary realism. On the other hand, the ethical implications of a naturalistic philosophy have been concisely and effectively assessed in the still valid essay by E. P. Lamanna, "Il naturalismo etico," *La Cultura Filosofica*, VIII (1914), 1-30.

For the sake of clarification and distinction as to our broader use of the term, and with specific reference to modern naturalism as centered in Zola's exemplary production, one may consult the standard studies of P. Martino, *Le naturalisme français (1870–1895)* (Paris, 1951⁵) and L. Deffoux, *Le Naturalisme, avec un florilège des principaux écrivains naturalistes* (Paris, 1929). Zola's naturalism consists of the deterministic reduction of man's behavior to his rapport with nature (his *milieu*) and heredity, while working toward a biological, physiological explanation of the "causes" of moral phenomena, in reaction against the metaphysical and the supernatural.

I am indebted to my colleagues Professors Nicolas J. Perella and Karl M. Birkmeyer for valuable suggestions concerning this study, which started with the help of a grant from the J. S. Guggenheim Memorial Foundation.

Unless otherwise indicated, all translations of quotations from foreign languages are mine.

The Problem of Nature

I

Virtutem definiunt secundum naturam vivere.
They define virtue to be a life ordered according to nature.
Th. More, *Utopia*

As a preliminary step, we have started to inquire whether it is possible, among the several meanings of this slightly amorphous term, to find and isolate the precise acceptation under which we want to use the category of 'naturalism.' To determine what is nature and what is not, obviously depends on a relative frame of reference. Nature (Lat. *natura* from *nasci*) was for the Greeks (φύσις) all the existent. There was, originally, only a metaphysical distinction between what has existence (= nature) and what has being (= God), the former being defined by accidental particularity (as everything that owes its being to something else, and whose 'nature' consists of the condition under which it has been 'born'), the latter by necessary, general oneness.[1] The Sophists later differentiated the 'conventional' from the 'natural,' the former being the result of human intervention, laws, institutions, and customs, all determined by historical circumstances.[2] Aristotle enumerates four nominally distinct meanings for the term "nature" in the *Physics*, and seven in the *Metaphysics*. Four of them distinguish the natural from the artificial, on one hand, and the immutable, on the other, or identify it with the material, containing the principle of movement. The remaining meanings equate the nature of a thing to its essence, principle, or main characteristics.[3]

But already by the time of Plato the term had begun to acquire a more precise content by contrast with the opposite concept of 'supernatural' (Platonically the World of Ideas, the Supercelestial Regions); and as a result of the dichotomy of matter and spirit, body and soul or mind, nature became practically identified with the material universe.[4] Such new conceptual meanings were inherited and reinforced by Christianity. This general attitude underlying all of Plato's metaphysics also informs that conception of Eros which was to have such a profound impact on much of Western culture. From the *Symposium* and, even more explicitly, the *Phaedrus*, one learned that the condition whereby one can only apprehend what comes in at the avenues of sense is inferior to the disembodied capability to contemplate the pure Forms. But in our mortal estate as it is, beauty operates the strongest suggestion on our senses, and we come under its direct influence when we fall in love. What we call unreason or madness in the lover is really his mystic power to attain the vision of, and union with, the higher values which common men ignore. This idealistic view of love was most powerful in indirectly determining many aspects of medieval love literature. It entailed a rather vague and ambiguous assessment of the role of sexual experience, as compared with this latter's explicit, unequivocal centrality in every view of love which we can consider consistently naturalistic. It was for good reason that the *Symposium* became the central text in Renaissance Platonism, that is, in the most typical non-naturalist tradition of the Renaissance.

Plato had postulated the purification of good men into disembodied souls after death and the metempsychosis of bad
ones into animals having the qualities corresponding to their
former vices. Specifically, the incontinent, those who yielded to
animal instincts, were logically destined to be turned into
beasts literally, for beasts they had been metaphorically.[5] The
Platonists (for example, Porphyry) further associated this view
with the myth of Circe, following the tradition of the Pythag-
oreans who saw in this myth the allegory of metensomatosis;
the philosophers thus allied themselves with the allegoristic
interpretation of Homer developed by the grammarians. At the
onset of the Middle Ages, Boethius, a key figure and parting
point for much of medieval culture, likened vicious men to
specific animals, and put to use the Circe myth to illustrate his
warning, not without adding the distinction that in reality,
unlike the cases of the myth, vices do thwart man's rational
power. Thus the libidinous are more like real pigs than Circe's
pigs, which, as Homer contended, did retain their reason.[6]

On the opposite end of the spectrum of classical metaphysics
and ethics, one could find the naturalistic, materialistic, thoroughly sexual view of love of the Epicureans, whose most frank
and brilliant exposition shines forth through the pages of Lucretius' *De Rerum Natura* (IV, 1030–1207). But, as it is to be expected within the framework of the fundamentally rationalistic
classical mind, this view brought Lucretius to condemn serious
passion, and consequently to recommend, as an antidote, the
volgivaga Venus, the occasional, mercenary outlet to be experienced as a rather frivolous *divertissement.* In this separation of sex and rational exercise of the human faculties we see
a typical pagan attitude which also contributed its share to the
Christian dichotomy of noble and ignoble in the psyche.

For the medieval Christian, as for the Renaissance reformer,
nature has degenerated with the original sin and has thus become the realm of Satan, although one can also identify a
medieval Christian stream at best represented by Thomas
Aquinas, which emphasized a view of nature as the realization
of God's creative activity in forms and patterns. But this latter

was, so to put it, an ontological aspect of the concept of nature, whereas the 'demonic' view of nature was part of the ethical approach to the conditions and role of our physical environment.[7]

The traditional use of the term received a serious blow by Pico della Mirandola's (1463–1494) contention that "the Great Artisan . . . received man . . . as a creature of undetermined nature . . . and said to him: 'You . . . shall determine for yourself your own nature, in accordance with your own free will. . . . Neither heavenly nor earthly . . . you may fashion yourself in whatever form you shall prefer.' "[8]

The naturalism or immanentism of Giordano Bruno and, more consistently, Spinoza, inherited and brought to final maturity the antisupernatural content of the classical idea of nature. But Pico's speculation was the first, epoch-making step toward the modern view whereby, in the wake of Darwin's evolutionism, the concept of "history" was introduced to break down the closed circle of the species. Furthermore the sharp distinction between the 'conventional' world of man's civilized behavior and a 'natural,' external world independent of man and possibly hostile to him also broke down, and gave way to the consideration that man's environment, physical and not, is historically conditioned, that is, shaped by man himself and continuously modified by his own activity. So that, in a way, a modern skyscraper is ultimately as 'natural' to man as a sequoia tree, and certainly a more fitting and logical environment for him to live in or under, when all has been considered.

Any historical discussion of naturalism in formal philosophical thought shifts the attention to technical levels on which the conclusions must sound somewhat remote from those based on literary viewpoints. Within the technical domains of Western philosophy (logic, physics, metaphysics) naturalism can hardly be considered a Renaissance innovation, as the thought of the Renaissance in these domains kept moving within the basic framework of the issues raised in the Middle Ages. The novelty of Renaissance thought generally depends on the penetration of literary methods and viewpoints into the thinking

habits of logicians and scientists. The philosophical changes of
this period were due rather to the influence of literature and,
even more, of philology than to a profound and truly creative
evolution from within.

A great deal has been made of the change from a fundamental Aristotelianism to a fundamental Platonism in the
fifteenth century (although P. O. Kristeller, among others, has
tried to prove the continuity of the Aristotelian tradition), but
the Platonic current in the Middle Ages is only in degree inferior to that of the Renaissance.[9] Medieval Humanism is also
an indubitable fact. But in fifteenth-century Italy a reference
to Plato or Aristotle implied an actual, philologically founded
and historically sound reading of the respective Greek texts,
instead of medieval commentaries on translations—and this
constituted a profound change. Furthermore, the Renaissance
study of antiquity was then grounded on and sparked by a full
awareness of the diversity of cultures, whereas ancient ideas
had previously undergone the same process whereby Greek
and Roman heroes appeared to the medieval imagination in
the garb of medieval knights (and this not only in popular
narratives, but even in the works of as great a humanist scholar
as John of Salisbury).[10]

If by naturalism is meant the recognition of physical nature
as an autonomous mode of reality to be studied and appreciated for its values and peculiarities, we shall find two distinct
but, to an extent, concurrent streams in the thirteenth and fourteenth centuries: the Aristotelian-Averroistic and the Platonic-
empirical. Generally speaking, Aristotle's teachings were the
most influential in establishing an attitude of interest in the
direct observation of nature, but the pure Aristotelian (that is,
non-Averroistic) school of thought was *de facto* developed into
the kind of rationalistic Scholasticism (best exemplified by
Thomas Aquinas) that tended to focus the attention on formal
logic and metaphysics. G. Toffanin had especially in mind the
Averroistic current when he attempted to identify (rather
abstractly) a continuous line of 'physical' thought as opposed
to the 'rhetorical' current. The former presented the several

aspects of naturalistic rationalism, Averroistic atheism, polemic emphasis on the *quadrivium* versus the *trivium, scientia* versus *sapientia,* the bare truth of philosophy versus the *ornatum* of rhetoric. It allegedly started in the twelfth century, prevailed in the thirteenth especially in France and Italy through the Arabic influences, returned in the fourteenth at the School of Padua, which continued to thrive through the fourteenth and sixteenth.[11] On the other side of the fence were the followers of rhetoric, whose standard bearer was John of Salisbury in the last masterpiece of the pre-Humanism of Chartres, the *Metalogicus;* their cause was powerfully revived by Petrarch and the *Cénacles* of Nicolas de Clamanges and Guillaume Fichet, and triumphed with the Italian humanists of the fifteenth century. For the Catholic-minded Toffanin this was the struggle of Roman-Christian-Classical *pietas* against the new pagans.[12] On the other hand, there was a significant strain of naturalism in the school of Chartres, to which we will have to turn our attention later (see pp. 33 ff.).

The other current, the Platonic-empirical, was perhaps even more influential for the establishment of scientific naturalism, and it was represented most effectively at the School of Oxford, from Roger Bacon through Duns Scotus to William of Occam —Boccaccio's contemporary. In spite of its mysticism in theology and metaphysics and a basic agnosticism in logic, it gave the most powerful impulse to the cause of empiricism for the development of what it considered the only legitimate field of knowledge for man, the analysis of nature in the concreteness of its individual manifestations. It had connections with the prehumanistic and vaguely Platonic center of Chartres, and in its ultimate results it marked the dissolution of Scholasticism, thus preparing the ground for the Renaissance and the empirical naturalistic science of the seventeenth century.

But this is not the main direction of Renaissance naturalism. Although both Humanism and medieval empiricism ultimately contributed to the shaping of the modern mind, the naturalistic aspect of Humanism is a dimension of the aesthetic and ethical spirit of the new culture, not a by-product of a critique of logic and rationalistic theology, as empiricism had been. It is not so much nature as an autonomous series of factual phenomena that interests the humanist, but nature as the set of circumstances of man's earthly existence, morally and psychologically. Cognition of the individual reality *(ecceitas)* was a password of the Oxford School: it was also a password of fifteenth century art according to the interpretation proposed by the art historian Georg Weise (an interpretation which I shall analyze in the Appendix to this book). But at Oxford *ecceitas* meant an extension of sensorial experience into the mechanistic world of physical nature (a meaning which could be applied to Flemish fifteenth-century painting), whereas the art of the Italian Quattrocento (painting, sculpture, and architecture) can be said to be informed with a naturalistic principle of cognition of individual reality only as a method of understanding, intuitively and rationally, the reality of man in his environment, microcosm in a macrocosm.

The term naturalism has been particularly applied to the Italian Renaissance to emphasize its contrast with the medieval preoccupation with values set above and against nature. In this sense the term becomes a part of the general concept of 'immanentism,' and 'naturalism' can then be best defined as the opposite of 'supernaturalism'—an acceptation which, in Renaissance historiography, was typical of the school of Giovanni Gentile. The opposition to supernaturalism can manifest itself through a militant defense of natural, that is, earthly existence with its self-sufficient values and ends. This attitude obviously characterizes the *Decameron*. The formula which opposed the *Decameron* to the *Divine Comedy* as its relative counterpart (the "Human Comedy") is acceptable and valid (in spite of Branca's somewhat tendentious, a priori objections) in the limited sense that, whereas Dante's realism is always (to use Auerbach's significant term) "figural," a representation of events and experiences as signs of an anagogical, suprasensorial truth, Boccaccio's realism (in the *Decameron*) resolutely eliminates the transcendental. At the same time—and this is for us the other, concomitant facet of naturalism—there is in the *Decameron* a conscious, even polemical attitude that shows in which direction "the conflict between the worldly will to live and the Christian sufferance of life" was to be solved.[13] Boccaccio undoubtedly is, though not exclusively, a realist, and so was Dante. But he is also a 'naturalist,' which Dante was surely not.

However, when we come to the question whether Boccaccio's naturalism belongs to the Middle Ages or to the Renaissance, the issue is bound to become foggy. I shall try to point out certain aspects of that naturalism which, in my interpretation, belong to the new culture, others which belong to the medieval tradition; but where naturalism, generically and *per se*, should historically belong, shall remain for us a moot question.[14]

French Mainstreams of
Medieval Naturalism

II

Amoris impulsio . . . culpae diminutio
Abélard, *Planctus Dinae filiae Jacob*

The thought of a largely unchallenged authority of
the Christian Church in the Dark Ages and a romantic conception of primitive life have somehow conspired to create the
image of a semibarbarian society essentially puritanic in its
sexual mores. It is known how wholesome and strict the Ger-
mans had appeared to Tacitus, and the closeness to the ways of
nature by which the Roman historian accounted for the barbarians' virtues was later to be replaced by the formal teachings
of the Church, and its consequent checking of the brutal instincts of savage peoples. Yet, the role of Christianity must have
been rather limited in conditioning the erotic life of medieval
man—especially among the ruling warrior caste. The practical

sense of legal rights, particularly in the form of property, must have been stronger and more articulate than a genuine feeling for moral proprieties. The chastity of a maiden or the honesty of a wife was undoubtedly more valuable as an assurance of legitimate offspring, present or future, than as a formal, ethical asset. To put it rather bluntly, virtue meant, so one feels inclined to assume, reliability as an authentic piece of property. And men were not really expected to be "virtuous" as their women were, but to let their natural instincts run relatively free as long as their satisfaction did not infringe upon other men's legal rights. Nor did the Church doctrine on sexual matters and even on the technicalities of marriage become clearly formulated and consistently enforced until the Council of Trent (1545–1563). Thus the expedient and the good had tended to be easily identified. A peculiar case of confusion of moral and biological prejudices appears to be a typical symptom of this state of affairs, namely the assumption that noblewoman's adultery with an inferior was bound to bear a progeny unworthy of the standards of nobility.[1] More generally, all adultery was supposed to result in a 'permanent' mixing of the generative blood in the mother, with the consequence of hybrid offspring unfit for high destinies.[2]

COURTLY LOVE

The appearance, then, in the early romance lyric, of a type of morality in obvious conflict with Christian teachings is to be regarded as the first recognition of a duality of standards, rather than as an indication of an actual change in the mores. Nevertheless the very fact that such a lack of conformity with the ecclesiastical viewpoint had not been openly, theoretically stated before entitles us to regard this literary phenomenon as a most impressive formal reaction, if not a revolution.

Shortly after the onset of our era's second millennium we witness a resurgence of the sense of nature's rights as a reaction to the stifling 'conventions' of an official morality which

tended to be theologically and socially carried to an extreme of
constraint. The rampant contrast between theory and practice
was bound to find a conscious recognition, which took place
within certain cultural movements impregnated with a sometimes latent, sometimes overt hostility to the rigid standards
left heretofore unchallenged. Starting in the South of France,
and quickly spreading throughout Western and Central
Europe, the theory and literary practice of *amour courtois* contained the seed of much naturalism to follow. As Rabelais was
to remark later in defending his humanistic ideal of broad
freedoms, constraint imposed from the outside tends to make
us worse, not better, for "it is agreeable to the nature of man to
long after things forbidden, and to desire what is denied us."[3]
Things forbidden must seldom have seemed sweeter than in
the eleventh century.

One effect, and not the least conspicuous, of the Provençal
school of poetry on later literature was to rejuvenate the cus-
tomarily stiff and stale world of medieval culture with a breath
of fresh air. It was a contagious lesson in freedom from prejudice, when man again looked at life and the world as a new
Adam or a child who first opens his eyes on reality, filled with
interested eagerness and naïve wonderment. The fact that
under that breath of novelty there remained the vital heritage
of Late Latin and Arabic traditions need not detain us here, for
the impression of a new start was none the less profound.[4] It
was the same basic feeling of spontaneity and authenticity
which later prompted Dante to define his own school of the
"sweet new style" in terms of an immediate response to an
inner urge from the heart.[5]

From the poetry in *langue d'oc* vigorous expressions of realism and naturalism unequivocally pointed the way to much of
later romance literature.[6] Guillaume de Poitiers (d. 1127), the
first great master of the troubadours, had not hesitated to sing
his passion in overtly and freely sensual tones. The Monk of
Montaudon (Peire de Vic, d. 1215) took the defense of human
weaknesses (especially women's vanities and his own earthy
pleasures with them) in libertine debates he imaginarily held

with God and the saints, while the severe and hypochondriac Peire Cardenal (d. 1272) even carried his private quarrel with God to the point of arguing that the best proof of God's merciful understanding of the world and man would be to do away with Hell and welcome everybody, virtuous and sinners alike, into His Paradise (*Un sirventes novel vuelh comensar*).[7]

The principles of courtly love as sung and practiced by the troubadours and their imitators (*trouvères, Minnesinger,* courtly lyricists and narrators of all countries) were effectively codified by the recognized theorist of this pervasive movement, Andreas Capellanus, in his *De arte honeste amandi* or *De Amore.*[8] Capellanus expounded the doctrine of love as a free union of noble souls, normally adulterous, fired by the contemplation of visible beauty and aiming at actual fruition to be logically granted by the lady as a reward for the various and strenuous tests whereby the lover has proved his loyalty and his merits.[9] Love is the sign of true nobility, above and beyond social rank: "Love causes a rough and uncouth man to be distinguished for his handsomeness; it can endow a man even of the humblest birth with nobility of character." (*De Amore,* Book I, chap. 3.) "For, since all of us human beings are derived originally from the same stock and all naturally claim the same ancestor, it was . . . excellence of character alone which first made a distinction of nobility among men and led to the difference of class." (Ibid., chap. 5. See also the whole First Dialogue.) Since Provençal culture stood in the background of the *De Amore,* this doctrine of nobility will seem natural among intellectuals who often (as, for example, Marcabru, Bernart de Ventadorn, Giraut de Borneilh, Peire Vidal, and others) were of humble origin, and had ascended to high social station by intellectual merits alone.[10] But it is of particular importance to find such principles in a theoretical work.

The frank admission of sensuality as a fundamental element in the sentimental adventure obviously ran counter both to the Christian commandments and to the classical philosophical ethics inherited from Platonism and Stoicism. In fact, the bishop of Paris, Etienne Tempier, eventually condemned the

De Amore in 1277.[11] Yet, it would be a serious error of historical perspective to overlook one important feature of courtly
love which keeps it within the boundaries of the medieval
mind and rescues it from any affinity with the materialistic
eroticism of our sex-obsessed age. As C. S. Lewis aptly put it
in commenting on the *De Amore,* "On the other hand, love is
not sensuality. The sensual man—the man who suffers from
abundantia voluptatis—is disqualified from participating in
it."[12] Thus limited, the naturalistic undercurrent in courtly love
remains nonetheless obvious, as shown in the telling though
demure terms of the following statement of principle in the
De Amore: "I do not believe that God can be seriously offended
by sins of love; for that which is accomplished *under the com-
pulsion of nature* can be cleansed through easy atonement."[13]
It is the very principle that, in a more light-hearted time, will
prompt Pope to ask the rhetorical question: "[Can] that offend
Great Nature's God / Which Nature's self inspires?"[14] But that
which seemed so logically to be answered in the negative after
Spinoza's identification of God and Nature (*Deus sive Natura*)
could very well be, and in fact usually was answered in the
positive by the medieval man, for whom nature frequently
appeared synonymous with the state of fallen man after the
original sin—hence the realm of Satan. The populace had never
ceased to hear stern and frightening warnings from the pulpit,
to the effect that, as Rousseau could still repeat at the middle
of the eighteenth century: "La force de l'âme qui produit toutes
les vertus tient à la pureté qui les nourrit toutes," and that,
conversely, lust was the father of all vices, the beginning of
the corruption of the whole soul.[15] I cannot refrain from con-
jecturing that Dante himself, when positing lust and incontinence as the least serious step in the scale of sins in the moral
structure of his *Commedia,* was heeding this courageous postulate of Andreas and the courtly schools more than Aristotle's
Ethics.[16] In fact, for Capellanus love was "an inborn [that is,
natural] passion . . . which rules the whole universe, and without which no one ever accomplishes anything good in this
world."[17]

As is well known, the courtly code, or, more broadly, "chivalry" found its application in many a pattern of real life. In its practice as a system of social fashions Huizinga has acutely revealed the sort of "cunning of reason" which marks the subtle triumph of nature over the repressive moral standards of the time:

> Knightly exercises and courteous fashions with their worship of bodily strength; honours and dignities with their vanity and their pomp, and especially love;—what were they but pride, envy, avarice and lust, all condemned by religion! To be admitted as elements of higher culture all these things had to be ennobled and raised to the rank of virtue.[18]

True enough, the more prevalent, official code of ethics took its revenge and attempted to take the entrenched stronghold of courtly society by storm when Andreas himself, with an uneasy and striking about-face, retracted his previous position in the Third Book of the *De Amore.* It was as though he had become aware of nature's ultimate coming to grips with the overpowering forces of society. This curious inclination to speak through both sides of one's mouth, affirming and denying at short distance, somehow paralleled Ovid's "recantation" of the *Ars Amatoria* in the *Remedia Amoris.*[19] Thereafter, it became a traditional feature of the love *canzonieri* through the Middle Ages and the Renaissance, with Petrarch's *Canzoniere* as the most influential example. At the beginning and at the end of the collection of his love lyrics, the poet became accustomed to condemn the very experience he was exalting in the body of his work. We find a similar contrast between Boccaccio the humanist and scholar and Boccaccio the author of the *Decameron.* At the end of the Renaissance Torquato Tasso, a poet of unusual, pathological seriousness, attempted to solve this dualism of nature versus morality—and failed at the expense of his mental balance.[20]

The courtly literature of France is usually classified along two major cycles, the 'classical' and the 'Breton.' The latter is typically represented by the Arthurian romances and by the

legend of Tristan. The tragic figure of Tristan polarized the
most radical developments of the courtly ideology. His cycle
appears to have gone through an evolution which we can re-
construct as follows. Originally it seems to have entailed a
tragedy in the Greek sense—a tragedy in which the driving
force, the 'natural' urge that breeds the catastrophe, is seen
as negative although the heroes are not morally responsible,
therefore not 'bad.' For, as we have seen, the romantic sense of
love passion (rights of nature against society) had no recognized place in the classical world, where passion was either
treated as inferior, an aberration of the enraged senses, the
cause of error and calamity, or rationalized by being directed
to a worthy intellectual goal (as in Plato's *Symposium*).

Similarly,

> the love-philter in Béroul and Eilhart is the marvelous
> but material origin of the passion, and inasmuch as we
> can recognize its effects, such effects are ill-fated and
> evil, since they engender hate and misery together with
> love (cf. Eilhart's "Der vil unseliger Trank," 'the most un-
> holy potion'). The philter is the excuse for a simple
> passion.[21]

Hence certain traditional judgments of Béroul's *Tristan* as noncourtly: "the lovers are conscious of their 'villainous folly'
(*folie et vileinie*): society retains its rights."[22] And in the *Tristan*
of Thomas "the very essence of the tale, the passion, is kept
outside human control, in sharp contrast to courtly love, made
of choice and measure."[23]

Concurrently, the social order had thus far maintained its
force in the form of the prevailing rights of the husband: "The
husband had the right to kill the unfaithful wife and her lover
as well, and Jonin advises us that all phases of Yseult's trial
[in Béroul] can be explained by contemporary customs."[24]
But soon the Tristan legend was further invaded and conquered by the 'immoralism' of the courtly philosophy. In turn,
the elemental, primitive, wildly instinctive violence of the
Tristan theme allied itself with the refined, sophisticated manners of the Provençal, while it transcended them in a powerful

tragedy undreamed-of in the worldly, elegiac poetry of the courts of Southern France. The climate of the legend turned into a 'mystic' apology of sin, the 'rightful' triumph of passion; [in Thomas] "Tristan and Iseult, united in their suffering as well as in their love have a grandeur that is lacking in courtly poetry."[25]

The romance of Tristan thus came, at last, to glorify the un-Christian, yet typically medieval preëminence of love as the supreme duty and right, even above loyalty to the feudal lord and respect for social order. It would now have been an act of grave guilt for king Mark to punish his unfaithful wife and her lover, even though this latter was his rebellious vassal. And when, at long last, Mark did take action against the adulterers, king Arthur made himself the indignant spokesman of public opinion and ignominiously punished Mark for his 'crime' (as seen even in the comprehensive Italian version of the legend, *La Tavola Ritonda*).[26]

As an enlightening parallel to this significant conclusion, one may recall that the role of Arthur was somehow fulfilled, in a purportedly real story, by the king of Aragon in the punishment of Raymond de Roussillon, according to the codices *A* and *B* of the troubadours' *Vidas*. In an addition to the (probably) Oriental novella of the eaten heart studied by Gaston Paris, we here see the 'crime' of Raymond as essentially a crime against the code of the courts. He had wreaked vengeance on his wife's lover, the troubadour Guillem de Cabestaing, by slaying him in an ambush and having his heart cooked and served to the adulterous wife. The latter, while the husband was threatening her, jumped from a balcony. But in the end Raymond died in the king's prison, whereas the lovers were buried before the church with splendid rites.[27]

As long as the Tristan legend remained within the framework of the courtly code, as part or at least an overgrown appendix of the Breton cycle, its excesses had potentially found a justification in the 'superior' (superhuman) ethics of chivalrous idealism. But as early as 1210 Gottfried von Strassburg gave a version of the epic (Wagner's source, let us remember) which seemed to isolate it once again from the orthodox courtly and knightly world by treating the latter with the irony and detachment of a sophisticated cleric.

There was in this medieval current embodied in the adulterous heroes from Cornwall a touch of latent anarchy, a strain of outspoken amoralism, an irrepressible bent toward a state of natural chaos, that has its roots in an outburst of primeval life forces only unstably checked by the artificial, unrealistic fetters of the knightly code. But Gottfried abstracted the motif from its chivalric context. For him there is one only norm in the world: Love, *Minne*. *Minne* is the absolute ruler of noble hearts, *edele Herzen;* everything must yield to it, all rights and duties vanish in its sight. He only sins who operates against *Minne*. One and a half centuries later Boccaccio will not speak otherwise, almost with the same quasi-mystic overtone.

Typically medieval as this phenomenon was, it can only be understood as a reaction against the official position, the guilt complexes, inhibitions, and restraints of all sorts that characterize in our eyes the highest, official levels of consciousness in that culture. Popular Tristan undoubtedly was but always one step removed from the acknowledged, acceptable standards. It seems as though Gottfried had realized the basically disruptive, heterodox potentiality of his theme. And this realization probably lies at the bottom of the ethical- and social-minded Chrétien de Troyes' apparent aversion to the Tristan motif. Indeed it did not fit with the position of Chrétien, the 'official' bard of *courtoisie.*

The story of Chrétien's contribution to the consolidation of *courtoisie,* and especially of its subtle moral casuistry, is too well known to need retelling. The cult of woman, of Provençal origin, found its boldest statement in *Lancelot,* the romance which, as E. Faral put it, "proposes as an ideal a sort of triumphant dictatorship of the lady."[28] But Chrétien's distinctive social sensitivity made of him the first great moralistic interpreter of *courtoisie,* in the noblest sense of the word, and, as such, the first great exponent of the tradition which attempted to reconcile the two great medieval codes of ethics, and ultimately resulted in the dissolution of *courtoisie* in its pure, original form.[29]

Courtly love arouses few or no moral qualms in the exquisitely feminine conscience of Marie de France. S. Painter has aptly summarized the brief and direct circle of Marie's intuition of love as follows:

> Her conception of love was simple—it was physical attraction exerted by youth and beauty. The niece of his lady told Guigemar "This love is most proper—you are both beautiful" (lines 451–453). Marie preferred to have her lovers find their solace in marriage, but if love and matrimonial obligations were in conflict, love always won. In one of her tales this doctrine was accepted by a wife. When she saw how beautiful her husband's mistress was she retired to a convent so that the lovers might marry (*Eliduc*, 1006–1144). It was axiomatic to Marie that a young wife could not love an elderly husband and would eventually be captivated and led astray by a young gallant (*Guigemar*, 209–217).[30]

HÉLOÏSE

In surveying the revisionist scholarship on medieval and Renaissance culture after Burckhardt, Eugenio Garin, a leading authority in this field, has pointed out the various efforts to trace back to the Middle Ages the basic characteristics attributed by Burckhardt to the Renaissance. In particular, he states, "a great deal of medieval *naturalism* has reportedly been uncovered by Nordström and Gilson in stressing, among other things, the significance of Abélard and Héloïse's story."[31]

With regard to this fascinating story, I hesitate to applaud Mr. Gilson's efforts unconditionally. In the famous lovers I do find an impressive mark of realism and an amazing capacity for self-analysis, but I believe that their individualism and naturalism must be more accurately qualified. To start with the question of individualism, this being conceived as self-awareness and self-assertion, we had better not exaggerate the

novelty and originality of this "rediscovery." Michelet had
already clearly realized the significance of the twelfth century
and, particularly, of Abélard's figure within his idea of the
civilization of the Renaissance which he himself, as is well
known, first defined as "the discovery of man and the discovery
of nature."[32] But I must add that the fundamental difference
between the individualism of Abélard (or Villon, or the medieval man in general) and that of Cellini (or Leonardo, Michelangelo, or the man of the Renaissance) is that the former was
regularly stifled, and eventually bent by the resistance of an
unfavorable environment. In fact, Abélard typically accepted
his mutilation and repented of his moral heterodoxy (although
his revolt against certain standards continued in the intellectual,
philosophical sphere); likewise Villon always returned, contrite
and humble as a prodigal son, to the consolations of the faith.
The Renaissance heroes rarely 'repented': they triumphed in
their very nonconformism.

As to the problem of naturalism in Abélard and Héloïse, a
number of qualitative, historical distinctions are imperative.
First of all we should, of course, not expect here the all-pervasive, conscious, fully stated naturalism that we shall find, for
instance, in the *Decameron*. At any rate, the naturalism we
find in some segments of medieval culture is not, by and large,
of the sort which is characteristic of the Renaissance as a
whole: the sort we do find in the latter is rather an aspect of
its general 'immanentism.' The appeal to the rights of nature
as distinct from and possibly opposed to the laws and conventions of society, with the implied defense of the senses against
the tyranny of reason, not only is not common to the Renaissance
generally speaking, but is not even typical of it in its more
essential manifestations. Likewise, although in a different context, Gentile correctly distinguished between Humanism (pre-
dominant in the Quattrocento) and the naturalism of the later
Renaissance.[33] Moreover, I feel that between the behavior of
Abélard and that of Héloïse a clear differentiation must be
made.

We have a witness of what must have been their contemporaries' common reaction to the extraordinary story of Abélard

(1079–1142) and Héloïse in Foulques de Deuil's unsympathetic judgment: "What, as they say, caused your downfall is the love of women [*singularium feminarum*] and the snares of desire whereby they catch libertines."[34] Gilson has made a great deal, and justly so, of Abélard's impressive autobiography (*Historia Calamitatum*), and even triumphantly compared it to Dante's *Vita Nova* and Cellini's *Vita*.[35] Now, Gilson himself concludes, quite correctly I think, that the *Historia Calamitatum* "is no love story, but the tale of the incontinence of Abélard, victim of the noonday evil" (p. 6), for the repentant Abélard "said he would have never fallen from the sublime apex of continence had not *ill fortune* offered him in Héloïse the occasion to fall from it" (p. 3). Abélard himself summed up his story as a tragic adventure in the destiny of a great man who yielded to an ugly temptation. "I . . . yielded my loins to lust," as he put it in his characteristically brutal, self-flagellating frankness.[36] In the absence of a more direct analysis of Abélard's feelings toward his unfortunate victim at the time of their sinful relationship, we are bound to rely on such statements, and conclude that, generally speaking, and as far as Abélard was concerned, this story presents nothing that is not typically 'medieval' in terms of prevailing ethics; we find no appeal to any ethical or psychological code that can in any way be termed naturalistic.

The question gains in complexity when our attention turns to the truer protagonist of the story, Héloïse. Unwittingly, thanks only to the unique sincerity of her passion, Héloïse eventually came to divest herself of the most tenacious prejudices of her age and practically became a heroic rebel to the unnatural features of the prevailing ethics. She thus became one of the purest embodiments of feminine humanity, 'eternal feminine' and 'ideal lover' in one, and to such a degree of authenticity, such an adherence of the literary representation to the experience of life, that she has remained one of those rare womanly figures with whom (as has been said of Chaucer's Criseyde) the sensitive male reader cannot help but fall inexorably in love.

Whatever defense of the inescapable laws of nature against

the rigid ethics of a puritanic and ascetic-minded society we
may find in Héloïse's story, it did not come about as a result
of a well-meditated experience. At the beginning, once she had
fallen prey to the unscrupulous ways of her seducer, and when
confronted with his reiterated proposal of marriage, she attempted to dissuade him from effecting a liaison that struck her
as an irregular status. This she attempted to do by offering the
opinions of Theophrastus, Seneca, St. Jerome in praise of
chastity!

After the marriage (and once his capability to make it good
had been removed by the cruel mutilation of the year 1119)
Abélard began to realize the extent of his error: "In marrying,
I was destroying myself; I was casting a slur upon my own
honour." He invoked nature in a context rather foreign to us:
"How indecent it is, how lamentable, that created by nature
for all mankind, I should go and consecrate myself to a single
woman and stoop to such shame."[37] Héloïse agreed. So far,
rather than the triumph of 'nature,' their story expresses an
ideal which "is nothing less than the heroic virtues of the
Christian life. Both of them speak in terms of these, not to sing
their personal victory but to mark the extent of their defeat."[38]
Their pleasures were constantly accompanied by a profound
sense of guilt, not naturally sought for and accepted. "Respect
neither for God nor decency . . . deterred me from wallowing
in the mire. When you objected to it yourself and resisted with
all your might, and tried to dissuade me from it, I frequently
forced your consent . . . by threats and blows."[39] This feeling
of guilt later made him accept his mutilation as a just and
providential punishment.[40]

If he had scruples, so, and even more, had Héloïse. She
repeatedly warned the cleric-philosopher to be continent "lest
you should come to prefer shameful pleasures to the divine
service, lest you . . . should destroy yourself in these obscenities
to the mockery of the whole world."[41] She compared herself to
Xantippe, Eve, Delilah, the wives of Solomon and Job, and
accepted her misfortunes in expiation for their sins and for the
tragedy she had caused to Abélard.[42] But if in such attitudes

we cannot fail to see a basic homage to medieval asceticism and puritanism, we must now turn to an aspect of the affair which, from the viewpoint of our particular inquiry, offers an enlightening contrast with all the preceding.

In his *Theologia Christiana,* II, Abélard seemed to have reduced the Gospel and the essence of true Christianity to the teachings of natural law: in particular, he had considered the virtue of continence an addition to the Gospels, therefore not indispensable.[43] Héloïse, the perfect pupil as well as the perfect lover, remembered that part of the master's thought, and to her it fell to remind him of it when he seemed to have changed his mind.[44]

When the tutor was still working on the education of his devoted pupil, they had both found inspiration in Seneca's ethic, which was based on 'nature' (the end of man is to live according to nature, "propositum nostrum est, secundum naturam vivere"), but preached a Stoic continence (*Epistola V, 4 ad Lucilium*). Héloïse had afterward learned the high price of continence at her expense, and was no longer inclined to plead its cause so unconditionally. In asking for a new rule for the 'Paraclete,' the convent of which Abélard had made her the abbess, she warned the master to proceed by the cautious principle of "discretion": "discretion is the mother of all virtues, and reason the measure of all goods."[45] In the same Sixth Letter she consequently criticized the use of imposing on novices duties that they do not know and may not be able to bear: "Zeal must be regulated by the very constitution of nature." In responding to this touching appeal, Abélard reiterated the sound maxim of Seneca, that nature must be followed, not forced and dragged along: "naturam sequens potius quam trahens" (*Epistola* VIII). But, though his moral doctrines might resemble those of the enlightened Erasmus, he applied them, in practice, with a Senecan rigor foreign to Erasmus' temperate and humane ways—as Gilson recognizes.[46]

The most important point for the purpose of our investigation is one of which Gilson makes no particular mention. I mean the striking contrast between Héloïse's former deter-

mination to persuade Abélard that he should be continent to
save his consistency as a philosopher, a theologian, a cleric,
and a teacher—all this before the marriage she insistently rejected—and her later firmness about her conjugal rights, to the
point of criticizing the validity of monastic continence, in a
desperate attempt to persuade him to keep on loving her after
having forced her into the Paraclete. Gilson paraphrases part
of her arguments in the following terms: "Are we to imagine
that the life of laymen like Abraham, Jacob, and David was
without value, even though they were married!"[47]

Abélard magnificently described the ceremony when Héloïse
took the veil: "And even while saying these words, in a minute
she hastens to the altar, and lo! she has taken the veil" ("Atque
in his verbis ad altare mox properat, et confestim [. . .] velum
[. . .] tulit," where that extraordinary clash between the present *properat* and the past *tulit* expresses all the surprise of the
spectator at the rapidity, almost rashness, of her action.—*Hist.
Cal.*, PL CLXXVIII, 136). Yet, if she had shown such prompt-
ness in obeying her husband's will, it was not out of any true
religious calling, but in a supreme demonstration of total submission. By that sacrifice she joyously took upon herself the
role of martyr—martyr not of religion, but of love, not to renounce the world, but her own will for that of her beloved.
She was taking the veil not to become Christ's spouse, but to
prove to her husband how deserving she was of his love, since
she unhesitatingly accepted his most absurd whims—with a
submission, indeed, more heroic than that of Lancelot entering
the criminal's chariot for the sake of pleasing Guenevere. Then,
there came upon her that change of heart which Gilson neither
underlines nor explains, but which can be reconstructed
through Héloïse's first letter. She had hoped to persuade
Abélard to love her without needing her body, hence her
campaign for continence before the marriage. After entering
the Paraclete she began to realize how important the sexual
factor had been for Abélard, and accused him of not really
"loving" her. We may assume that, unconsciously, she was
herself attracted more and more to the thesis of the indissolu-

bility of sentiment and sex, the heart and the senses, and finally came around to criticizing the ideal of continence on an ideological ground (*Epistola* VI). In the meantime she cried: "Alas! It is concupiscence that attracted you to me; it is the ardor of the senses rather than love; this is why, once your desire was extinguished, all demonstrations of affection that such desire had inspired vanished with the latter." She had felt ready to give her body because she had given her soul, and claimed the same right on Abélard's body because he had pretended to love her with his soul. But now she felt deceived. For there was in this woman that perfect harmony of spirituality and naturalism that is the hallmark of medieval love literature at its best, and the condition for all truly great love between man and woman: body and soul in unity without quarrel. But Abélard was no match for her. He had first been overwhelmed by the sensualist in him, then, thanks to Fulbert's knife, had decided that, after all, the way of the perfect life and sublime wisdom did have to be paved with the mortification of the body.

His mind once made up, he could no longer understand Héloïse's obduracy in refusing God's grace, he could not abide the revolt of a woman in love, even if it was he who had sparked that all-consuming passion. Public opinion was against this woman in love, and the time had not yet come for public sympathy toward great sinners. The sympathy of some of her contemporaries (for example, Peter the Venerable) for Héloïse was purely a movement of exquisite hearts and humane understanding, and did not imply recognition of her revolt, rather strove to cover it up officially. In a famous letter Peter reported to her the death of him "to whom you were joined first in the flesh and then by the stronger and more perfect bond of divine charity"; a noble piece, indeed, of wishful thinking on the part of the great abbot of Cluny, clearly contradicted by the evidence, since Héloïse never appeared to have undergone such a conversion to true "divine charity."

Rather than a spontaneous expression of her inner personality, we must assume that Héloïse's expressions of guilt had been an unconscious reflection of her feminine dedication and submission to Abélard's viewpoint. But in her second letter her true personality bursts out. Immediately after accusing herself of sinning and inducing Abélard to sin, she expresses her perseverance in the enjoyment of those "sweet" memories, and rejects Abélard's "flatteries" by confessing to her "hypocrisy." She is *not* virtuous, she defiantly avows, since "virtue is a matter of the soul, not of the flesh"; her flesh is now perforce chaste, but her mind is not. She does not repent and does not reject her past. Yet she considers it *sinful* not from her viewpoint, but from that of Abélard, who has been brought to ruin by their mutual passion.

We do have here an extraordinary piece of implacable self-analysis, but not the serene, whole-hearted, and naïve acceptance of the natural ways of the flesh that we can regard as coherent naturalism. She admits that she cannot change her attitude, but does not really defend it from the charges which a different approach to her condition could bring against her. Doggedly, with the blindness of a man determined not to be swayed, Abélard turns Héloïse's literal statements into the allegory of the Scriptures. Would she have chosen to be Abélard's concubine rather than his wife, as she has emphatically stated? This was the destiny of the black woman in the *Song of Songs*. "Such a bride will seek the intimate gratification rather than the public joys of marriage." (*PL* CLXXVIII, 201–202.) She was black from her tribulations, hence more fit for the secrets of the royal bed than the white woman, more fit for the pomp of the palace. The bones of the black one are ever so much whiter, expressing her inner virtue, like Héloïse's.

One feels inclined to conclude that there was a touch of masochism in Héloïse's persistence in the conventual life without vocation, while there was perhaps jealous, ungenerous egotism in Abélard's tyrannic deliberation to send her to the convent and keep her there for life. But who are we to judge, when the object of our indiscreet attention is a Héloïse? Had it taken all the folly and suffering within mankind's power to produce the experience of such a love, the achievement would have been worth it all. Héloïse, we may assume, would not have changed her lot.

All in all, this case remains absolutely exceptional and isolated, and too serious in its reality to be mixed with fiction and literature. Nevertheless, at the risk of sounding somewhat irreverent, I venture to postulate an ideal relationship with the world of *courtoisie*. Granted that Abélard, as a postulant who suffered from *abundantia voluptatis*, would not have qualified for membership in a 'love court.' For her part Héloïse, great lover but no sensualist, would have passed with flying colors. For a good start, the book that lies at the origin of all *courtois* speculation, Ovid's *Ars Amatoria*, was one of their favorite readings in the period of their "sweet sighs and dubious desires," and may well have played between them the role of Gallehault which Francesca da Rimini attributed to the romance of Lancelot. I suspect that Héloïse's motives for rejecting the marriage proposal were not so far removed from certain tenets of courtly love. The transition from the exalted role of a worshiped mistress to the total submission of a wife to her husband's unchallenged authority was an unattractive loss, not a gain, in the mind of a medieval woman of quality. The refined and cultivated Héloïse, whose extraordinary mental qualities and scholarly attitudes prompted her to place herself and her teacher on the highest pedestals, explicitly manifested a genuine horror at the thought of Abélard and herself prosaically engaged in the mean chores of housekeeping and family upbringing, which would have irreparably stifled their freedom of spiritual and intellectual development. She wanted to picture herself as the future fountainhead of Abélard's inspiration and *probitas* (even to the point of persuading him to continence)— and was this not another basic precept of the courtly ideal? Nonetheless, the poetic knight chose to become a prosaic lord. Then, compelled by Abélard to become his wife, Héloïse's ideal shifted from that of the courtly lady to that of the Griselda, that is, to joyful, irrational obedience and total self-sacrifice ("ad altare mox properat . . . ," and in her first letter: "I would rather have been your courtesan than Augustus' wife": "Deum

testem invoco, si me Augustus universo praesidens mundo
matrimonii honore dignaretur, [. . .] charius mihi et dignius
videretur tua dici meretrix quam illius [Augusti] imperatrix."
PL CLXXVIII, 185), but she insisted on her rights, including
sexual rights. It seems to me a pity that C. S. Lewis should
have made no mention of Héloïse in his masterful study of
courtly love, and that Gilson should have made no reference to
courtoisie or to the Griselda ideal. This latter was a deeply
rooted reality in the medieval mind, and after Héloïse had offered an immortal incarnation of it, it found its great literary
expressions in Chrétien de Troyes (*Érec et Énide*), Boccaccio,
and Chaucer.[48] The humanists' general hostility to engagement
in marital bonds is reflected in the early case of Héloïse's motivation, and whatever the influence which acted on her, classical or Stoic or vaguely *courtois,* we can safely conclude that
she kept moving in a cultural and psychological climate alien
and hostile to Abélard's final goals, until they ended up by
speaking two different, reciprocally uncommunicable languages.

The cultural and social factors that influenced Héloïse must
also have partly erased in her eyes the inconsistency and abnormality of a sensual liaison with a cleric. Capellanus excluded
nuns from the service of love, but not *clerici*—nor did he consider love completely incompatible with religiosity; on the contrary, the ideal lover was expected to show Christian piety and
reverence for the Saints.[49]

The breaking of the more restraining ties of the medieval
mores and mental attitudes is, with all its historical limitations,
the profound challenge of Héloïse's story. This difficult triumph
of woman's deep, unfettered nature without and against the
medieval God must have been of paramount importance for
the interest of later humanistic circles in the dramatic lesson it
had to offer. It cannot be without meaning that two of the
three best extant manuscripts of Héloïse's and Abélard's letters
belonged, one to Francis Petrarch (now MS 2923 of the Bibliothèque Nationale), and the other to Roberto de' Bardi, the
Florentine Chancellor of the University of Paris from 1336,

who in 1340 invited his friend Petrarch to be crowned in Paris with the poet's laurel, and in 1346 purchased the MS now of Troyes 802 from the Library of the Chapter of Notre-Dame. Coluccio Salutati, the successor of Petrarch and Chancellor of Florence, in 1395 asked Jean de Montreuil for a manuscript or a new copy of the famous correspondence. This manuscript was sent to him in the following year, and is now lost.

THE ROMANCE OF THE ROSE

"Let the peoples know that the goddess grows in power when she seems most neglected": thus, in the verse of an early medieval poet, Venus reassured Cupid upon hearing his warning that virginity had conquered the world.[50] The confident, never-setting goddess could certainly be pleased with Héloïse as her splendid witness. Indeed, the deity of Venus never shone more brightly than in the ascetic-minded Middle Ages, when her triumph was carried on with a challenging smile, since her naturalistic campaign was fought as a direct attack on religion, ethics, and society.

Nevertheless, another school of naturalism was contemporaneously being developed with the seed of the Renaissance in its bosom. From this new vantage point nature appeared to teach men to be whole, well-integrated human beings in a well-ordered society. Such an attempt to harmonize all human faculties characterizes the new Platonism of the School of Chartres. In its context one begins to perceive the ripening of a naturalistic current which had stemmed from late Latin literature, and developed during the Middle Ages independently from, and in constant rivalry with the 'Gothic' spirit of the time as embodied in the two chief manifestations of this 'Gothic' spirit, the religious and the *courtois*. Such rivalry evolved both from within and from without, since at times it appears that naturalism is allied to courtliness as an integral part of it, at other times it is obviously set upon dissolving it as its constitutional enemy. The heart of the matter is, from a sociological viewpoint, that the religious and courtly attitudes were the most direct expressions of the two ruling classes, the clergy and the nobility, whereas the naturalistic spirit throve in the wake of the progressive affirmation of the new *bourgeoisie*, the third estate.

Bernardus Sylvester's (fl. 1140) *De Mundi Universitate* was based on Chalcidius' commentary on the *Timaeus* and dedicated to Thierry of Chartres, the master who had reconciled *Genesis* and Plato's *Timaeus*. Sylvester's message was carried further by Alanus de Insulis (Alain de Lille, d. 1203) in his *Anticlaudianus*.[51] Here a middle point was struck between the theological ethics and the courtly ethics, with direct attachments to classical allegory.[52] The perfect man, accordingly, was to be fashioned with qualities of goodness that is not ascetic, knighthood that is not adulterous. "Honestas" warned man "to revere Nature in order to avoid vice, condemning that which is born by criminal habit and which is brought about by ill will, and embracing all that Nature created."[53] Nature thus seemed to criticize the "unnatural" in *courtoisie*. Even more important is Alan's *De Planctu Naturae*, a complaint of Nature about the breaking of her laws.[54] Here, as part of a theme which was also derived from Bernardus Sylvester, Nature pleads the cause of natural love versus both the celestial Cupid (the god of 'Platonic,' suprasensual or purely spiritual love) and the infernal Cupid (the god of sinful and adulterous love).

Alan's naturalism is a position whereby nature, that is, the source of physical life, was assumed as a norm of moral value.[55] Averroes (Alan's contemporary) distinguished between *natura naturans* (the active creative principle) and *natura naturata* (the totality of things created). The former is the goddess Nature in Alan's work, as it will be in Jean de Meung's. Alan speaks of a "power contained in natural things, which procreates like from like, whence something is said to be made according to nature."[56] Now the Catharists (attacked by Alan in his *Contra haereticos*) believed matter (*natura naturata*) to be evil, the realm of the devil who brought it into existence. Alan countered with the tract "Substances are good *qua* existent, though not goods in themselves" (*Quomodo substantiae in eo quod sint, bonae sint, cum non sint substantialia bona).* In thus opposing the radicalism of a Manichaean spiritualism, representative of the most prevalent and typical trend of the time, Alan made himself the defender of the inherent goodness of creation in the context of an explicitly naturalistic polemic. He proceeded further to make the distinction between the natural as good and the unnatural as evil, the latter being man's own subversion of the moral harmony of the cosmos by sexual perversion and vices.[57] These are defined as excesses and are discussed in terms which foreshadow the technical approach borrowed by Western physicians from the Arab philosophers. Love can degenerate into furor, an illness crying for immediate remedy:

> I do not deny the essential nature of love honorableness if it is checked by the bridle of moderation, if it is restrained by the reins of sobriety, if it does not transgress the determined boundaries of the dual activity, or its heat boil to too great a degree. But if its spark shoots into a flame . . . the rankness of the growth demands the pruning knife, and the swelling and excess requires an assuaging medicine; for . . . the pride of unhealthy extravagance fattens, so to speak, into imposthumes [*apostemata,* 'abscesses'] of vices.[58]

Thus, in the end, Alan assumes an anticourtly role: in his moral scheme there is no logical place for passionate love. In the fifth "Prosa" of the *De Planctu* we learn that Venus had two sons: Cupid from Hymen (the god of nuptials), Jocus (Play, Mirth, "by antiphrasis") from the adulterer Antigamus (the Enemy of Marriage). And Hymen is Nature's brother (Wright, II, 474–482). Alan was, then, engaged in that reconciliation of Christian morals and courtly naturalism whose development through English letters has been brilliantly investigated by C. S. Lewis, with a particular stress on Spenser. Seeing the matter in a new light, the master from Lille forcefully interpreted the traditional, pagan and Christian ethics in a freshly original naturalistic context; but, thanks to his humanistic and ecclesiastical background, he succeeded in avoiding

the typical tension of medieval vernacular naturalism, and his
speculation found its conclusion in orthodoxy. Reason remained
theoretically triumphant over the senses: "And just as the army
of the planets opposes with contrary motion the fixed rolling of
the firmament, so in man is found a continual hostility between
lust and reason." Such is the analogy which shows reason as the
superior force, the 'circular,' perfect movement versus the 'rectilinear,' imperfect motion of things material.[59]

Alan soon found a long series of admirers, among whom we
must mention at least Jean de Meung, Dante, and Chaucer. In
the very years of bishop Tempier's condemnation of Capellanus (1277), the process of dissolution of courtly love was carried much further by Jean de Meung in his continuation of the
Roman de la Rose (ca. 1275–ca. 1280), the most popular text of
French medieval literature, and the very work that Guillaume
de Lorris had started as a supreme allegorical hymn to courtly
love. From the school of Chartres, Jean de Meung learned the
principles of his reëlaboration of courtly love into naturalistic
love, but he remained completely within a medieval framework
by departing from the process of "pouring the sentiment which
the Middle Ages had created into molds that the law of Reason
can approve."[60]

In Jean de Meung's portion of the *Romance of the Rose* the
adventure of *Amant*, the Lover, is, quite significantly, antagonized by *Raison*, as it was in Guillaume de Lorris's portion.
But the remnants of that mystic love with which Guillaume's
Reason could still have agreed to ally itself are now unharmo-
niously juxtaposed to an unabashed defense of sex, in a way
that is typically medieval for its disregard of overt contradiction and paradox.

Raison and *Amant*, the latter being abetted by a host of allies and advisers, are decidedly on opposite sides of the fence,
and no sophism can reconcile them. The poet does not even
attempt a serious reconciliation; he prefers to leave the two
parties on two levels, without real communication between
them. And the author takes his stand in unequivocal terms
speaking through *Amour*: "And then will come Jean Chopinel

[de Meung] who will be my [*Amour's*] servant all his life, and will be such a truly wise man that he will have no use for Reason."[61] Yet, this statement, direct as it may sound, cannot be taken too seriously, for there are other good reasons to consider Jean de Meung an earnest student of *Raison*, as most critics are inclined to do. More than any systematic, unilateral philosopher, however, the poet is a brilliant master of paradox with a rich scholastic foundation to his polymorphous personality. We cannot really expect a 'rational' justification of the irrationality of love before the *Decameron*—for Boccaccio was, in a way, the first who openly defended the "rights of the irrational." Yet Jean de Meung is closer to the world of the *Decameron* than to that of courtly love.

The dissolution of the courtly code rings through the speech of Friend (*Amis*), who instructs the Dreamer in the unholy art of deception: "Only let them not perceive that you aim to deceive them."[62] The loyalty, trust, and exclusiveness preached by Capellanus have vanished as delusions for daydreamers. Furthermore, nothing is lost by sharing the source of our pleasures: "It is silly to spare it; it is like the candle in the lantern: its fire can well be used to kindle a thousand others without any loss to itself."[63] *Amis* says this against *jalousie*, the villain of many a popular story from Jean de Meung to Boccaccio and well beyond. But jealousy itself, in the person of the *Jaloux*, is well convinced of such an undeniable truth. *Jaloux* states that all women are constitutionally unfaithful, and have a good time with their lovers, whenever they can (vv. 9133–9137).[64] Yet, jealousy is the inevitable companion of marriage. In his famous, masterful retelling of the pathetic story of Héloïse, of which he was particularly fond, Jean de Meung's conclusion was: Do not marry, if you wish to avoid trouble (vv. 8759–8832). Abélard's jealousy, we can infer, and her own absurd faithfulness were the true causes of Héloïse's undoing.

The traditional maxims on inner nobility as the warrant of true love, as codified by Capellanus, found fertile ground in the *Roman* (vv. 18607–18896) in the very years when this theory was passing into the hands of the Italian *stilnovisti*, who,

on their part, revived it in an elaborate and systematic doctrine
soon to be inherited by Dante. According to Jean de Meung
the rich and powerful are not thereby more noble or *gentil*
than the laborer. Only virtue and true valor bestow nobility
(*gentillesse*), which is more easily found in clerics and knights
than in kings, and is not hereditary. The sons of noblemen who
go astray are all the more to be blamed.

In Alan's *De Planctu Naturae,* Nature had introduced Venus
as her *subvicaria;* Love was at Nature's service.[65] In comparing
Jean de Meung's views with those of Alan of Lille, Gérard
Paré has appropriately concluded by contrasting the spirit of
the two authors: even while they managed the same themes,
Alan ended with an apology of Christian virtues, whereas in
Jean's context "chastity and continence are regarded as vices,
and it is indeed against continence that Genius's accents are
most inflamed."[66] Similarly, if we turn our attention to the
theory of love expounded by both *Raison* and *Nature* in the
Roman, we find love to be conceived as a natural phenomenon
(Venus is Nature's friend, *amie*), whose justifying end lies in
the propagation of the species. As such it is good and necessary.
This biological approach marks the defeat of the sentimental
tradition, which had viewed love as the blind play of pure,
dreaming passion, its goal being made of mystic, more-than-
human sublimity and happiness. Such disenchantment was, and
had always been, the logical outcome of a consistently naturalistic mentality, from Lucretius to Jean de Meung. Only Boccaccio will reconcile the most crude pagan and medieval naturalism with the loftiest *courtois* sentimentalism, the materialistic with the spiritualistic streams (but without asceticism),
rationalistic positivism with romanticism.

Genius, Nature's priest in the *Roman,* confirms Nature's com-
mandment before Amour's army: "Arez, pour Deu, baron, arez
. . ."[67] Yet, in spite of this practical justification for its social
ends, love is free and intolerant of conjugal bonds. Love re-
quires equality, whereas marriage subjects one to the hierarchy
of the family. "He who wants to be regarded as the master cannot be loved by his wife, for love must die when one lover becomes the lord of the other. Love can only last and thrive in

free hearts."[68] Let us, then, follow the pagan examples of refined free love: "Hence, my friend, the ancients enjoyed sweet
companionship untroubled by servitude, formal ties, or dis-
courteousness."[69] To conclude with the words of a recent student of the medieval 'naturalistic' style, "Raison, indeed, first
launches the naturalistic ideas which are passed down the
poem to become with Genius a doctrine of procreation and
with the Duenna a philosophy of promiscuity."[70]

In the famous episode of Vulcan and Venus, a masterpiece
of nonconformity whereby the *Vieille* tries to persuade *Bel Accueil* to welcome the lover, we are made to side with Venus
against her husband. The installing of the net designed to catch
Venus and Mars in flagrant adultery was plain silly, and truly
worthy of a husband's stupidity.

> A great fool he was in daring to do this, for he who pre-
> sumes to have his wife all for himself is a man of little
> wisdom. Women were born free, the law has disenfran-
> chised them of the freedom Nature had given them. Na-
> ture is not so foolish as to bear a Lucy just for a Larry.
> All women are made for all men, each for each in com-
> mon, female for male and male for female.[71]

It is, therefore, only natural for women to break away from the
fetters imposed on them by society. "They try all means to return to their original freedom—ladies and young ladies alike."[72]

The only good matches are those which result from free
election, and their only rule is the pursuit and attainment of
pleasure. Once caught in the web of social conventions, human beings aspire to break away just as the bird in a cage longs
after the freedom of woods and prairies, and the fish caught in
a treacherous net struggles toward the water.

> Nature can never lie, she makes them feel the call of
> freedom, as Horace himself who knew this matter well,
> tells us: "You may defend yourself from Nature and
> drive her out with a pitch-fork; she will always come
> back." Indeed, Nature will always hasten back, nor will
> she delay because of any costume. Overwhelming is the
> force of Nature; she is even stronger than upbringing.[73]

In conclusion, wisdom should have taught Vulcan to keep his secret to himself and continue to enjoy Venus by sharing her, instead of losing her in addition to making his shame public.[74] But this is not the sort of wisdom one learns at the school of theory: the Duenna, in fact, has learned so much by hard practice and lifelong experience.[75]

Friend had advised the Lover to deceive the guardians by feigning abstinence. In this manner were eventually introduced the allegoric figures of *Faus Semblant* (False-Seeming) and *Contrainte Astenance* (Constrained Abstinence). This was admittedly part of a technique—the technique of wooing by deceiving—hence such 'allies' were never openly recognized, for the strategy must, of course, be covered. It has been said that the poet has a spokesman in the person of *Male Bouche* (Bad-Mouth), who reveals all the ignominious truth about women. But, since this unsavory truth might hinder the natural course of things, Bad-Mouth is duly strangled by False-Seeming at the assault of the Castle. Thus hypocrisy unofficially helps the cause of Love by removing a serious obstacle; after all, some degree of esteem toward the woman is necessary for wooing her. This compromise, or happy medium between the absurdities of romantic illusion and the sterility of objective truth amounts to the dialectic of Nature, whose theory as also expounded by Reason contemplates the employment of man's instinctive search for pleasure (Venus) for the ends of the triumph of life over death. Finally, it is precisely under the martial guidance of Venus and Nature that *Bel Accueil* is liberated from his imprisonment. The way to the Rose is now open. Thus the plea of courtly sentimentality, on one hand, has been rejected as effectively as that of morose asceticism, on the other, asceticism being a possible result of pessimistic, antifeministic 'realism.' For sentimentality led, through self-deceit, to the same danger as asceticism did through Constrained Abstinence: the denial of sex *or* nature.[76]

As in France and elsewhere, the *Roman* also became very popular in Italy, as attested by at least two notable Tuscan versions of it, *Il Fiore* and *Il Detto d'Amore*. The most pointed traits of Jean de Meung's unconventional message were not lost for the Italian reader: in *Il Fiore, Amor* spoke to *Amante* in such clear terms: "You shall worship me for I am your God; lay all other faiths aside, believe neither Luke nor Matthew nor Mark nor John."[77] And in the advice of the *Vecchia* the supreme law of nature (*franchezza*) was very effectively set off against the artificial laws of society, whose prison we have the same right to flee as the bird his cage.[78] Significantly, the obscure allegory of *Dangier* was rendered by the unknown imitator by the quite explicit *Schifo* (= fr. *pudeur,* modesty, almost prudishness): Danger, may I recall it, was one of the most formidable obstacles the Dreamer must remove in order to pluck the Rose.

During the Hundred Years' War, against the popularity enjoyed by the prose *Lancelot* on account of its chivalresque appeal, it dawned upon certain audiences that the *Romance of the Rose* supplied a sort of bourgeois gospel. Jean de Meung's new popularity arose in the wake of his fresh rationalistic appeal to the mentality of social groups not directly touched by the courtly sentimentality. But he also aroused a critical reaction. It was particularly against his cynical attacks that Christine de Pisan took the defense of women in her *Epître au Dieu d'Amour* (1399) and *Le Dit de La Rose* (1400). This gave origin to a famed correspondence between Christine, Jean de Montreuil, and Jean Gerson (?). The *Querelle du Roman de la Rose* swept more widely through the intellectual circles as Gontier and Pierre Col joined Jean de Montreuil's camp in defense of Jean de Meung.[79]

F. Simone has expressed reservations as to the traditional interpretations of the *querelle's* historical significance, since he wants it to be placed not within the struggle of the new humanistic spirit against the lingering medieval prejudices, but as a clash of two equally medieval traditions to be viewed, broadly, in the secular development of the *querelle des femmes* —a *querelle* which goes from the Roman schools of rhetoric through St. Augustine, Abélard and Héloïse, and Alan of Lille, to Rabelais.[80] A. Coville interpreted it in the light of a contrast between the theologians (Gerson, on Christine's side) and the humanists (Montreuil), but if so, as Simone points out, it was the 'theologians' who, in this case, were looking forward, in defending the dignity of womanhood. Simone's position shows some affinity to that of Huizinga, for whom the whole affair amounted to a clash between the two medieval conceptions of love, the chivalresque and the libertine—this latter being a re-elaboration, operated by the *esprit gaulois*, of the ancient, freely erotic approach. Yet, I should like to add that in this fifteenth-century debate on feminism versus antifeminism one sees a development within the new bourgeois spirit of two contrasting viewpoints and dialectical poles of that same spirit. The glorification of womanhood in a chivalrous climate had been, so to say, 'a poetic convention': now one was taking a pensive, realistic look at the question of woman's dignity, in the light of a moral awareness and in a more practical mood. Thus the humanistic current (of the Northern type, not the 'civic' type which prevailed in the early Italian Quattrocento) found inspiration in Jean de Meung's pessimism in order to defend the ideal of the independence of the sage-scholar and his non-engagement on a social plane (the ideal of Abélard, Petrarch, Erasmus). The theological milieus, instead, reflected the practical preoccupations of the Catholic traditions, which had stressed the social function of the family and of its sacrament, marriage, if and when it was realized in an orderly, hierarchical relationship of husband-master and mother-housewife (radically, the 'Griselda-ideal'). Thus, after the decline of the stylized, idealized figure of the *midons*, the exalted and distant lady (Beatrice or Laura, typically), one could find, on the one hand, the amoral, dissolute female, instrument of the devil (the widow of Boccaccio's *Corbaccio*), on the other, the submissive, humble, 'functional' Griselda.

FURTHER DISSOLUTION OF THE COURTLY HERITAGE

The fabliau (from the end of the twelfth century to the beginning of the fourteenth) is the most impressive storage of literary realism in the Middle Ages. This vast and varied body of stories offers the best opportunities to 'loose' naturalism. Nevertheless, this genre (if one can speak of genre for such a composite ensemble) is far from being of substantial interest for the explicit and articulated forms of conscious naturalism with which we are here concerned. Furthermore, whereas the naturalistic spirit as such can be considered a reflection of the growing independence and awareness of the middle class, the same cannot be said of realism in general, nor of the realism of the fabliau specifically.

Edmond Faral, for one, denied the bourgeois origin and character of the fabliaux, which he defined, on the other hand, "realistic."[81] They were most probably produced, according to this distinguished literary historian, in the same milieu as the seriously sentimental, romantically aristocratic literature of the *matières de Bretagne* and *de Charlemagne*. The victims of the fabliau are people from all classes, but no important personages, no princes or bishops, nor any class in particular.[82] Peasants are looked down upon, but also, occasionally, glorified for surprising, unexpected talents. Bourgeois and knights are "sensiblement plus maltraités que les vilains."[83]

The *farces* of the fifteenth century (with their masterpiece, *Pathelin*) somehow are the heir of the medieval fabliaux and correspond to the Italian literature of wit unprejudiced and triumphant.

A notable general affinity to the fabliaux marks, for our purposes, the *Roman de Renart*, where the Fox (Renart) and the Ass (Bernart) do not hesitate to expound a most befitting animal philosophy based on the doctrine of sexual intercourse as the end of life, a sufficient reason for being alive.[84] This would be all right, the speakers being what they are. But sometimes and somehow the (human) reader could not help but feel that the sermons were also addressed, of all animals, to him. And when the Ass pleaded to the King to proclaim that those who abstain from using their organs for their intended physiological end shall go to Hell, the reader was again entitled to wonder whether it was only the Hell of Asses that was meant here. All this notwithstanding, the tales of Reynard are chiefly for the fun of a varied and uncommitted audience, wanting a moment of good, free, full laughter. The 'doctrine,' if there is any, has the function of a light, good-humored parody and is without the weight of serious consequences.

We should turn to a more serious level than the fabliau if we wish to follow the evolution of the naturalistic spirit from *courtoisie* to the intellectual climate in which the *Decameron* was born. The *courtois* literature had enjoyed its prime in the twelfth century. The following century saw its incipient dissolution in the second part of the *Roman de la Rose*. But the most serious objections to the courtly ideals in their original, radical purity were not so much those which could come from the cynic naturalism of a Jean de Meung. They lay rather in the type of responsible attitude which one can notice in the moralizing of the school of Chartres, in the intellectualizations of the Platonists, and in the theologizing of the *stilnovisti*. The heart of the matter was that, if it is true that Nature cannot be chased from Man, neither could Reason be long kept in the background, for an agreement or, at worst, a compromise between the two goddesses was, in the long run, imperative.

"The very nature of courtly love—once again to quote C. S. Lewis—demanded that the perfect love poem should end with a recantation. The claims of the objective moral law—of *Resoun* as the Middle Ages said—must, in the end, be faced. Hence the last book of Andreas, and the conclusion of *Troilus and Cryseide* [sic]."[85] Thus a younger contemporary of Boccaccio, John Gower (ca. 1330 –1408) ended his "Confession of the Lover" (*Confessio Amantis*) with the acceptance of hard, cold reality under the guidance of experience, conscience, and reason: "Homeward a softe pas I went." Typically medieval was this sudden realization of a tension ending in a clumsy attempt to reconcile the erotic code with the moral code, the a-social and irrational laws of love with the superior and ultimately inescapable laws of moral reason. It was not so, as we shall see, with Boccaccio, who did realize the irrationality of passion, but *not* in order to renounce it in the name of *resoun* and "go where vertu moral duelleth." He will go home to "reason" only

after the *Decameron,* in the *Corbaccio* or rather with the crisis
of 1362. The *Decameron* celebrates the (temporary) victory of
pure naturalism in its vigorous counterattack against all attempts by "reason" to defeat it. And it came, characteristically,
shortly after the most formidable attack on naturalism the Middle Ages had witnessed: the triumph of Dante's Beatrice over
Francesca da Rimini, the heroine of *amour courtois.*[86]

The process of reconciling sentiment with reason and morality flows, ideally, from the school of Chartres into the Platonism of the Renaissance, thus forming, so to speak, a current of
basic intellectualism and rationalism alongside the fundamental
romantic irrationalism which runs, ideally again, from some of
the Provençal, Héloïse, Capellanus, Tristan, Lancelot, Jean de
Meung, to the Portuguese nun, the Chevalier of the *Liaisons
Dangereuses,* Des Grieux of *Manon,* or, in Italy, from the *Decameron* to the *Aminta.* And the same 'Platonic' rationalization
of love which invoked the rule of reason to reconcile nature
and morality, is, though historically distinct from it, ideally
akin to the 'Gothic' rationalization operated by the *stilnovisti,*
with Dante at the extreme end of the school.

But together with the naturalistic idealism of the Platonists
and the theologizing idealism of the *stilnovisti,* the new realistic
spirit also was conspiring to bring about the final dissolution of
courtoisie. In spite of a basic idealism, chivalry and courtly
literature had begun, may I repeat, in a naturalistic key. They
ended, however, in a moralistic vein which was almost in direct
opposition to that beginning. The courtly casuistry of the Burgundian *Grands Rhétoriqueurs* of the fifteenth century is the
literary mirror of the abstract, moralizing idealism which informed the chivalric attitudes and mentality of the society of
Philip the Good and Charles the Bold, and which found its
counterpart in the disenchanted, individualistic realism of contemporaneous France, shaken and sobered by Azincourt.
Georges Chastellain and Philippe de Commynes are the ex-
ponents of the two opposed worlds—and the future, the 'renaissance,' lay in the path trodden by the latter.

One outstanding example shall suffice to illustrate the decay-

ing of *courtoisie* into *grande rhétorique,* the original Gothic into
Flamboyant Gothic. Olivier de La Marche, the representative
courtier of the dukes of Burgundy, rhapsodizes about his being
struck dumb, one December night, by the sight of a beautiful
lady: it is love at first sight. But let us not be deceived. What
he wants from her is the chance to contemplate a shining mirror of moral perfection; accordingly, he will tailor for her a
new, wondrous accoutrement, made of slippers, stockings, gar-
ter, girdle, and so forth—that is, out of allegory: humility, dili-
gence, perseverance, and so on and on through the edifying cate-
chism of precious virtues.[87] The approximate date of this subtle
allegory is 1492 or 93. The battle of Nancy was now far from
memory, and Charles VIII was ready to set foot in Naples.

The other camp deserves more examples: here the new,
realistic spirit was slowly but relentlessly undermining the
foundations of the fortress of chivalry, until it could take it by
storm from within and convert its structures to new uses for
its own ends. In the *Cent Ballades,* lyrical masterpiece of the
fourteenth century, wanton love had found an ironic spokesman amidst a casuistic debate on the merits of faithfulness.[88]
Another foundation of the time-honored doctrine, namely the
principle that the lady's love is what lends the knight true
worth, was wittily criticized by the author's wife in the *Livre
du Chevalier de la Tour Landry,* of the same century.[89] In the
early years of the following, the somewhat hypochondriac
Eustache Deschamps pours the glum vein of his old age into
the ever more vehement satire of his society and its institutions, in particular, women and marriage, as in his *Miroir
de Mariage.*[90] Sure enough, this work finds its place in a long,
persistent tradition, and Deschamps owes something to
Mathieu's *Lamentationes* (end of the thirteenth century). But
the inspiration is clearly contemporary.

The first time, perhaps, in which the idyllic and once proud
chevalresque ideal comes out pathetically defeated from a
confrontation with the new, brutal bourgeois realism occurs in
Antoine de La Sale's *Petit Jehan de Saintré* (ca. 1456).[91] Here
a story of *'éducation sentimentale'* comes to an unexpected

denouement: a big, strong, vulgar abbot replaces the gentle, naïvely devoted Jehan in the favor of a lady who has educated and polished him. But our sympathy no longer goes to the defeated party in Jean de Bueil's *Jouvencel,* composed between 1461 and 1468.[92] This work shows the ripening of the new spirit, realistic and naturalistic, against the backdrop of the anachronistic ideals and formalistic conventions of chivalry. The author, one of the most brilliant captains of Charles VII, recalls the principal military events of the time; but, far from the established image of the feudal knight, unaware of any responsibility, answerable to God alone and to his honor, the hero is now engaged in a serious struggle in which one can destroy or be destroyed, regardless of the means employed—a struggle in which it is essential to win, rather than to fight well and according to the rules.

The Decameron

Ch'Amor de' far gentil un cor villano,
E non far d'un gentil contrario effetto.
Ariosto, Orlando Furioso XXXII, 93

THE DECAMERON *AND MODERN CRITICISM*

Most modern criticism on the *Decameron* has been concerned with correcting the rather unilateral approach of Francesco De Sanctis who, in his epoch-making *Storia della Letteratura Italiana* (1870), had focused his attention on the problem which constitutes the main purpose of my investigation. De Sanctis' fault was not that he identified the essential inspiration of the *Decameron* incorrectly, but that he stressed it unilaterally at the expense of other elements which are almost equally important for a fair and complete critical picture. For him the world of the *Decameron* was a world whose only law was nature.[1] At the same time he failed to recognize this

'naturalism' (which he conceived as an essentially 'new' attitude, in direct and complete reaction against medieval spiritualism, asceticism, and mysticism) as a *serious* value for the
author. De Sanctis obeyed in this his well-known prejudice in
favor of a literature reflecting and influencing the civic and
social ideals of the people or nation. Hence his judgment of
Boccaccio as, fundamentally, an 'aesthete' ("L'arte è la sola
serietà del Boccaccio") distorted the picture of the author's
true personality and worth, since he was seen as a great realist
lacking an ideal that might give meaning and direction to the
events he could so powerfully describe.[2] Incidentally, this
position of De Sanctis' somehow contradicted his previous
statement that "there are in these novellas two serious elements: the apotheosis of intelligence [*ingegno*] and knowledge [*dottrina*], which impose themselves on the most powerful lords, and a certain bourgeois pride."[3]

The ground for De Sanctis' stressing of the *Decameron*'s
naturalism had been prepared by Edgar Quinet, in the chapter on Boccaccio ("L'art pour l'art") of his *Les Révolutions
d'Italie* (1848–1852). Quinet emphasized the secular fight
against medieval clerical asceticism and forcefully underlined
the naturalism and realism of the *Decameron*.[4]

But there was also, in De Sanctis, the distant heritage from
which Quinet had departed, that is, the moralistic, puritan
severity of the preceding Romantic criticism, which had
blamed the *Decameron* for a lack of morality and spirituality.[5]
What a Romantic 'spiritualist' like Cantù could no longer
understand was the sort of naturalistic ethics that Marguerite
de Navarre had so subtly and felicitously expressed by defining *honneur* as "une gloire et cruaulté, par qui elles [i.e.,
women] espèrent acquérir nom d'immortalité, et ainsy se
gloriffians de résister au vice de la loy de Nature (si Nature est
vicieuse), se font non seullement semblables aux bestes in-
humaines et cruelles, mais aux diables, desquels elles prennent
l'orgueil et la malice."[6]

After De Sanctis these two poles of his interpretation, the
moralistic and the naturalistic, were duly dissociated from

each other, and the former was impatiently brushed aside so
as to allow the latter's uninhibited triumph. "Historical criticism was, then, all permeated with naturalism and anti-cleri-
calism."[7] Adolfo Bartoli authoritatively summarized the position of this movement (namely, the positivistic school) in an
essay in which he strove to insert the *Decameron* in the spirit
(not the letter) of the fabliaux—the battle cry, in his view, of
the new, antimedieval, antiascetic, and irreligious spirit of the
bourgeoisie.[8] This in spite of his stern warnings against the
exaggerations of the then fashionable search for direct literary
sources (for he believed in the popular substratum) and the
"nationalistic" claims of priority of French sources.

The positivistic approach, with its intemperate stress on a
naturalistic, irreligious campaign as the substance of the
Decameron, caused a widespread reaction to set in, which
was partly justified by the fact that a basic truth had been
either overstated at the expense of other factors, or inaccu-
rately stated in terms of a detailed historical perspective. The
attention shifted, then, to an intrinsic, loftily aesthetic reading of the text. Attilio Momigliano's intervention marked the
turning point almost forty years ago by throwing the *Decameron* open to the new, 'impressionistic' methods (appropriate to the age of hermetic, surrealistic poetry, Crocean
aestheticism, and Anglo-Saxon 'New Criticism').[9] Momigliano
claimed that the *Decameron* must be read in an abstract
state of mind, unpreoccupied with history, psychology, morality, and philosophy: the book itself and it alone had to be
the object of our attention. For it was not a book of prose,
but poetry. Croce, who had announced the new, postromantic
and postpositivistic reading of the *Decameron* with a historically oriented study of the Andreuccio da Perugia story,[10] followed up with the statement of principle that not in the relationships with its age, but in its very transcending of its age
was to be found the peculiar value of the *Decameron* as a
work of poetry.[11] Of course we might object that, although this
is true of any great work of art, our appreciation of this 'tran-

scending' is made possible and eventually heightened by our
acquaintance with the culture from which the particular work
grew and ultimately detached itself as an *unicum.*

In particular, under the powerful influence of Croce, Italian
criticism has been concerned with the identification of the
center of inspiration of the *Decameron,* its aesthetic 'unity' to
be defined with a philosophical formula; but the *Decameron*
has come out of this most earnest and worthwhile methodo-
logical effort as one of the least 'definable' works of art, somewhat alike, in this, to the *Divine Comedy.*[12] The various
formulas proposed centered on the ideas of love or intelligence or both. Umberto Bosco first proposed the theme of 'intelligence.'[13] In the wake of this tentative solution Giuseppe
Petronio has claimed to have tackled the problem with the most
systematic awareness, and solved it by redefining this 'intelligence' or rather *saviezza* ('wisdom') in terms of 'generic
sympathy for intelligence.'[14] The reaction to De Sanctis' position was carried further by Mario Bonfantini, who did not
hesitate to assign to Boccaccio "the attitude of a moralist."[15]
This bold, almost revolutionary statement has enjoyed some
success, as witnessed in an essay of Salvatore Battaglia,[16] but,
aside from the fact that here Bonfantini probably used the
word 'moralist' in its French literary acceptation, I find it acceptable only if the message that Boccaccio is supposed to
have preached was that of naturalism and no other.

Natalino Sapegno has broadened the quest of the unifying
element from the single work to all of the author's production,
and has consequently claimed that 'realism' is the fundamental
aspect of Boccaccio's personality, the "only constant element"
of his work being his "realistic disposition." This despite the
fact that throughout his literary career one finds a running
struggle between this realistic tendency and the need for an
academic, 'literary,' abstract aloofness.[17] More specifically, this
realism becomes in the *Decameron* what I call naturalism: "If
one wants to fathom Boccaccio's true importance, one must
be able to sense . . . the human leaven which makes his work

ferment and rise: the warm and serene affirmation of the rights of our instincts and passions [affermazione dei diritti degli istinti e delle passioni]."[18]

Guido Di Pino has focused the attention on the 'polemic' implicit in the *Decameron* and made explicit in the Proem to the Fourth Day, but resolved as a living poetic motif in the development of the stories.

> The polemical context of the *Decameron* develops along two main directions consisting of the theme of love and the theme of intelligence. . . . Love in the characters of the stories is always a proclamation of freedom: freedom against the conventions of a conservative and revengeful society as well as against any inhumane acceptation of sin.[19]

Di Pino describes Boccaccio's artistic parable as a movement away from the literary "fable" of the Middle Ages toward the historically conditioned, contemporaneous reality which triumphs in the *Decameron*.[20]

Ultimately Vittore Branca has concluded the parable of the reaction to De Sanctis by stressing the medieval heritage in all of Boccaccio's career, so that he reclaims in the *Decameron* the keen responses to the deep and wide suggestions of traditional *courtoisie*, until the masterpiece, couched as it is in medieval stylistic rhythms and ringing with echoes of a businessman's society ("the epic of the Italian merchant") is all but bodily subtracted from the area of the Renaissance.[21]

More recently Mario Marti has newly tried to focus the realistic orientation of the masterpiece: "The original and essential unity of the Decameron, its *soul* is to be perceived, in my opinion, in the author's constant, continued, unwavering attention to the very manifestation, viewed *per se*, of the reality of man and of nature."[22] Indeed of the reality, as I should rather put it, of nature, and of man within its framework.

In conclusion, it might seem as though the pendulum were, after a wide oscillation, swinging back to De Sanctis: the painstaking reassessment of his views has led the critics, perhaps not without a certain embarrassment, back to statements which have a familiar ring. But even though some critics tend to overdo their disapproval of De Sanctis, they are basically right in stressing the novelty of their approach. In fact, the realism they now attribute to Boccaccio no longer implies a sudden, unexpected, and rather puzzling revolution against the culture and spirituality of the Middle Ages, but moves within the horizon of a medieval realistic tradition (in the treatment of the human subject matter as well as in poetic theory), although one feels compelled to note that its impetus is more direct than ever before in medieval times, and carries with it farther-reaching implications.[23]

THE NOVELLA

Let us now take our own look at the masterpiece. The first question about a book concerns its form, and the *Decameron* is, in form, an unusually systematic collection of novellas. A good deal of realistic literature had developed in the Middle Ages within the framework of the short story, from the Latin forms (variously called *exemplum, parabula, fabula, historia, legenda*), to the French *contes* and *fabliaux* (*fablel, fableau*) and the Italian *novella* (*conto*). Of the literature that lies at the formal origin of the *Decameron* one must distinguish two types: firstly, the parable or tale with a moral (*conte à queue*, as the French used to call it), closest to the ecclesiastical milieu, frequently used by priests in sermons; such paradigmatic stories could occasionally be gathered into allegedly edifying collections, with a general ethical or satirical purpose, such as the *Disciplina clericalis* and the *Novel of the Seven Sages* in the various languages. Secondly, the fabliau or *conte à rire*, pure divertissement without serious afterthought. A number of items of the first type derived from the Orient, a few from classical literature (for instance, from Aesop, from the ancient comedy and novel). What Boccaccio did to all this production was to treat the first type in the spirit of the second, and invest the second with the paradigmatic,

'symbolic' value of the first. In addition, the idea of a systematic collection produced with him for the first time a truly
homogeneous and balanced ensemble.

At the outset, this imaginative representation of everyday
experiences, in a spirit of close, keen observation of human
nature, had explicitly shown a transcendent purpose, quite
akin to the moralistic raison d'être of the Indian narrative (regardless of the extent to which we are prepared to accept the
derivation of the European novellas from Indian sources).[24]
The 'naturalism' of the Indian story, as well as of the early
medieval European novella, is only one of method: in sharp
contrast with the first appearance, inspiration and purpose lie
in the ascetic refusal of worldly existence, whose basically evil
nature is unmasked by the substance of the realistic incidents
related by the narrator, amusing as such incidents are on the
surface, ridiculous and disgusting in the last analysis.[25] But
from this beginning the novella genre gradually evolved toward
an expression of immanent wisdom: the acceptance of reality
as is. When we think, in later times, of what the genre was to
become in the hands of a La Fontaine, we clearly realize how
thoroughly the cycle of this metamorphosis has been consummated. Most typical of the general process had been the
novellas dealing with sexual adventures; the unmistakably
misogenous aim of the Indian storytellers was obvious in the
exemplary treatment of lascivious aberrations intended to
show the inner vulgarity of a life dominated by the senses, in
a chaos of contradictions breaking all social and moral rules,
at the mercy of the insatiable, basely corrupt instincts of
womankind.[26]

Prompted by a deeply pessimistic view of human nature,
the ascetic-minded male had preferred to close his eyes to the
impenetrable and unavoidable evils brought by womanhood
into our lives. As Saint Bernard warned, "De feminis tuis sus-
pectis quid agant ignorantiam queras. Postquam sciveris crimen
male uxoris a nullo medico curaberis." "Should you have reason
to suspect your women, you had better profess ignorance of
their doings. No physician could cure you once you found out
the mischiefs of a bad wife."[27]

In fact, the medieval consciousness constantly swings like a pendulum between two opposed yet complementary views of womanhood: the religious-monastic (woman is sin, crime, error, folly, wickedness, in brief, the eternal Pandora) and the courtly (woman is the embodiment of all the best in life and the world). The one is the result of a realistic approach, the other of an idealistic one, but they are in actuality both abstractions, or, to put it differently, the realism of the former view is the way of looking at reality of one who searches for an ideal perfection irreconcilable with any given reality; while the 'idealism' of the latter view is the hypostasis of a good that one recognizes in reality but projects upon a screen of perfection without which that limited good would not seem satisfactory. Boccaccio's naturalism is, in its coherence, something different and new. He takes reality and woman as they are, in all their polyvalence. His women characters are both, and even simultaneously, interested and disinterested, loving in order to give and loving in order to take, safe and dangerous, self-centered and generous, in brief 'good' and 'bad.' They are *real* according to *nature,* not to a superimposed schema of man-made, mentally construed and idolized, supraworldly, suprahuman, and supranatural perfection. From them can come happiness, as for Federigo, or extreme suffering, as for the scholar, for they can behave, according to the situation, like Monna Giovanna or like the widow respectively. They are not all of one mold, and the same woman may vary according to circumstances. The absolutism of the Middle Ages, both in the positive and in the negative direction, is gone. Man is finally able to face the play of natural instincts and take them for what they are.

The two viewpoints could be occasionally found side by side in medieval literature: witness, above all, Jean de Meung's noted antifeminism at the same time that he was completing a poem-treatise on courtly procedure wherein the pursuit and conquest of the beloved lady was the way of all happiness. But in Jean the two attitudes are essentially juxtaposed, in a singularly medieval texture of unwitting and partly unconscious contradiction.[28] In the *Decameron* this juxtaposition gives way to harmonious and organic fusion. To be sure, we must not forget that the *Decameron* represents a unique moment of equilibrium in Boccaccio's career, standing as it does at an ideal middlepoint between the early attempts to follow the lead of the *stilnovisti* and the outburst of rampant misogyny in the *Corbaccio*.

Medieval naturalism is ordinarily disorganic; at times we encounter it, not without surprise, side by side with opposite elements, like the concern for the "figural," allegorical value of the event, or those sudden, arbitrary flights of fantasy so typical of the medieval mind but so charmingly conflicting with the occasional, though intense observation of reality. By contrast, the 'organic' coherence of the *Decameron* (not all of Boccaccio's fiction!) deserves to be emphatically stated, especially as it seems to extend to all aspects of the work. And even in the style the organic concentration of all traditional rhetorical devices contrasts with the typically 'centrifugal' construction of medieval prose, where the general impression is one of division, 'segmentation,' articulation into constitutive elements.[29] This distinctive characteristic appears to have escaped V. Branca in his investigation of the medieval foundations of Boccaccio's work. And I should not hesitate to maintain that this 'organic composition' is as typical of Italy's Renaissance literature as it is of its Renaissance art, in contrast with the Northern art (including Flemish fifteenth-century painting).

But to get to the more obvious center of Boccaccio's naturalism one has to start from his conception and treatment of love. And as a preliminary to a close discussion of such questions, we must go briefly over the basic developments of the early Italian love literature.

FROM THE 'SWEET NEW STYLE' TO THE DECAMERON

When, around the middle of the thirteenth century, the Italian vernacular began to emancipate itself from Latin to generate a new literature, the chief attitudes of

French culture (the hegemonic culture of the time in Europe) were being rapidly assimilated. But the various forms which can be subsumed under the general category of *courtois* literature never appeared in Italy without profound modification. The treatment of love, all in all the paramount literary motif in early Italian letters, was conditioned by a situation which we can simplify as follows.

Throughout Western and Central Europe the tradition of the Schoolmen had impressed in medieval consciences a typical Christian concept and corresponding sentiment, namely that of "charity," a cosmic bond between the Creator and His creatures, on the one hand, and among the creatures themselves, on the other. This was the true, sublime, and virtuous love for the Christian. Sensual love tended to be regarded as the prototype of sin, and was looked upon with suspicion even as a legitimate marital bond: marriage was the sanctification of sex in the face of its social function for the perpetuation of the species, but beyond this practical goal sensuality as such and its sheer gratification remained condemnable.

Accordingly, the society of the courts, as we have seen, had in the wake of the Provençal poets developed a spiritual, "Neoplatonic" cult for the lady of exception, under the name of *fin amors;* this sublimated attitude, whether literarily fictitious or actually practiced, was essentially suprasensuous, noncarnal. But the same school also admitted an intermediate form between this *fin amors* and *fol amors, amor purus* and *amor impurus.* Capellanus called it *amor mixtus,* and it was disguisedly or quite overtly fleshly, and programmatically exempt from the conventional, social and moral sanction of marriage.

With all the debts he owed to his French models and their Italian imitators from Sicily and Tuscany, Guido Guinizelli (ca. 1240–ca. 1276), the founder of the *Dolce Stil Nuovo,* marked a turning point of far-reaching consequences in love lyricism. He laid the foundation of a metaphysical-minded school of poetry in which the lady, viewed as an angelic being (*la donna angelicata*), was the path to the knowledge and enjoyment of God through one of His creatures. The role of the

sexes was therefore conceived as a necessary stage in the ascent from the world of the natural to the world of the supernatural, thus bridging the gap between philosophers and
poets, the Church and the pagan Court.[30] Guido Cavalcanti
(ca. 1255–1300) represents a moment of hesitation in his resistance to this process of abstraction of a sentiment into a concept. His love is human and worldly, clearly sensual, recognizes no duties toward any other human faculty and makes no
concession to supernatural causes.

Dante, on the other hand, chose to follow Guinizelli's lead,
and actually theologized his metaphysics. Dante's Beatrice
was more than an angel, she was Grace itself, while his Francesca da Rimini, a feminine embodiment of earthly love as
conceived by the courtly tradition, was unequivocally rele-
gated to her place in hell, all human sympathy notwithstanding. The way was thus being prepared, by long hand, for sub-
sequent developments. At last the Florentine Platonic Academy firmly ensconced the lady in the system of Platonic love,
made of intelligences and souls, cosmic derivations and in-
fluxes; this comprehensive experience was conceived as evolv-
ing through the three stages of the sensual, the fantastic, the
abstract, according to a process fundamentally intellectual.
'Sentiment,' that had been discovered, as one could say, in
eleventh-century Provence, thus ended by being again chased
into the background, at least in Italy.

Dante's extreme effort in the sublimation of love, and Cavalcanti's renunciation of the Sweet New Style's attempt to reconcile the medieval need for spiritualism with the newly discovered value of the erotic sentiment, both stemmed from the
basic problem of courtly love: the secret realization of the
conflict between the supernatural and the natural, of a gap
between the postulates of reason and those of the senses, between the order of reason and the chaos of passions.

We have seen (Chapter I, note 2) how, within the frame of
reference of the ancient Alexandrian and Pergamenian
schools, 'nature' could be differently assumed to conjure up,
respectively, a fundamentally rational orderliness of things

(under the category of analogy) or the irrationality thereof
(category of anomaly). In the Middle Ages the concept of nature could vaguely imply the recognition of a realm of reality
on which rationalization could be artificially superimposed by
human will without altering its profound irrationality. Given
his view of things, it may appear to us that the medieval man
was in this respect attempting the impossible—somewhat the
reverse of Terence's witty hypothesis of a person wanting to
go mad in a planned way, that is, to be reasonable in love:
". . . haec si tu postules / Ratione certa facere, nihilo plus agas /
Quam si des operam ut cum ratione insanias." (*Eunuchus*,
I, I, 16.) Love belonged to this realm. How could one be truly
in love, and still be rational about it? The orthodox medieval
mind had been utterly unable to explain and control this most
important phenomenon without either raising it to a purely
spiritual, essentially intellectual experience (divine charity), or
reducing it to the unromantic, practical contract of marriage
as a social and biological act. On the other hand, no serious
attempt was possible to justify on a rational basis the heterodox theory and practice of courtly love in its pure form (romantic and openly adulterous), although it had given origin
to the best medieval lyricism. The sensible Chrétien de Troyes
appeared to feel guilty (or at least uneasy) about his *Lancelot,*
and implicitly tried to place the blame on the patroness who
had commissioned it.

   Boccaccio courageously grabbed the bull by the horns, and,
speaking through Fiammetta, started by defining love as an irrational, fateful force (*Filocolo*, Book IV, 7th Question). Fiammetta
had then concluded that love was to be avoided as an evil, whereas Galeone (presumably Boccaccio's mouthpiece) had limited
himself to contradicting that conclusion implicitly.[31] Later, in the
Decameron (X, 7) the humble Lisa will justify to the king the
absurdity of her having fallen in love with him by stating that
not by guarded choice do we fall in love, but according to our
appetite and instinct ("niun secondo debita elezione ci s'innamora
ma secondo l'appetito ed il piacere").

   This sort of irrationalistic definition of love was traditionally

allied to Aristotle's terminology, a source from which is derived both in Cavalcanti's 'canzone' *Donna me prega* and in
the *Filocolo* (11th Question), as well as, later, in Leo Hebraeus'
Dialoghi d'Amore, the axiom of sight as the starting point of
the amorous experience (the eye is the window through which
beauty enters the soul and kindles its desire for union with
the beautiful object).[32] The threefold Aristotelian distinction
of "amore dilettevole, utile e onesto" is also found in the
Filocolo (p. 340) as well as in the *Dialoghi d'Amore.* But it is
only the first that interests Boccaccio, for practical usefulness
and moral or spiritual honesty are, for him, outside the proper
sphere of true love.

THE ILLNESS CALLED LOVE

There is an area of medieval culture in which philosophy, literature, and medicine are intimately intertwined.
Official doctrine and science (specifically, medicine) agreed in
condemning love as a sort of disease or madness. Indeed,
Plato had spoken of love as a form of madness or excess of
affectus, μανία, but he had distinguished a bad from a good
μανία: the former is truly a disease, νόσημα (Lat. *aegritudo*),
while the latter is a God-inspired frenzy which does not hinder, but helps philosophical speculation. One kind of this μανία
he attributed to Venus and Eros as 'erotic mania,' and of such
love furor which fosters our *beatitudo* rather than preventing
it he treated in his *Phaedrus* (XXII, 244A f., XLVIII, 265A-B),
followed by a long tradition from Plotinus to Leo Hebraeus
and Giordano Bruno.[33] Of course, physicians were concerned
with the love-*aegritudo,* a deviation of the faculty of imagination (*imaginativa*) overriding reason by the stimulus of the
senses. Halyabbas (Alì ibn el 'Abbâs, d. 994) showed the physical effects and symptoms of the illness in a famous description
of the lover that was paraphrased by Avicenna. Halyabbas
and Avicenna as well as the Catalan Arnaldus suggested the
classical remedy already advocated by Lucretius: to divert
love by offering a physical outlet in lower pleasures, merce-

nary or other.[34] In other words, medicine agreed in regarding sex as normality, passion as illness. Not the animal instinct or appetite was considered the enemy, but the psychic super-structure built on it by the imagination. Matter was healthier than the spirit.

In desperate cases, doctors were even advised to favor the meeting of the lover with the object of his passion, for this would end his infatuation and cure him.[35] The obvious danger of incurring inflexible moral censure was lightly disposed of by formally recommending a restriction of these methods "within the legal and ecclesiastical rules" ("secundum modum permissionis fidei et legis")—which was obviously no more than a verbal palliative, since no such rules would admit of the sort of rendezvous that might cure an 'infatuation.'

This 'scientific' naïveté of curing the lover by pandering for him is, after all, not too surprising (though Boccaccio, himself no physician, simply by his psychological intuition could have easily perceived the alleged 'remedy' of intercourse as perhaps the most assured way to strengthen and perpetuate the disease). But aside from this, it will be even less surprising to find the same conception of passion in poets who spent their whole literary career in singing the praises of this frightful 'disease.' The most pessimistic, even tragic note, was struck, in Italy, by Guido Cavalcanti, the best poet before Dante, who also stated his doctrine of love by "natural dimostra-mento" in the obscure and much-discussed 'canzone' *Donna me prega*.[36] Here the erotic love of the courtly poets, sensual and 'fantastic,' was defined as passion issuing from the sensitive faculty, not the rational, causing an inevitable deviation of the judgment, feeding on the natural instincts but beyond the natural boundaries and the natural sense of measure. The fire of the senses is sparked by the ideal and fantastic elaboration the object of desire undergoes in the intellect of the lover. It is a physical phenomenon, but it feeds on the imagination. Its very excess (the angry Mars within us) guarantees its short duration, without hope of gaining any degree of wisdom by its experience. Because of opposition from the rational faculty, and because of the jeopardy in which it places the delicate and unstable balance of the faculties, the erotic experience is bound to end in unhappiness when not in tragedy. No obstacles can stop it, they can only make it all the more deadly if they are insurmountable.[37] We are here confronted with a sharp dualism: the poet knows that there is no salvation outside the rational good and the control of reason over our passions ("Ma quanto che da buon perfetto tort'è / Per sorte, non pò dire om ch'aggia vita, / Ché stabilita non ha segnoria"), yet he sees love as an irrational but natural, hence irrevocable movement ("non perché oppost'a naturale sia").

Another poet of the same school, Lapo Gianni, concluded his 'canzone' *Amor, nova ed antica vanitade* by sadly dismissing love as a mishap which darkens the mind and sickens the body.[38] Some aspects of this 'doctrine' will be echoed as late as in Leo Hebraeus' *Dialoghi d'Amore* in the full bloom of the Renaissance, but certain particular motifs found an effective restatement in the philosophical naturalism of the *Quaestio disputata de felicitate* by Jacopo da Pistoia.[39] In this Aristotelian treatise with Averroistic overtones, the problem of sensuality is treated with apparent reference to Cavalcanti. First Jacopo admits that passions are the most natural result of inborn inclinations. Yet they are said to conflict with the balance of the faculties, since they are caused by a disproportioned development of the organs of the fantasy or imagination, thus hindering the operation of understanding. The conclusion is, not unexpectedly, that in order to attain the contemplation of the supreme intellectual objects, man will have to stifle the venereal passions, or at least regulate their process.[40]

This relative parallelism between medical and literary language as well as basic attitudes extends, in the *Decameron*, beyond the specific treatment of love. We need read no further than the famous Introduction to be confronted with a first impressive case of general import.

The presence side by side of realism and flight from reality is notoriously characteristic of the 'primitive' psychology of the medieval man. But, in spite of our first impression, we must conclude that the striking contrast contained in the introduction to the *Decameron* is not really part of this dualistic attitude. The transition from the terrifying spectacle of the plague to the idyllic withdrawal for a lofty enjoyment of the best things of life sounds to us like an implicit, though conscious, reaction against a then current inference: namely that the evils of earthly existence should teach us that the world of nature is nothing but a valley of tears, and must be rejected or at least transcended for something radically different and superior. If, as L. Di Francia suggested, Jacopo Passavanti's stern warnings from the pulpit of Santa Maria Novella were occasioned by the Black Death of 1348, the striking contrast between the friar's and Boccaccio's lessons derived from that same experience is most enlightening.[41] But even more characteristic is Boccaccio's specific agreement with the instructions of the famous physician Tommaso del Garbo—an agreement which appears to seal a sort of alliance between the author's pre-Renaissance mentality and the naturalistic orientation of Tommaso's science.[42] Consider the baseness of our existence, let this ever-present spectacle of death lead you to forsake the lust and greed of earthly pleasures, says the eloquent preacher. Forget the death that surrounds you, do not let it contaminate your mind and body, flee all this sadness and give yourselves to gay entertainments and pleasant company, says the doctor. But, just as Boccaccio does, he adds the warning to do this with the measured restraint of good taste, orderliness, and moderation. Thus will health be preserved, in keeping with the remedy prescribed by science. Death is, accordingly, courageously challenged by Boccaccio's *brigata*, and toward the end of this adventurous vacation the author will have to exclaim, evidently pleased with his characters' performance, "Either they will not be vanquished by death, or they will meet it in a gay mood!" ("O costor non saranno dalla morte vinti o ella li ucciderà lieti." Introduction to the Ninth Day, as the party comes back in high spirits from country-outing at dawn.)

Humanism will speak in similar terms through L. B. Alberti's warnings not to endanger the life of a living man by the hopeless attempt to cure a dying one, no matter how dear to us.[43] The modern sensitivity, whereby we feel compelled to share the misfortunes of our fellow-humans and try to help them at any price, could not find room at times when the reasonable remedies in common disasters were so much more limited and risky.

The place itself chosen by the youthful *brigata* for their salvation—and for the very setting of the *Decameron*—must retain our attention briefly for another important consideration as to its specific function. The *villa* in the countryside was a middlepoint between sophisticated city life and the pastoral simplicity of the peasant's world. The peculiar way of life of Boccaccio's *brigata* during their retirement in the *villa* may appear to the present-day reader as a curious transposition of extraordinary rational discipline to a place where the senses and the imagination might be expected to have free play. We must, then, remember that in the Middle Ages the *villa*, the *locus amoenus*, or the garden are, indeed, an occasion for escape from the closed life of the walled city or the fortress-like house, but without quite plunging into the perturbing disorderliness, the 'wildness' of open nature. Places of this kind represent a compromise, a fusion of elements of city and wilderness, symbolical of a harmony between reason and the forces of the subconscious. A fitting climate, then, for naturalism as revaluation of instinctive life in a rational framework; or (to be more precise, if we deal with the *Decameron* in particular) an appropriate introduction for a gentle opening of the mind—without a direct, sudden, and drastic exposure— to those subterranean phenomena of life, those forces of matter and of the unconscious, which, in their full bloom, could but frighten and repel the medieval mind.[44] Besides, one ought not overlook the medieval fondness of enclosed gardens as allegorical settings wherein to stage the exclusive, aristocratic scene for actions of courtly love. To this effect the enclosed garden has been regarded as a symbolic place of refuge from the morality of the church. The Introduction to the Third Day, in fact, presents us with an enclosed garden, a true model of an Italian medieval garden retreat. It provides an illusion of nature with the security of privacy and, above all, the reassuring, urbane quality of the "bello ordine" which graces its design. Similarly, the "Valley of the Women" (Conclusion of the Sixth Day), a typical *locus amoenus,* is described as a place which looked like a work of nature, though it was artificially landscaped ("quantunque artificio della natura e non manual paresse," Branca II, 190). Although they are often built on suggestions from the literature of Provence or of the *Dolce Stil Nuovo* (for example, Dante's Earthly Paradise), Bosco has confirmed previous judgments to the effect that Boccaccio's landscapes are the first humanistic landscapes.[45] On the other hand, Grabher has indicated an interesting (though somewhat meager and vague) rapport of such landscapes with Capellanus' descriptions, whose lesson for Boccaccio would lie in a stylized vision and syntax.[46]

LOVE AND INTELLIGENCE

For an ideal relationship with Boccaccio's outlook it is worthwhile to recall two famous *contes.* First the tale of *Richeut* (ca. 1170), the earliest medieval example of *astuce* in action, where a courtesan teaches her son Samson the arts that will later enable him to emulate his mother for success in life. But we may be even more interested in the *Lai d'Aristote,* a fascinating tale justly popular at its time (as witnessed by a medallion on the portal of Lyon's cathedral).

In the type of literature to which these little masterpieces belong one can witness the flashing forth of certain motifs that were destined to find their full development in the art of the Italian Renaissance. Such was the motif of the triumph of intelligence in the form of cunning, as expressed in the vast fabliau literature of practical jokes. It appeared to revindicate the rights of the bourgeois view of life against the pseudo-aristocratic view that was still officially prevalent. From the

Decameron (rightly though not exhaustively defined by some critics as a 'Hymn to Intelligence,' as we have seen) through the anonymous *Grasso legnaiuolo* and Pulci's *Morgante* to Folengo's *Baldus* and the sixteenth-century novellas, this motif found a fertile ground in Italy. Of Boccaccio's novellas of jests I will have something to say later. The masterpiece of the *genre* is perhaps the fifteenth-century tale of the *Fat Ebony Carver* (*Il Grasso Legnaiuolo,* translated by Th. Roscoe). One finds in this literature, as it developed in Italy, an aspect of the attack of the new bourgeois spirit on the medieval sense of excellence as a kind of valor that could ultimately be reduced to mere physical force. This *reductio ad absurdum* of the chivalric ideal appeared in Pulci's genial introduction of the pair of the giant Morgante and the anti-hero Margutte into the Carolingian epic, with all the impact of parody, semiconscious as it may have been. The knight had been the medieval hero, whose image stood for everything that was right and good. If, then, the poet seems to imply, you have to be strong to be a hero, the giant has the best chance to qualify. Hence the sympathetic but humorous introduction of Morgante. But Margutte rejects that ethics altogether. He lives by one value only, his cleverness; he confides only in the power of his brain, and otherwise he is a confessed coward who boasts of all his negative qualities.[47] We cannot help but recognize in Margutte the transfigured embodiment of the chief values and modes of life of the new class, the *mercatanti.* The introduction of this new 'myth,' packed with so much symbolic significance, into the chivalric genre, the popular medieval genre *par excellence,* was a far-reaching development. But the motif of *ingegno* (even as pure cleverness, so uncompromisingly condemned by Dante through the *figurae* of Guido da Montefeltro and Ulysses) having the power, therefore the right to prevail against any other value, as a natural force inevitably destined to triumph beyond good and evil, had already brilliantly stated its case in the *Decameron* and, even earlier, in the French fabliaux (for example, in *Les trois aveugles de Compiègne* and much of the *Roman de*

Renart). Furthermore, both in the *Decameron* and, to a lesser degree, in some fabliaux, human ingenuity had found a godly master to serve with exultant readiness: love. In the realm of the fabliau, Henri d'Andeli's *Lai d'Aristote* may well be the masterpiece of this theme allying intelligence and love. The young Alexander (the 'Great') has taken a fancy to a bewitching girl, but Aristotle's stern warnings make him hesitate. Then, to rid herself and her target of the importunate old master, the girl sets a trap into which Aristotle most gladly falls. As the amazed Alexander watches his tutor play horse and horse rider on the grass with the girl happily riding on his back, the dreaded influence of the austere philosopher has instantly vanished, and Aristotle himself is all the wiser by the good lesson he has learned. The sympathy of author and readers goes without the least hesitation to the charming, carefree wench who puts Philosophy in person to shame in order to free Alexander, her target, and thereby proclaim the rightful triumph of nature.[48] This is the sort of love that the *Decameron* tirelessly sets before us: direct, unhesitating, charmingly youthful, and amorally determined to win its case with all means, specifically *ingegno*. The *Dolce Stil Nuovo* had preached that love reveals true nobility, and, at best, makes us noble by developing our hidden, dormant virtues. Boccaccio's love even makes his characters *ingegnosi,* and the intelligence thus developed has one supreme goal: the satisfaction of the sensual instinct, a right of nature.

More than just 'naïve,' spontaneous, natural, Boccaccio's love is 'naturalistic' inasmuch as it is an urge that engages the whole human being, body and soul, muscles and mind, senses, will, and intellect, all at the service of natural desires. In two of those inspired essays that could perhaps only be written in the atmosphere of the Romantic movement, Heinrich Heine analyzed the genesis of medieval civilization in terms of a spiritualistic revolution against the materialistic naturalism into which the pagan world had fallen. But this Christian culture, that had found its roots in the Platonic, Gnostic, and Manichaean distinctions and oppositions of body and soul, the material and the spiritual, went to the other extreme of mortifying nature and the flesh for the sake of the supernatural and the purely mental, the real for the sake of the ideal (see *Die Romantische Schule,* 1836, and *Religion und Philosophie in Deutschland,* 2d ed., 1852). One of the assets of the Renaissance was the reëstablishment of an equilibrium between the body and the soul, thus restoring the harmony that characterized the days of the best flowering of classical art.

In the movement toward this goal the *Decameron* sounded like the battle cry against the excesses of the Middle Ages. If the majority of its stories seem to go overboard in underscoring the newly realized rights of the senses, this is not simply due to the characteristics of the genre, the low-style comedy that had claimed such privileges from Aristophanes and Plautus through the rich tradition of the fabliaux; the *Decameron* is, indeed, a conscious revolt against prevailing standards, as the Proem to the Fourth Day will show. Nor could the 'balance' be restored without temporarily going overboard in the opposite direction. Briefly, the excesses of spiritualism had to be corrected by an outburst of naturalism.

LOVE, NOBILITY, AND SOCIAL PREJUDICE

The new gospel of love as a supreme force and law of nature places it above every social convention. De Sanctis had appropriately pointed out the peculiar moral and social orientation of the *Decameron:* "Nature, that in Dante's world had meant sin, has now become law, and its enemy is society as ordered in that complex of conventions called 'honor.' "[49]

For De Sanctis Boccaccio had no serious intentions to reform the mores, his 'laughter' was to be kept distinct from the 'comic' of Rabelais and Montaigne, which expressed their reaction to an artificial and conventional world.[50] The truth of the matter is, rather, that the *Decameron* is, to use Croce's famous distinction, a work of 'poetry' not 'oratory.' Yet, all filtered and purified as it is into the lofty lyricism of his tales, there remains in Boccaccio's naturalism a basic attitude of reaction against society and its prejudices.

Boccaccio was not completely insensitive to social distinctions, although he holds his honorable place in that Italian
tradition which, from the *Dolce Stil Nuovo* and Dante (*Convivio,* IV) to the humanists (as in Buonaccorso da Montemagno's *Disputatio de Nobilitate*) so effectively criticized the
medieval concept of aristocracy and defined true nobility not
in terms of birth and blood but by identifying it with moral
and intellectual virtue, whose highest test lies in the capability
of loving. Indeed in one form or another the criticism of nobility can be traced back to antiquity, and in some literary
schools it had been a regular *topos,* sometimes allied to the
theme of avarice or corrupt wealth.[51] As we have seen, even
in the aristocratic climate of Provençal poetry both social station and wealth were deemed subordinated to sentiment.
Cercalmont had sung the theme that was to become central in
the Italian Sweet New Style: "For a woman has no worth
either by riches or by nobility if she is not inspired by joyous
love."[52] Authorities as differing as Capellanus and the unsenti-
mental Jean de Meung had emphatically concurred on this
point. In the words of the great Suger of Saint-Denis, It is the
heart that makes one noble ("Nobiles efficit animus").

In spite of having been exposed to the environment of the
Neapolitan court, upon his return to Florence Boccaccio took
pride in being the son of a city which "under plebeian law
curbs the wanton pomp of the nobles . . . and thrives in glory
and readiness to greater things, if envy, avarice, and pride will
not hinder her, as some fear."[53]

But even while in Naples, and as early as in his first work
of importance, the *Filocolo,* Boccaccio had Florio argue against
his father for the true nobility of his beloved Biancofiore, on
account of her superior "virtue," and despite her social rank.[54]
And in the *Filostrato* Troiolo thus spoke to Cassandra: "A true
king is he whose worth stands on his virtue, not on his power"
("Re è colui il qual per virtù vale, / Non per potenza" VII, 99).
If sometimes a noble ancestry makes a woman disdainful and
unapproachable, her prospective suitors were warned to be-
ware of such baseness: "O loathe these, youths! Hold them for
mean and vile, / For they are beasts, not gentle ladies free

from guile! / A perfect lady hath more true desire / To be
beloved, and to love doth delight."[55] Indeed, the position of
Capellanus on nobility has been likened to Boccaccio's principle whereby the plebeian may, even must, love a lady of
nobility (see the 'autobiographic' story of the Neapolitan Fiammetta, the *Amorosa Visione*, Idalagos and Galeone in the
Filocolo, the Introduction to the same *Filocolo*).[56]

Boccaccio felt all the fascination exerted by medieval aristocratic literature, but nobility for him was an inner value, not
a simple matter of social station. The story of Ghismunda's
love for Guiscardo, "a man of very humble birth but noble by
virtue and manners," rings with this determination to love
only a person made truly worthy by personal valor.[57] The
heroic woman firmly replies to her irate father: You blame me
"for giving myself to a man of lowly station, and you do not
realize that you so blame not my sin, but that of Fortune, who
far too often raises the unworthy, leaving the most worthy
down below."[58] And she proceeds to state, in terms that remind us of Capellanus' *De Amore*, that all men were created
equal by God ("all flesh comes from the same stock, and one
and the same Creator made all souls and endowed them with
equal faculties, equal powers, equal virtues"), but in the exercise of virtue we distinguish ourselves from one another;
nobility was originally a mark of distinction to sanction this
operative excellence of some of us, and this must remain its
true meaning in spite of its degeneration in the vulgar opinion.[59] This principle is forcefully restated, without reference to
love, in the case of Cisti, a living proof of the fact that "the
two ministers of the universe, Nature and Fortune, often hide
their dearest things in the shadow of the most lowly trades,
so that they will shine more brightly when the opportunity
brings them into the open" (VI, 2).[60]

When other forces come into conflict with love and interfere with its course, Boccaccio takes an unequivocal stand. He
never hides his condemnation of obstacles raised by the families on the account of social differences, as in the case, just
seen, of Ghismunda, or that of Pietro Boccamazza, the scion
of a noble Roman family who elopes with l'Agnolella, a girl of

humble origin (V, 3). In at least one case, however, the conflict is represented with unusual objectivity, as if this particular type of conflict had been especially close to the author's
experience. This occurs in the story of Lisabetta ('the pot of
basil,' IV, 5), where the three merchants with the coldest busi-
ness-like efficiency carry on the suppression of their sister's
lover because they simply cannot afford to weather the threat
represented to their business interests by such a mésalliance.
Love takes its revenge and has the final word with Lisabetta's
dying of heartbreak. Yet, no explicit blame is cast upon the
brothers. It would seem that Boccaccio, a son of bourgeois
and democratic Florence, was more prepared to understand (if
not approve) strong practical, economic considerations such
as those of his merchant friends, than mere social prejudices.

The *tour de force* which crowns the whole book, the story
of the patient Griselda, centered as it is on the typically medieval ideal of the absolute submission of wife to husband, closes
on a significant note: "Even into the households of the poor
the heavens let fall at times spirits divine, as into the royal
ones souls that are fitter to tend hogs than to have lordship
over men."[61] In fact, the author's position is far from unconditional approval of the Marquis' behavior; Dioneo, the storyteller, considers it foolhardy and excessive to the point of in-
humanity ("non cosa magnifica ma una matta bestialità," II,
p. 644).

In spite of the fascination that the courtly literature (all, at
least potentially, aristocratic in character) exerted on him, in
essence Boccaccio can be said not to have made a real distinction between aristocracy and middle class. At times his
merchants, or even his commoners, behave with splendidly
noble manners; but more typically, some of his noblemen are
portrayed in the bourgeois, realistic circumstances of their
everyday existence, with a sympathetic smile for their good
common sense, if they happen to possess any. Lizio di Valbona
and Ricciardo Manardi, for example, in the 'nightingale story,'
behave in delightfully bourgeois fashion, yet they can boast
of a *specchiata nobiltà* sanctioned by no less an authority than

Dante (*Purgatorio*, XIV, 97). Federigo degli Alberighi (V, 9) will have gained an unmedieval wisdom after the splendid excesses that brought him to financial ruin by following the precepts of the aristocratic and courtly tradition. His romantic career terminates with a smile of subtle, sympathetic irony on the part of the author, when he makes allusion to Federigo's having become, at last, a good, economy-minded administrator after the lucky marriage ("miglior massaio fatto"). But Boccaccio always has his arrows ready for the misplaced ambitions of *parvenus* and social climbers. In VII, 8, Arriguccio Berlinghieri "foolishly, as we know by daily experience to be the way of merchants, thought to compass gentility by matrimony."[62] So he did, and dearly did he pay for it—which was well deserved, the author seems to comment between the lines. But his punishment also shows something else: namely, that the nobility into which he has unwisely married can be just as vulgar in manners as the vilest stable hand (II, pp. 269–270).

All in all, Boccaccio shows a basic equanimity in his impartial treatment of social classes. He has not set about elevating one status or humiliating another (as it might seem in III, 3, where a woman "d'alto legnaggio," married to a wealthy wool manufacturer "di bassa condizione," seeks a lover "assai valoroso"). His aim is an aristocracy of the spirit. Socially speaking, we all start equal before love, but our performance in love's service differentiates us by the degree it shows in our inner nobility. Hence certain expressions of scorn for the "gente meccanica," for instance, must be taken not as a social judgment, but with reference to a superior discernment of the authentic values, regardless of social groups. And when an unfaithful wife scorns her husband as socially inferior, we may presume that the real inferiority lies in the inner, individual worth.

At any rate, social distinctions must completely disappear before love, an irresistible force capable of overthrowing any obstacle.[63] "Love's power is so much greater than yours and mine," says Guiscardo to Tancredi, and he states it in a tone that raises the naturalism of this ethic to a heroic level.[64] The loving pair are at the same time heroes and victims of love, and they accept all its consequences without hesitation, with a tragic determinism. Nor is age, in this respect, a legitimate source of authority in Boccaccio's eyes: he finds "the reasons of the elders" ("le ragioni dei vecchi") quite preposterous ("once they are no longer young, they refuse to remind themselves that they have been young").[65] Let us listen to Giannotto, Madonna Beritola's son, justifying his affair with Currado Malespini's daughter as follows: "Currado, . . . if I dealt with her after a fashion which to the mechanic mind seems hardly honorable, I did but commit that fault which is ever congenial to youth . . . and which, if the aged would but remember that they were once young and measure the weaknesses of others by their own . . . would not appear so grave as you and many others would make it."[66] Even religious vows do not hold good against love: the sins of nuns appear monstrous only to the bigots who in their prejudice subvert all the rules of common sense, as if the very obedience of nature were an unnatural crime: "they feel so deeply disturbed, as if a most heinous crime had been committed *against nature.*"[67] Another misconception due to the lack of understanding of nature's ways and forces is that of the many who "blindly believe that, what with the hoe and the spade and coarse fare and hardship, the carnal propensities are utterly eradicated from the tillers of the soil, and therewith all nimbleness of wit and understanding."[68] Another social distinction thus breaks down: the realm of love and nature knows no internal barriers, it is a most 'democratic' one.

The total surrender to the erotic instinct is, generally speaking, the aspect of Boccaccio's world which was more easily grasped and appreciated by the public and by the romantic critics as well (including De Sanctis), to the prejudice of others. Hence recent criticism has tended to overdo the correction in trying to reveal the richness and openness of Boccaccio in other directions. The heart of the matter is, it seems to me, that Boccaccio's naturalism does not necessarily involve cynicism toward the spiritual ideals (*courtois,* epic, or ethical), although his inspiration in the highest spheres of spirituality is often stale and *forcé*—as in the larger portion of the Tenth Day. The structure of the book, dialectically ordered as it is to give a well-integrated picture of reality where every basic attitude finds compensation in its opposite, reveals that the coexistence of opposites is not, for Boccaccio, the absurd contradiction of our existence, but the cosmic balance of the chain of being: dramatic contrast is part of the beauty of the universe, for "more beauty is added to the sight of a flock of white doves by a black raven than by a candid swan."[69]

Women can be as changeable as the wife of Riccardo di Chinzica (II, 10), but also as steady and faithful as Zinevra, wife of Bernabò da Genova (II, 9). Gone is the medieval radicalism whereby the severe intransigence of misogynous condemnation was a natural consequence of having placed the ideal of womanly virtue too high, above and against nature. Boccaccio as the new man is precisely the relativist who can appreciate and defend a woman with all her human frailty and natural needs, even though he is still sensitive to the medieval (*courtois* and religious) abstraction of the Griseldas. This partly explains the author's striking but not quite abrupt about-face in the *Corbaccio* (clearly foreshadowed in the *Decameron,* in the story of the widow and the scholar). Even when the practical behavior of a feminine character appears to remain the same as that which inspired (or was expected to inspire) moral disgust in earlier literature, in the *Decameron* we look at her with different eyes, as we do in Canto XXVIII of the *Orlando Furioso* (the Giocondo story, which shows particularly evident connections with Hindu and Arabic literature).[70] Both here and in the *Decameron* the wayward woman, rather than deserving condemnation for her incorrigible lasciviousness, is to be applauded as a living example of that golden rule, "naturam expelles furca, tamen usque recurret." And the sympathy of authors and public for the spectacle of nature taking its revenge will keep finding its expression

through all of French Classicism, with La Fontaine and
Molière as standard bearers.

FREEDOM OF CHOICE VERSUS THE FETTERS
OF FAMILY AND MARRIAGE

In the curious encounter between the judge, Riccardo di Chinzica, and Paganino da Monaco, the corsair who
kidnaped his wife (II, 10), Boccaccio shows all the genuine,
straightforward freshness of his approach: it was 'natural' for
the young and vigorous corsair to take the pleasure-starved
woman with him and offer her the fun that was due to her age
and sex. Even the husband will, later, implicitly recognize this.
It had been his own fault; he had almost asked for it: "thinking to satisfy a wife by the same resources which served him
in his profession, he sought a beautiful and young woman for
his wife, which he would rather have eschewed, had he been
able to counsel himself as well as he could others."[71] One had
seldom witnessed such an explicit *prise de position* on the part
of a narrator toward his characters. No doubt is left as to
where the reader's own sympathy must be placed. When, after
the kidnaping, the two men come to meet, the judge "soon
assumes a very familiar and friendly air."[72] Then, most courte-
ously ("il più piacevolmente"), he asks for his wife to be returned. No apparent offense or indignation toward the other
man. The corsair warns him: "it would be villainous of you
to want to take her away from me" ("voi fareste villania a
volerlami torre") if she did not freely consent to go back to
him (p. 299). In fact she won't, as Riccardo soon finds out, and
astonished but not really indignant, rather "knowing his folly
to have taken a young wife while he was exhausted," he will
leave, all but acknowledging the 'natural right' of the other
to keep the woman whereof he can take better care.[73] Indeed
a drastic upsetting of the laws of society! The humorous effect
is heightened by the curious introduction of the *courtois* psychology: "villania," "questo gentile uomo in casa cui noi

siamo." After the wife's confession, it is the judge who is humble and understanding. He begs her to come back to him; now that he has seen her "disorderly appetite" "he will constrain himself" to satisfy her ("appetito disordinato," "si sforzerà"). The moral sermon issues not from his, but from the woman's lips: "I rather wish that my parents had been concerned with my honor when they gave me to you."[74] Bartolomea inveighs over the poor husband's head with cruel determination that admits of no reply, so sure is she of her good right, that *diritto del senso* which forbids a beautiful woman "giovine e fresca e gagliarda" to end up in the hands of a "tisicuzzo e tristanzuol" of a bookworm, "out of whom, by squeezing hard, one could never wring one single cupful of sap." The judge, annihilated, returns to Pisa, where "he lapsed into such madness for his grief" ("in tanta mattezza per dolor cadde"), that he died.

After the excesses of romantic exegesis, the critics have justly grown reluctant to admit ideological programs in Boccaccio, and conversely tend to underscore the author's attitude to represent reality for the pure fun of it.[75] Nevertheless, a mere comparison of the extraordinarily lively and eloquent figure of Bartolomea with the relatively cold portrait of Zinevra (Bernabò's virtuous, heroically faithful wife in the preceding story that Dioneo is here trying to slight by telling the story of the corsair) undeniably shows in which direction the artist's heart was more inclined to beat. Furthermore, the ten storytellers underline the author's sympathy with their conclusive comments: "and the young ladies unanimously acknowledged that Dioneo was right, and pronounced Bernabò a blockhead," like all husbands who "imagine that the women they leave behind at home will not suffer their hands to stray from their girdles" while they, the husbands, are having their fun abroad.[76] Boccaccio's mind is open to all experience, including the noble and purest ideals of conventional virtue, but when singing hymns to the freedom of the senses his inspiration waxes incomparably warmer and livelier. Even in a serious story (of a seriousness more elegiac than tragic, as

Bosco pointed out) like that of Ghismunda, we have the frank
confession of the heroine: "I am a creature of flesh and blood,
and still young, and for the one reason and the other doubly
fraught with fleshly appetite."[77]

All this is a psychologically natural reaction within a civilization which, to express it in Montaigne's effective words, had
forgotten that "il n'y a rien en nous, pendant cette prison
terrestre, purement ny corporel ny spirituel, et que injurieuse-
ment nous dessirons [= déchirons] un homme tout vif," that
is, by dividing so sharply and unnaturally the spiritual from
the material.[78] And the reaction was especially in order in a
land where the social situation was such that, to borrow Montaigne's words again:

> Leur coustume [namely, in Italy] donne communement
> la loy si rude aus femmes, et si serve, que la plus es-
> loignée accointance avec l'estranger leur est autant
> capitale que la plus voisine. Cette loy faict que toutes
> les approches se rendent necessairement substantieles;
> et, puis que tout leur revient à mesme compte, elles ont
> le chois bien aysé. Et ont elles brisé ces cloisons, croyez
> qu'elles font feu.[79]

In describing methods of courting, Boccaccio deploys the
widest range of approaches, from the brutally direct one to
the interminable longings of the subtle souls or the trembling
hearts. But, regardless of the method, in the *Decameron* the
love adventure is always sensual, the final aim is almost in-
variably one and the same, and sex is never left out of it—
when, exceptionally, it is not explicitly mentioned, we have no
reason to assume that it is really absent (as in the story
of Federigo degli Alberighi). Neither the 'Gothic,' 'transcendental' love that had flourished for two hundred years before
the *Decameron,* nor the 'Platonic,' 'immanent' but still spiritual
love that rose with Petrarch and ran through all the Renaissance, have any place in this book, varied as it is. We find in
it all sorts of feminine characters (from the *courtois* to the
bourgeois and the popular type), but not one 'Gothic' woman,
no Beatrice, and no Laura.

Love, then, is omnipotent, inspired from heaven (that is, from the stars), all-pleasant if wisely favored, tragic and fatal if antagonized. It extends its rule over all of mankind, from the royal palaces to the humblest huts. Such is the theme of the Fourth Day. The sixth story, in particular, is an idyllic, elegiac commentary on this principle, and its tragic development is, once again, at least partly caused by the social inequality that raises a barrier between the lovers. Andreuola was the daughter of a "gentile uomo," while her lover, Gabriotto, was "uomo di bassa condizione ma di laudevoli costumi pieno" (p. 432), like Lorenzo (IV, 5), Pasquino (IV, 7), and, the following day, Martuccio (V, 2). Public recognition of his worth comes to the dead Gabriotto when "not in the guise of a plebeian but in a lordly fashion . . . he was taken to the burial place on the shoulders of the noblest citizens with the greatest honors."[80] The following novella reproduces a parallel situation but with popular characters and in a colloquial, slightly caricatured tone, as another variation on the same motif in a different key.[81]

Finally, the storyteller of the eighth novella comments on the preceding one by some 'programmatic' remarks:

> Some there are . . . who deem themselves wiser than the rest of the world, and are in fact less so; and by consequence presume to measure their wit against *the nature of things*; which presumption has from time to time been the occasion of most grievous mishaps, whereas nought of good was ever seen to betide thereof.[82]

The warning has a serious tone, and quite categorical: to obstruct the normal course of love is a sin against nature, a terrible sin if the obstacles are created by human intellect (*senno*); it is a double evil to operate against the god of love with that very faculty which of that god should always be a humble servant. Intellect becomes, then, 'false wisdom' ("si credon sapere, e sanno meno"). Of this Neifile, the present storyteller, will give a further example: that of a mother who caused the death of her son, foolishly presuming to work for his good by eradicating from his heart an 'unworthy' passion. Girolamo, the son of "un grandissimo mercatante e ricco" loves Salvestra, the daughter of a tailor. Girolamo's 'unwise' mother deserves a severe judgment, for she ought not to have ignored that "of all the natural forces, that which less than any other brooks to be schooled or thwarted is love. Whose nature is such, that it sooner consumes itself than allowing anyone to stifle it by some device."[83] In other words: not only does it tolerate no interference from reason (*consiglio*), but it will destroy its bearer rather than retreat in the face of a serious impediment. The reference to 'nature,' 'natural,' occurs as a true *Leitmotiv* through this page. And again in the story of Martuccio and Gostanza (V, 2) we shall witness the willful triumph of human affections over and above the established order of things.[84]

No doubt our author would have wholeheartedly applauded Chaucer's eloquent way of expressing such an attitude when, in a story significantly derived from an early work of Boccaccio's (the *Teseida*) he had his Arcite thus proudly speak to Palamon:

> For paramour I loved hire first er thow.
> What wiltow seyen? Thou woost nat yet now
> Wheither she be a womman or goddesse!
> Thyn is affeccioun of hoolynesse,
> And myn is love, as to a creature;
>
> . . . .
>
> Wostow nat wel the olde clerkes sawe,
> That 'who shal yeve a lovere any lawe?'
> Love is a gretter lawe, by my pan,
> Than may be yeve to any erthely man;
> And therfore positif lawe and swich decree
> Is broken al day for love in ech degree.
> A man moot nedes love, maugree his heed.
> He may nat fleen it, thogh he sholde be deed,
> Al be she mayde, or wydwe, or elles wyf.[85]

Chaucer's splendid lines give us in a nutshell—besides the revealing 'naturalistic' protest of loving a woman as such (and passionately, *paramour*), not as an angel or goddess, that is, the bearer or symbol of transcendental values—the statement of faith in the superiority of the *natural* law of love (an irre-

pressible passion) over the conventional *positive* laws of men
and societies, that is, moral and social (specifically including
the chastity of maidens and the honesty of wives).

Concurrently, in Boccaccio's radical subjecting of all human
faculties to the tyrannical, uncompromising rule of love, with
impatient disregard of all constraints, be they individual (*senno*)
or collective (social distinctions and conventions, morality itself), one can sense a certain potential 'anarchism.' By *common*
standards it seems safe to comment that Boccaccio shows a
rare lack of moral discrimination. Even more than in the later
Decameron, this lack appeared overt and 'shocking' in the
Ameto. Here the idea of adultery was all-pervasive, and it was
made more impressive by the biographical references to cases
of real Florentine ladies. Although this was a consequence of
the courtly tradition, the courtly atmosphere was notably at-
tenuated by the naturalistic conditioning of such cases. The
apparent justification for the sexual behavior of the characters
was to be found in the unchallenged law and right of free
choice in love, as dictated by the senses, the sight of beauty,
the expectation of genuine pleasure; and all of this was bound
to prevail against the social ties arranged by practical opportunity. But we are confronted by much more than problems of
sexual behavior. In the *Decameron* Boccaccio's latent anarchism best comes to the fore in the story of Cimone and Efigenia
(V, 1). Boccaccio's conception of values, his outlook on rights
and beauty is so thoroughly naturalistic that all laws and poli-
ties are on the verge of crumbling under the sovereign tyranny
of love, the only law. Cimon is the brute turned into a miracle
of refined civility (even "valorosissimo tra' filosofanti divenne,"
II, p. 10) by the spectacle of the sleeping Iphigenia.[86] The re-
mainder of the story displays an adventurous string of kid-
napings and forced separations, crowned by success as the
lovers are finally united.

We modern readers, fastidious as we have become on the
subject of civil rights and nonviolent, fair play in achieving
individual ends, may feel that, after all, Cimon has not
changed so radically from the big beast he was (*bestione,*

montone, insensato animale) if, to bring about his union with
Iphigenia he sees fit to break a wedding, turn pirate, kidnap,
team up with a governor equally bent on violence as he is,
finally kill and have his loot to keep. But we are obviously too
remote from the 'ways of nature.' Lysimachus, the governor
who has imprisoned Cimon for the kidnaping, faces the same
problem as his prisoner: he also loves a girl who is about to
marry another man. He has, therefore, a constructive tête à
tête with that novel paragon of wisdom and all virtues, Cimon,
and frankly discloses to him his conviction that the gods are
on his, Cimon's, side on account of his unparalleled virtue:
"Essi [gl' iddii] hanno della tua virtù voluta più certa
esperienza."[87] They had better join forces, arm themselves, together assail the double wedding party, take what they want
and kill whoever is in the way. So they do, all too successfully,
and the gods remain with the good governor and the virtuous
Cimon, who have it their way—"and long and blithely thereafter lived they, each well contented with his own wife in his
own land."[88] The author has shown us a sort of Machiavellian-
ism where love replaces the 'reason of state.' Cimon is indeed
for Boccaccio what Caesar Borgia was to the Florentine Sec-
retary.

Without referring specifically and directly to this story,
Emilia's introductory comment to the following one is revealing of the attitude of the *brigata*, hence of Boccaccio: "Meet
and right it is that one should rejoice when events so fall out
that passion meets with its due reward; and as love merits
rather joy than suffering" etc.[89] We have no doubts but that they
all side with Cimon and the governor, since they were true
lovers, and lovers deserve, without any question, success and
happiness. There is not a shadow of moral judgment on the
antisocial means used by the characters in securing love's due
triumph. Consequently, it was only logical that the contemporaries should regard such examples as more dangerous for
morals than the occasional obscenity of the book. For one of
its most evident characteristics, if we choose to turn from
matters of legality to matters of conscience, is the complete

absence of the sense of sin. Boccaccio's heroes even out-
spokenly react against the possibility of remorse for yielding
to our appetites. If a tender-hearted fair lady happened to feel
any hesitation, she only had to remind herself of Tedaldo's
'sermon,' a most methodic, unhesitating attack aimed to dis-
pel the qualms of a lover and undo the work of her con-
fessor.[90]

IV

Morality as Conciliation Between Nature and Society

Nature, my lady, is immoral.
I blush for it, but I cannot help it.
G. B. Shaw, *Man and Superman*

I have used Tedaldo's sermon to illustrate the absence of the sense of sin from the *Decameron,* but I may have been guilty of an injustice. For the reader must recall that there *is* a sense of sin in the book, and Tedaldo's eloquence is there precisely to propagate a religion of which he is priest and apostle. In this religion it is sin, a most grave sin without remission, to be untrue to nature. Boccaccio's position betrays itself in this (artistically) rather preposterous sermon against the mortifying morality preached but not practiced by the monks and in favor of a curious ethics of sexual freedom, the only rule being that of remaining true and loyal to the object of one's passion and, we may add, of observing the time-

honored maxim, "Amor [che] a nullo amato amar perdona."[1]
At the most, "intimacy between man and woman is but a sin
of nature," but being cruel to the one we love and who loves
us is criminal, and "proceeds from wickedness of the mind,"
because we belong body and soul to our beloved.[2]

On this account Arturo Graf accused Boccaccio of sophistry,
for in the tales "it is repeatedly stated that it is a most serious
sin to discontinue a dishonest affair; whereby the concept of
sin is actually turned upside down."[3] Quite so indeed, turned
upside down. Bosco subtly argues against this interpretation,
on the assumption that, differently from such cases as that of
Nastagio, where the author is serious, one cannot always
attribute to the author the specious reasonings of his characters.[4] Of course not. When, as especially here in VIII, 7, and
then again in II, 3, in VII, 3, and finally in X, 8, the rationalization of the erotic instincts seems captious and sophistic to
the readers, it is only fair to recognize that the writer intended
it to be so, as a demonstration of the principle that we are not
guided by our reason, but use it to justify the desires of our
senses and of the heart.

Evidently, in no civilization can a naturalistic view of life
ever be thorough and fully consistent. Although nature can
well be self-sufficient and find its physical and animal balance,
when seen from the vantage point of a civilized state the perspective of a life entrusted to the unfettered play of the instincts, that is a true 'return to nature,' cannot but frighten us
as a blind leap into chaos. Compromises with the 'conventions'
of artificial organization are, then, inevitable, since nature
(conceived as the mere obedience to primeval instincts) and
society (the artificial order brought about by custom and
'reason') are distinct and partly opposed realities. The compromise betrays its actual latitude precisely in the reservations
with which the naturalistic *forma mentis* limits its acceptance
of social (especially moral) values. The greater these reservations, the purer the faith in nature remains. As moral values
are accepted more and more unconditionally, nature is left
further and further behind.

Love, Nature, and the Poet
From the MS *Oeuvres* of Guillaume de Machaut (ca. 1370)

Garden of Love
From the MS *Les Echecs Amoureux* (ca. 1500)

Cimon and Ephigenia
Miniature, late fifteenth century

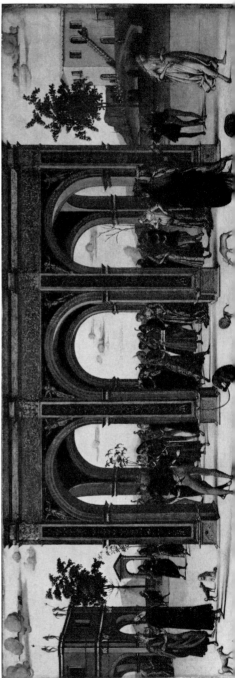

Master of the Story of Griselda, *The Story of Patient Griselda* (ca. 1500)

First page of the *Decameron*, 1492 edition

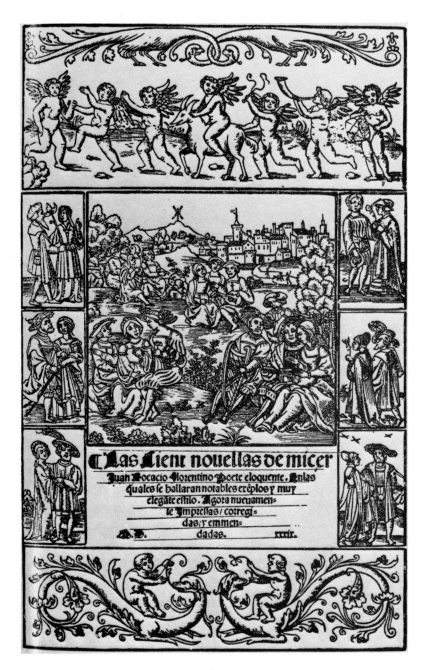

Frontispiece of Spanish translation of the *Decameron*, 1539

Meister der Liebesgärten, *Garden of Love* (ca. 1450)

Now Boccaccio's concepts of honesty, virtue, wisdom (*onestà, virtù, saviezza, senno,* and so on) are delimited and defined by his idea of 'discretion'; *onestà* tempered by *discrezione* results in operative wisdom (*senno*), an inward virtuous habit allied with an outward decorous personality.[5] As Boccaccio's 'virtue' reminds us of Machiavelli's concept and term, his 'discretion' might remind us of Guicciardini's.

It seems to me that greater attention should be paid to Boccaccio's moral terminology, for it would appear that he is at times surprisingly close to the language and semantics of later authors who are usually, and justly, admired as important innovators. For example, in the passage quoted above concerning Cimon's virtue, the word *virtù,* as frequently with Boccaccio and later, systematically, with Machiavelli, carried the Roman connotations of virile determination and capability to effect what is good and right (*virtus, vir, vis* = virtue, man, force—just as in Greek ἀρετή, ἀρείων = virtue, stronger), not the medieval Christian meaning. Pagan virtue was always active, the medieval, at times, passive.[6] The former was eminently defined by what one should do, the latter by what one should not do, as we could be tempted to put it. *Virtù* also carries in the *Decameron* (for example, Vol. I, p. 93 *10;* Vol. II, pp. 319 *7* and 320 *8,* "pietre virtuose") the naturalistic meaning of *vis vitalis,* efficient quality or faculty, the power to operate in such a manner as to bring about intended effects. This acceptation is known to have been common to medieval science, especially medicine.

Even since the early *Filocolo* we have clear evidence of Boccaccio's general aptitude to transcend the traditional Christian connotations of moral terminology, as seen in a characteristic passage which embodies a reminiscence from Dante's Ulysses, a most fitting model of pagan 'virtue.' Florio was urging his companions to help in his quest for the beloved Biancofiore with the following reminder: "We were not born to live like beasts, but to pursue a life of virtue."[7] This virtue, of course, lay in the firm and heroic determination to achieve a lover's goals.

A passage I have already quoted contains a striking example of the ambivalence of the term *virtù*, for it is there used twice, but with two different meanings, separated only by one word. Ghismunda to Tancredi: "tu vedrai . . . tutte l'anime con iguali forze, con iguali potenzie, con iguali *virtù* create. La *virtù* primieramente noi, che tutti nascemmo e nasciamo iguali, ne distinse." As the reader will remember, Ghismunda is telling her father that we are all born equal in our basic vital faculties, but that some are endowed with an aptitude to great things which distinguishes them from the vulgar. This is the only rightful ground for nobility, as it also was its historical genesis. There are, then, *virtues*, that is, faculties (= *vires vitales*) that are common to all men, but *moral virtue,* the true nobility of the soul, the heart, and the mind (= Roman valor) is a personal quality of the heroic few, regardless of their family origin. As to the concept of *discrezione,* it is the basic condition for the new wisdom (*saviezza*), which consists of being able to understand the world and accept it as it is, not without drawing from it one's greatest possible profit—the opposite, all in all, of the ethical principles underlying the philosophy of the Indian and medieval novella.

In VIII, 8, Spinelloccio steals Zeppa's wife, but the 'wise' Zeppa is not the sort of man who lets useless resentment and anger spoil his equanimity and cause a harmful scandal. Instead of seeking violent revenge, he returns the game to Spinelloccio by persuading the latter's wife, with an appropriate trick, to chastise the unfaithful husband in the most direct way. The experiment works so well that everybody remains satisfied, and henceforth each husband will have two wives. Zeppa's humorous 'wisdom' is made of calm reflection and aptitude to get his advantage out of the most uncomfortable situations, while remaining in good harmony with the friend and the wife who have betrayed him. The comedy of the finale is sedate and detached in its sharp humor; the affair ends in a paradoxical lesson in how to adjust oneself to the hard facts of life, and we ultimately witness a humorous triumph of solid, down-to-earth common sense.

In the tale of Agilulf (III,2), a groom from the king's stables lies with the queen. The king cuts the groom's hair in the dark in order to recognize him in the morning, but the groom outwits the king by cutting the hair of all his companions sleeping in the stable. When all the grooms are called before the king in the morning, the latter, instead of losing his temper and betraying himself, decides to use his *senno* and *discrezione* (p. 328 3), and thus saves his honor even in the eyes of the adulterer by simply saying: "Whoever did it, let him not do it again"; "Chi 'l fece nol faccia mai più, e andatevi con Dio" (p. 335). Boccaccio, or the storyteller on his behalf, waxes enthusiastic over this brilliant display of wisdom and praises the king (and the groom) for it. This is, for him, true 'virtue.' Instead of having disorder, anger, shame, and suffering, here everybody is left contented: groom, queen, and the king too, for he has well managed to stop the affair. This, after all, was the best he could do, since a thing once done cannot be undone. The term 'discreet' is, then, broader and carries a more positive connotation than in our usage. It not only means circumspect prudence, but, at best, a superior discernment. In a less specific context, it can be unequivocally complimentary, as when the author addresses his readers as "discrete donne," for instance, p. 450 5.

Boccaccio's own youthful love, for instance, is said to have met with the approval of the *discreti:* "although, among the people of discernment to whose knowledge it had come, I enjoyed much praise and higher esteem than ever before"[8]—and yet, that love lacked discretion in our sense of the word, first in having been aimed too high, and then in being rather unruly and excessive: "out of excessive fire conceived in the mind by effect of a rather uncontrolled appetite" ("per soperchio fuoco nella mente concetto da poco regolato appetito"). The function of *senno* and *discrezione* is not, as we would assume, to regulate the violence of passion, but only to serve its ends.[9] For Capellanus himself had defined love as "inborn suffering derived from the sight of and an *excessive* meditation upon the beauty of the opposite sex."[10] *Saviezza*, on the other hand, is made of rational control and well directed will. 'Discretion,' then, must not be confused with a moral concept typical of much medieval literature, but absent in the Boccaccio of the *Decameron:* I mean the sin of excess in pride, greed, desire, or passion, which Dante called *dismisura* from the French *desmesure* (the pride of Roland, or the uncontrollable passion that drove the hero to tragic doom in *Raoul de Cambrai*).[11] It appeared, for instance, in Hartmann von Aue's *Iwein* as *unmâze*, and was evidently related to the classical, and particularly Aristotelian, conception of moral virtue as a happy medium between extremes (a conception which informed the whole moral structure of Dante's *Inferno*). But Boccaccio's bowing to the sacred right of true love to disregard and transgress all boundaries, is characteristic of his naturalistic ethics and quasi-mystic religion of love.

It is not unfair to ask ourselves why the ten charming youths of the *brigata* do not adopt that behavior which they so repeatedly approve and admire in their characters. The content and the frame of the stories, the behavior of the characters and that of the storytellers, move on two different levels. Why? The hypocrisy of keeping up appearances would be an easy but superficial answer. Another solution, also not completely satisfactory, could be found in the appeal of practical considerations, since Boccaccio must have realized that the shock for the puritanic part of his public would have been too direct and less bearable without the decorum of the *brigata* functioning as a screen between the readers and the characters. I prefer to suggest that the freely restrained standards which prevail among the *brigata* must be understood within the framework of reasonable honesty and decorous wisdom in which Boccaccio believed. *Onestà* and *discrezione* recur throughout the Introduction like keywords. Filomena is said to be "discretissima" (p. 34 73), the three young men are "discreti giovani e valorosi" (p. 36 80), and the whole company is called "una onesta brigata" (p. 6 13). This independent honesty is no mere lip service to society; concerning the *qu'en dira-t-on* the "discretissima" Filomena proclaims: "this is of no consequence; as long as I live honestly and my conscience is at rest in everything, let whoever will, asperse me."[12] But their very discretion warns them that it simply would not do not to be strict about their actions; they had to form a little republic, a free state of their own, and if theoretically they believe that what is pleasant must be legitimate, their practical sense tells them that a certain amount, indeed a great amount, of restraint is imperative if they are determined to coexist in an orderly social organism, were it only for fifteen days.[13] Inevitably, some tension still remains between the two poles of this reality. It will suffice to read attentively the exchange of remarks occasioned by the lecherous story of Alibec and the 'devil in hell' at the end of the Third Day. For a moment the party seems to stand on a razor's edge: the young men and women express their eventual readiness to follow the teachings imparted by Rustico to Alibec or by the nuns to Masetto da Lamporecchio (III, 1), respectively. But such resolutions remain mere statements of principle. Indeed, desires and temptations must be so strong on these elegantly unprejudiced characters, that only the difficult art of self-control seems to keep the party from being thrown into chaos and anarchy. Nevertheless this serene equilibrium is preserved, almost miraculously yet in an easy, effortless manner. One strong support for the equilibrium is, we venture to surmise, the aesthetic sense. The morality, the 'honesty' of the company also takes on an aesthetic coloring. Does this ultimately seem to verge on hypocrisy? Indeed, no matter how we turn it around, a touch of hypocrisy cannot be denied in this moral system, but it is only fair to add that the hypocrisy of Boccaccio's characters is a superior form of sincerity (like that of the Epicurean in Valla's *De Voluptate*): it is *their* way of being sincere. They raise, after all, no claim to being virtuous in the Christian sense.[14]

Boccaccio's profound, and for his time striking detachment from judgments and feelings that result from social conventions and moral prejudices can be seen in II, 7, where Alatiel, the daughter of the king of Babylon, is sent in marriage to the king of Garbo. Through various accidents she successively comes into the hands of nine men, but at last reaches her fiancé and

is wedded for virgin. The lyrical proverb that closes the story—
the most beautifully phrased proverb I know—underlines Boccaccio's sophisticated attitude and serves as a befitting conclusion to that tragicomic series of delightful misadventures:
"Bocca baciata non perde ventura, anzi rinnuova come fa la
luna" ("A mouth, once kissed, hasn't lost its chance: nay, as the
moon it renews its course"). Alatiel is implicitly praised for taking
the advice of a man of discreet wisdom, namely, to keep her
secret to herself. After all she has lost nothing except an adjec-
tive and gained a lot of not unpleasant experience, all to the
good of her future husband. She has done no harm to anyone,
and it would undoubtedly be a great loss for her fiancé to miss
such a beauty for his wife. On her part, she surely does not
deserve to suffer ruin for no crime committed. But, of course,
this superior wisdom does necessitate a bit of ingenuous lying
and superficial hypocrisy, for the gross minds of the public
would not understand all these incontestable truths should she
dare to reveal the bare facts.[15]

At other times the conventional rules are broken by Boccaccio's characters with so much delighted determination that
the author seems to have an earnest lot of grudges against his
society. One could find vague, yet not entirely unwarranted
analogies with later authors who waged campaigns for the
cause of nature and free love against society: one thinks of a De
Sade, the Romanticists (Schiller's *Kabale und Liebe*), D'Annunzio. But Boccaccio rather seems to be guided by a consideration
of the kind expressed by Montaigne (to mention again one of
the truly great analysts of the psyche) as follows:

> Inique estimation des vices! Nous et elles [that is, les
> hommes et les femmes] sommes capables de mille cor-
> ruptions plus dommageables et desnaturées que n'est la
> lasciveté; mais nous faisons et poisons les vices non selon
> nature, mais selon nostre interest. . . . L'aspreté de nos
> decretz rend l'application des femmes à ce vice plus
> aspre et vicieuse que ne porte sa condition, et l'engage
> à des suites pires que n'est leur cause.[16]

In the story of Lizio di Valbona (V, 4) another slippery situation is solved with surprising ease thanks to the discretion of a

wise and practical father who knows the ways of nature and of young girls, and does not forsake his precious knowledge simply because it is his daughter who is in question. The mother is scandalized and ready to cause trouble, were she not stopped in time and brought to reason by the old man's calm words of understanding; whereupon "the lady felt reassured, seeing that her husband took the affair so quietly and that her daughter had had a good night, and was rested, and had caught the nightingale. So she kept silent."[17] The powerful artistic effect of the main motive (the "nightingale") humorously developed into a stylistic *Leitmotiv*, does not suffice to confine this eloquent moral lesson of higher humanity to a place of only marginal importance within the story. And the lesson amounts to little more than the wise, yet so difficult art of accepting 'nature.'

In Agilulf's or Alatiel's cases to give away the secret would have been foolish; but when a revelation can also damage others the sin against *discrezione* becomes, in Boccaccio's mind, criminal and unforgivable. Tofano, the jealous husband of VII, 4, is portrayed under an unsympathetic light both for his jealousy (one particular target of Boccaccio's) and his doltishness in wanting to make his cuckoldry public. He shouts to his wife, whom he has locked out of the house: "Thou shalt never recross this threshold, until I have done thee such honor as is meet for thee in the presence of thy kinsfolk and neighbours."[18]

But Monna Ghita handles the situation so cleverly that Tofano is forced to make peace, and, what is more, on her conditions: "He promised her never again to be jealous, and moreover gave her leave to amuse herself to her heart's content, provided she used such discretion (*saviamente*) that he would not be aware of it."[19] *Saviamente* (as correctly understood by the translator) is here equivalent to *discretamente*. The woman was *discreta* from the beginning of the story ("discretamente con lui—her paramour—s'incominciò ad intendere"), and the story ends when Tofano, too, has become *discreto* in his turn.

Occasionally, discretion will ally itself to a sort of evil genius: then, as with Lodovico and Madonna Beatrice (VII, 7), an illicit encounter can be so ingeniously arranged that love-making becomes a fine art—one of the wicked fine arts, such as De Quincey's or Poe's murders, if one considers the twisted *tournure d'esprit* in the rather queer stratagem to which the husband falls victim. In fact, the concentration of Boccaccio's attention on the absolute rights of nature sometimes turns to the detriment of the rights of humanity, as of any ties that are alien to the direct development of love's impulses. In VII, 9, the author thoroughly enjoys the cruelty with which Lidia performs Pirro's whimsical and gratuitous requests at the expense of the innocent husband, Nicostrato, simply to prove to the lover how genuinely she cares for him (she kills Nicostrato's favorite sparrow hawk, plucks a tuft from his beard, and pulls a healthy tooth from his mouth!). More than the merry wickedness well known in Florentine literature, there is in Boccaccio a touch of sadistic cruelty that strews the *Decameron* with authentic *fleurs du mal.*[20] Ironically, the *brigata* expresses no regret for the mishaps of the poor husband, but only "pitied greatly the pear-tree that had suffered through no fault of its own."[21] To the case of Helen, the widow (VIII, 7), the women of the *brigata* react with restrained pity, as the punishment seemed only partly deserved ("albeit they censured the scholar as severe, intemperately relentless, and indeed cruel in his vengeance").[22] But the reader is well aware of the complacency with which that sadistic punishment has been related. Nevertheless, lest the uncautious reader of Boccaccio should jump to rash conclusions about his amoralism, I feel a general consideration is here in order.

It would be unfair to put Boccaccio in the same class with the numerous narrators of cruel and unwarranted jests which thrived in the Cinquecento.[23] The stories of jest for its own sake (such as the Calandrino series) are tempered and balanced by other stories where the practical jokes are a well-deserved punishment, and by a general statement of principle implying that not all jokes are to be commended, some are to be blamed: "He is not severely to be censured who bestows a flout on one that provokes it or deserves it."[24] Thus in VIII, 8 (already considered for the 'wise' exchange of wives) Zeppa had played a justified jest on Spinelloccio, "who well deserved it" ("la si guadagnò"). The storyteller even commended this case as an example of distributive justice, inasmuch as the revenge was operated with moderation and fitted the offense.[25] The hilarious case of Maestro Simone offers an example of "one who truly asked for it, wherefor those from whom he received it, were rather to be commended than condemned."[26]

Such calculated remarks contribute to the moral equilibrium of the *Decameron* and introduce a sense of values which will almost completely disappear in the Cinquecento novella, lacking as this latter is in the human, psychological, and moral dimensions. The preposterous moralism of the medieval novella, incoherent with the subject at hand, has given way to Boccaccio's discreet, temperate, and pertinent moral comment, destined in its turn to disappear in the late Renaissance. As regards the well-deserved jest in the *Decameron*, the tale of "Salabaetto e la bella ciciliana" can be considered the masterpiece of the genre (VIII, 10, the masterful conclusion of the day of practical jokes). It marks the apotheosis of the moral warning: if you are out to turn tricks on your neighbor, watch out for the cleverer fellow who will finally trick you, and when he comes along, do not complain; you asked for it. It is an ethic that would have pleased the austere Dante, who in fact had expressed the same basic principle in the episode of Guido da Montefeltro and Boniface VIII (*Inferno*, XXVII). Such stories remained popular in the Cinquecento (for instance, Lasca's story of Geri Chiaramontesi), but their full value was then lost in the lack of context, since they were not explicitly related, as their corrective, to other stories of wanton tricks, as they were in Boccaccio.[27]

Love is a delightful and playful experience (*sollazzo*), but not in the sense that it is mere frolic, nor is it to be taken lightly. The fact that love in Boccaccio so often ends in a serious manner, in tragedy or in the permanent tie of marriage, deserves meditation. If, on one hand, love in Boccaccio is no longer the mystic and sublime experience of some of his predecessors, for

it neither comes from God nor leads to Him, neither is it ever
sheer, light-hearted sport, for it ends sometimes in durable happiness, more often in death (as with the *Filostrato*'s Troiolo) or
despair (as with the Fiammetta of the *Elegia*). This had been
true in Boccaccio's earlier production, and true it remains in
the masterpiece.[28] The scene of the *Decameron* is not a natural
habitat for playboys, even in the oversized garb of Don Juans
or Casanovas. On the other hand, and not only in the *Decameron*, Boccaccio showed the powerful realism of his psychology of love by justifying our need for change as part of our
nature. In *Filostrato*, VIII, st. 30, we had read that "A young
woman is changeable, and desires many lovers" ("Giovane
donna è mobile, e vogliosa / È negli amanti molti."). And this
whole work was, indeed, a realistic study in the delusion of
faithfulness and the need for sentimental change, as Chaucer
well understood. In *Teseida*, XII, we had witnessed the easy
oblivion of the dead hero by his fiancée Emilia, and her rather
nonchalant settling for a new, festive wedding with Palemon.
This apparently excessive capacity of adjustment to the circumstances of life was, more deeply, a lesson in the sympathetic
understanding of what had traditionally been disposed of as
chronic, criminal wantonness. The lesson was well put to profit
by Chaucer (on Emelye, Palamon, and Criseyde) and Boiardo
(on Tisbina).[29]

But once all this has been given its due consideration, one
must further acknowledge that, although women are described
as wanton characters more frequently than men, even among
women (not considering harlots, a rewarding subject for comedy
at all times) fickleness of character is rather the exception.
Such is VII, 6, where Madonna Isabella is about to be caught
by her husband with two men in the house. The desire for
change may often be in the background, but comes to the fore-
ground only occasionally (as *ibid.*, beginning: "E come spesso
avviene che sempre non può l'uomo usare un cibo, ma talvolta
disidera variare").[30] The extraordinary pains the lovers frequently have to endure in the pursuit of their goals, the in-
tricate stratagems they have to enact, are not mere exercises in

virtuosity or the comical manifestation of a perseverance worthy of a better cause; they are the tangible proof of the dead seriousness of the business they are in. There is a heroic tone to this comedy of love, that seems to purify even the bawdiest adventures, if the protagonists are willing to risk so much, and do not hesitate to put up with anything. Love is no business for the pusillanimous: it is for the likes of Madonna Filippa, "endowed with a great soul, as those who are truly in love usually are."[31]

This position of the author is all the more interesting in a genre traditionally dedicated to light-hearted scepticism and indulgence, in contrast to the lofty ideals of absolute, ever-lasting, and unique passions dear to higher literary forms. Despite his sympathetic intuition of the basic inconstancy of the human heart ever since the *Filostrato*, Boccaccio never strayed far, even in the *Decameron,* from the idea of faithfulness which had dominated his juvenile production, the *Filocolo,* the *Teseida*, the *Fiammetta.* This last novel deserves more than a passing mention in this context. Recent scholarship has justly insisted on the classical inspiration of this work, which, far from being a story "in reverse" of the author's personal adventures with Maria d'Aquino, as Crescini too successfully put it, was intended as a tragedy in competition with the great pagan classics, a work, therefore, 'exemplary' in the rhetorical sense.[32] As a result we have here an apotheosis of absolute, unconditional faithfulness, of which Fiammetta is the proud, fully conscious heroine. Here is the positive element of this tragedy without any joy but this proud feeling of a heroic, incomparable achievement. Indeed Fiammetta, through the long mythological comparisons which so much irked De Sanctis, wants to state the grandiose uniqueness of her suffering, so as to place her epic case above all the other great loves of history. She wants to be remembered forever as the heroine of unfortunate love. Similarly, in the *Decameron* the endless betrayals of husbands are not, in the last analysis, changes of heart and mind, but rather the actual rejection of a conventional bond that has never meant anything deep for the heart and the senses.

A *CONCLUSION ON THE* DECAMERON

I have shown how Boccaccio's intuition of nature evolves out of the world of courtly love, not juxtaposed to it, as it appeared to De Sanctis, who, therefore, had to assess the *courtois* tales as 'rhetoric.' Momigliano started a new approach that did justice to the courtly element, but could not go to the end of the new path (see Petronio, *Il Decamerone*, pp. 30–31). Consequently Bosco excessively emphasized the element of *courtoisie,* and Croce saw the "senses" and "chivalry" together, but without fusing them into a unity. This Petronio proposed to do (see p. 32, *op. cit.*). I have tried to do it in the name of 'naturalism,' which is, as I see it, not a historically new phenomenon in Boccaccio (as De Sanctis made it appear), but an old one in new form.[33] Boccaccio sides, with unconditional sympathy, with all manifestations of the senses against conventional morality (see VI, 7), with adulterers and sinning nuns and monks, and condemns only when hypocrisy attempts to hide nature (VII, 3; VIII, 4; IV, 2), or when venality contaminates the free choice guided by nature (VIII, 1), or finally when men stoop to "perversi piaceri contro natura" (V, 10, and the attacks in the Epilogue).

Petronio has appropriately warned against a 'romantic' misreading of the work: Boccaccio's, as he puts it, is not "the romantic world of passion unrestrained (*sbrigliata*), slave and, at the same time, proud of itself."[34] It is, rather, the world of 'sentiment' serenely fused with reason and the will. Love is, indeed, irrational, but reason follows and serves it, without being quite subjugated by it. Thus love and 'intelligence' appear not really distinct, but united in mutual coöperation, or more exactly love is accompanied by intelligence, a thriving force even by itself.

When seen in this light, it appears that such an attitude is already part of the Renaissance, no more of the Middle Ages, where love could well be pure romantic passion. But it is not the mature Renaissance, in which love will work more for the ends of reason, its rightful guide, than vice versa. Yet, the danger of Petronio's interpretation, as I see it, is in the extent to which one is ready to posit the control by reason over the senses and the heart. Serene coöperation there is between them, but we must never forget that it is a coöperation of opposites.

We may now feel ready to conclude that taken singularly, almost every feature of the *Decameron's* ethics of free love finds its antecedent in the courtly tradition, and particularly in its most significant codification, Andreas Capellanus' *De Amore*.[35] The exalted praise of adultery and the consequent scorn for marriage were conspicuous pivots of Provençal poetry, and were embodied in the manual of Andreas. Andreas had singled out jealousy as the inevitable pest of marriage.[36] He had also insisted on true nobility as an inner moral virtue (*probitas*) that found in love its 'fountain'; and such a principle had been developed in an original way by the School of the Sweet New Style, in the most favorable social environment.[37] Some of the stories, and all of the conclusive Tenth Day, move in an explicit courtly environment. More particularly, Branca has likened the position of Capellanus to Boccaccio's principle whereby the plebeian may, even must, love a lady of nobility.[38] And C. Grabher has traced some significant elements of the Nastagio story (V, 8) back to Capellanus.[39] This celebrated tale was suggested to Boccaccio by Vincent de Beauvais (*Speculum historiale*), who was echoing a long tradition reflected in the *Flores* of Elinandus and finally in Passavanti's *Specchio di Vera Penitenza*, where the tale of the coal dealer from Niversa may have served as a close reminder to our author. But Grabher calls our attention to the pageant in Andreas' palace of the God of Love. There the dead women are divided into three groups: the good lovers dwell in the region of *Amoenitas*, the harlots in *Humiditas*, and the cruel ones in *Siccitas*. This last region is "almost like hell," and eternal (p. 122, Battaglia ed.). This idea was found in a similar cavalcade in the *Lai du Trot*, which Boccaccio was not likely to know.[40] The women sinners in this scene, which Grabher compares to a Bosch fantasy, are said to be of remarkable beauty, and this trait is common only to Andreas and Boccaccio. A marked difference between the two

versions, however, is in the fact that Boccaccio's description
exudes a pagan sense of health which is no counterpart to the
hellish, medievally morbid, 'decadent' atmosphere of Andreas'
scene. The Italian storyteller, then, "turns the religious concept
of sin upside down," after Andreas' suggestion, but he also
eliminates the religious horror of the 'sin against love,' and
reduces Andreas' hell to Passavanti's purgatory, where the
women will spend as many years as have been the months of
their cruelty in love. The purpose of the tale remains, nevertheless, the same, namely to exhort the cruel to be humane,
and return the love they receive (for, as Dante put it, "Love
exempts no loved one from loving in return"). Besides, Grabher
maintains, the amenity of the place where Nastagio witnesses
the punishment of the cruel lady cannot derive from Dante
(*Inferno*, XIII) or Passavanti, but only from Andreas.[41]

Yet, besides particular noncourtly elements, the general atmosphere, the spirit itself of the *Decameron* cannot be thought
to have emanated from the courtly tradition. The feminine type
that sweeps triumphantly through the work is eminently remote from the *midons* (= my lord) who had polarized the
feudally conditioned idealism of Provençal society.[42] Above all,
Boccaccio originally presents all precepts and attitudes, old or
new, as willed and imposed by nature, far from the stylized and
conventional ideology of the chivalric world. Furthermore, he
surpasses the inflexibility of the courtly 'heresy' in its most
consistent expression, as he significantly seems to forget a relevant corollary of Andreas' doctrine. The granting of favors by
the lady, including the ultimate *guerdon,* was necessary and
valuable inasmuch as it increased the lover's *probitas*, as a *free*
reward for his true merits.[43] Hence true love could not be found
in marriage, where favors are to be reciprocally returned as a
duty. In such an atypical manner, on the contrary, marriage
does end many of Boccaccio's love stories, because marriage
by free choice and mutual consent is, for him, the logical
crowning of love, whereas it is to be scorned as love's enemy
when it comes about by social imposition. Wherever they conform with the natural order, Boccaccio is ready to accept social
institutions.[44]

Just though it may be to insist on Boccaccio's dependence on courtly ideology in the *Decameron* as a reaction to the neglect of this important element by Romantic criticism, I feel that enough has been made of this issue by recent critics. After all, to Boccaccio the appeal of the world of chivalry lay especially in its naturalistic substratum, on one hand, and, on the other, in its possibility of providing examples of magnanimity, that is, grandiose, heroic virtues—in other words, the sort of thing that indirectly served his humanistic cult of classic greatness. But he was uninterested in the more technical aspects of chivalry *per se*. One significant testimony 'by omission' may suffice here. The poignant story of Guiglielmo Guardastagno and Guiglielmo Rossiglione (IV, 9, the novella of the eaten heart), derives from the "Vida" of the troubadour Guillem de Cabestaing (see our Chapter II, p. 21), but Boccaccio disregarded the very element which was most revealing of the courtly ethics of this story, that is the punishment of the revengeful husband by the king.

But in order to keep our notion of Boccaccio's naturalism in its proper focus, it is important to bear in mind that Boccaccio's true conception of love, like that of all great poets of love who preceded him (including the troubadours), must not be equated with eroticism. Di Pino has made some penetrating observations on the dialectical, polemic tension between the Diane symbol and the Venus symbol in Boccaccio. In each of his works starting with the *Caccia di Diana*, the goddess of chastity reappears in order to be confronted and, every time, eventually defeated by Venus. She still bears her name in the *Ninfale Fiesolano*, but in the following *Decameron*, even in the absence of this name, the motif that was hidden behind it reveals itself stronger and clearer than ever: "social convention." The movement toward reality which seals the literary evolution of Boccaccio's career has now reached its apogee, and the symbol is no longer needed. However, the "Venus" who wins out against Diane is not, literally, the terrestrial Venus, the goddess of pure sense: she personifies the new, antiascetic hence typically antimedieval ideal of operative life. The courageous engagement of our emotions, and the determined activity for their fulfillment, is as sacred as it is a duty. To conclude with Di Pino's keen words: "The prevailing of love over chastity does not signify a triumph of the senses. It is the triumph of an active and dramatic principle against sluggishness and re- nunciation." In the *Decameron* "noble love is courage and drama, tragedy even, but always action which elevates."[45] This fine distinction, if I am not mistaken, amounts to the most effective defense against the possible charge of obscenity or pornography. In the *Decameron,* in spite of all appearances, the real accent is not on sense and sex. Boccaccio's message is naturalistic, not erotic.

On the other hand, the triumph of naturalism marked by the *Decameron* was premature: our author could not help revert- ing, sooner or later, to a medieval awareness of the incompati- bility of a consistent naturalistic view and the superior rights of the pure spirit; and the result was the rejection of the *Decameron* as an error of his 'youth.' It was not before the sixteenth century that a coherent naturalism could inform the whole life of a man, without hesitation or crisis. Because he ushered in a new culture, in a somewhat dramatic way and at the price of his inner equilibrium, Boccaccio could not find, as an artist, that sublime though precarious harmony between spirituality and naturalism which had been the hallmark of certain medieval experiences, such as that of an Héloïse in actuality or, more fictionally, those of courtly literature at its best.

The Movement to and from Naturalism in Boccaccio's Career

V

The only way to get rid of a temptation is to yield to it. Resist it, and your soul grows sick with longing for the things it has forbidden to itself, with desire for what its monstrous laws have made monstrous and unlawful.

O. Wilde, *The Picture of Dorian Gray*

A NATURALIST MANIFESTO

In one sense at least, Humanism, in the broadest philosophical implications of the term, can be said to have been restored by Boccaccio even more than by Petrarch: namely as an open, unprejudiced appreciation of all that is human inasmuch as it is part of human nature, however good or bad ethically, right or wrong rationally it might be. Were we looking for a slogan to attach to the more polemical aspects of Boccaccio's works, we could recall Terence's *homo sum, humani nihil a me alienum puto,* or Epicharmus' θνατὰ χρὴ τὸν ϑνατὸν φρονεῖν ("it behooves a mortal to have a mortal's thoughts"), or Pindar's ϑνατὰ ϑνατοῖςι πρέπει ("mortal things are meet for mortals," *Isthmian* V, 20). And indeed such maxims could be most appropriately affixed in front of the author's self-defense in the *Proemio* to the Fourth Day and in the Epilogue to the *Decameron*.

Even before the hundred stories were completed, Boccaccio had released parts of his *Decameron* for circulation among his friends. Thus he had early met with bitter opposition from certain quarters, as was to be expected. In the Proem to the Fourth Day, a piece of extraordinary directness, sincerity, and introspective power, the author replied to the book's critics in words addressed to his feminine public. Petrarch seems to have approvingly looked upon this eloquent 'apologia,' which he significantly singled out for an implicit mention when, in the last of his *Seniles* (1373), he complimented Boccaccio for having dealt with his literary detractors as they deserved: "This very book had been attacked by the teeth of vile dogs, but you defended it with the stick of your very effective words."[1]

As Boccaccio expounds them, four charges had been thrust upon him: immoderate attachment to the feminine sex ("che voi mi piacete troppo"); deviation from truly worthy literature ("farei più saviamente a starmi con le Muse in Parnaso"); inability to make a living by his frivolous literary activity ("farei più discretamente a pensare dond'io dovessi aver del pane"); and unfaithfulness to the originals of the stories ("in altra guisa essere state le cose da me raccontatevi," pp. 450–451). He answers the objections in a very orderly manner, point by point, after having induced the right mood by one more novella, that of the women called *papere,* goslings ("devils" in *Barlaam,* Iacopo da Varazze, Jacques de Vitry, Vincent de Beauvais, the *Novellino,* and others). In this witty anecdote the departure from the medieval *exemplum* is quite drastic, and in such respect one can find here the best demonstration of the evolution which I have already discussed in general terms. For this purpose we must briefly retrace the background of the story in its essential lines.

Barlaam et Joasaf was the life of the Buddha turned Christian saint, in a spontaneous alliance between Buddhism and Christianity.[2] It contained an apologue (the tenth) wherein women were shown to be the best allies of the devil—rather devils themselves who deceive men. By this apologue a courtier had persuaded the king to send a wench to his young son (the prince Josaphat) as the surest of all temptations to turn him away from a life of religion. A young man, as the story has it, had been kept in the wilderness since his earliest years to ensure his dedication to a life of innocent asceticism away from all temptation. But at his first accidental glimpse of real women he suddenly and irrevocably grew so fond of them that, after learning of their being "devils," he decided he could no longer do without the devils' company.

The anecdote has a long story of popular derivations and transcriptions, through which one expediently notices the typical process whereby the originally moralistic, ascetic *exemplum* was irrevocably turned into a thoroughly immanent affair, naturalistic in inspiration and purpose.[3] In retelling the story, Boccaccio followed the example of the English Odo of Cheriton and dropped the nickname "devils" for the women to call them "goslings." La Fontaine, the rightful heir of Boccaccio and Ariosto as a storyteller, in his turn completed the transformation by divesting the background of its medieval tone: in his "conte" *Les oies de frère Philipe* the ascetic atmosphere surrounding the hermit is obliterated in the constant, consistently sceptical smile of the narrator. We are not even aware, any longer, of any connection with a medieval environment. Along the same lines, La Fontaine's *contes* had appeared to brush impatiently aside the traditional feeling of horror for womanly treachery by presenting the delightfully shocked reader with an "éloge du cocuage" as a fitting introduction to such stories as that of the "goslings"![4]

The dissolution of the medieval *exemplum*, outwardly naturalistic, inwardly ascetic, is one of the phenomena which mark the transition to the Renaissance, since, as a rule, the Renaissance novella does away with the 'moral,' that more or less consistent appendix to the short story which had officially justified its existence in the religiously inspired literature of the early Middle Ages (formal sermons or concealed ones as the case may have been). In this sense Boccaccio appears already immersed in the climate of the new culture. But his particular treatment of the "women-goslings" motif is indicative of something even more important. His naturalism is not the naïve, spontaneous, unconscious delight in detailed realistic representation which characterized so much of medieval realism. It is a conscious program, intellectually formulated and presented in a polemic, militant, aggressive tone, in explicit reaction to medieval prejudices. The attitude of conscious defense of the 'rights of nature' in a learned, intellectual art, must be placed into sharp focus and distinguished from the mere taste for the realistic, picturesque detail, the latter being characteristic of most late-medieval art.[5] Erich Auerbach has rightfully recognized this polemic consciousness in Boccaccio's "un-Christian" (as he regarded it) doctrine of love and nature, and in his being so fully "certain of himself" in his views on earthly love.[3]

To recapitulate, then, the traditional moral purpose of the women-devils motif has been completely overturned: instead of a warning to avoid the all but irresistible temptation of 'Pandora'—since the only way to prevent the world from ensnaring us is asceticism, complete withdrawal from the world—the anecdote is treated as a demonstration of the ineradicability of man's attraction to woman, *therefore* of the goodness of the sexual instinct as part of nature's plans, and the unavoidable defeat of all attempts to stifle nature by escape. The antiascetic intention is made quite evident, though discreetly concealed in subtle irony, when the young hermit remarks to his father that the girls he has just seen for the first time "are fairer than the painted angels that you have so often shown me."[7] Finally, the story is bodily subtracted from its traditional setting, as though to confirm even in the material details the rejection of its previous edifying character. In addition to what has been pointed out before, this is also achieved by the attribution of the incident to a well known Florentine merchant family, the Balducci (agents of the Bardi, like Boccaccio's own father), thus making it psychologically close to the reader's experience.⁸ This is particularly noteworthy in a context where the author is preparing to reject the charge of being untrue to his sources. He is obviously aware of the meaning of certain deliberate changes, and takes full responsibility for them. He does not deign to linger on lengthy and dialectical justifications of his behavior. He simply admits that his tastes and standards are not those of the past, nor those of his critics. For these latter, for instance, as for the Filippo Balducci of the anecdote, women are bad things, *mala cosa,* devils who should better be named after some insignificant thing or animal—like *papere.*⁹ Well, Filippo's son made up his mind without hesitation: "Why, is this the way naughty things are made?" "O son così fatte le male cose?" (p. 455). Naughty things they may well be, and let them be. For he does like naughty things, if they look better than painted angels, as these do. And he wants to take one to the cavern, where, with most loving care, he will see "that she have whereon to bill": "Deh, se vi cal di me, fate che noi ce ne meniamo una colà su di queste papere, e io le darò beccare—. Disse il padre: —Io non voglio; tu non sai donde elle s'imbeccano!— È sentì incontanente *più aver di forza la natura* che il suo ingegno." So this is the new moral: the hermit suddenly realized that *nature* was stronger than man's will to thwart it.¹⁰

Now to the particular censures. The one he takes more time to discuss is the first: Does he like women too much? Perhaps so; but he has no intention of retracting himself. "Le quali cose io apertissimamente confesso, cioè che voi mi piacete e che io m'ingegno di piacere a voi" (p. 455). He and his adversaries belong to different worlds: they are scandalized by the very things which are for him the finest part of life. He will not even try to persuade them. If they are surprised that some people, like him, cannot help but be charmed by intercourse with women, by their kisses and embraces, by their "ornati costumi e la vaga bellezza e l'ornata leggiadria," plus their "donnesca onestà"; if his adversaries are "persons who have neither feeling for, nor notion of the honest pleasures of

natural affections" ("Sì come persona che i piaceri né la virtù
della naturale affezione né sente né conosce," p. 456), his only
reaction will be to leave them to their destiny: "io poco me
ne curo." Nor is it a matter of age. They should know "perché
il porro abbia il capo bianco, che la coda sia verde." At any
rate, and leaving jokes aside, he is proud to "devote himself
to those matters to which Guido Cavalcanti and Dante Alighieri, on the threshold of their old age, and Cino da Pistoia
even in his advanced old age felt honored to minister."[11] Of
course, at least as far as Dante and Cino were concerned,
Boccaccio knew full well that their ways of caring for the same
objects were not quite the same as his; but we cannot really
blame him for neglecting to underline it. In one way or another,
Boccaccio seems to imply, all true poets are on the same level,
they all must love life—and life's quintessence are love and
women—, for poetry is 'aesthetic' activity, feeling for earthly,
sensorial and sensual values. This Boccaccio knew, or at least
felt intuitively, and he dared bring it to the open fore with a
frankness unexpected at his time, and with a clarity of consciousness of which Dante would not have been capable, no
matter how much greater he may have been as a poet and as
a man.

As to the three remaining objections, the gist of his replies
is the following: Muses are women too, and he reckons that
precisely for the sake of women they have helped him to write
the *Decameron,* contrarily to his enemies' scorn for this book;
he is quite confident that he will find greater riches in literature than many a wealthy man does in his treasures, metaphorically and, a little, even literally; let them produce the
originals and show him that he did not respect their integrity.[12]
In conclusion, from now on he will be more determined than
ever to tread his path, for all objections in the end amount to
nothing more than charging him with operating *according to
nature:* "altra cosa dir non potrà alcun con ragione, se non che
gli altri e io, che vi amiamo, *naturalmente* operiamo" (p. 459).
Of course, some people have—or pretend to have—the strength
to resist nature. Well, he doesn't. As a matter of fact, if he had

it, he had rather lend it to someone else than use it for himself. Boccaccio then cuts his eloquent self-defense short by summarily rejecting any concern on his part for 'supernature,' and he rejects it with irony and sarcasm. He takes the goodness of life's pleasures for granted. Actually, everybody does so in practice, Boccaccio hints on the sly in closing. It is only a matter of choosing the good or the bad pleasures, the natural or the unnatural ones: "Wherefore let my detractors [*morditori*] hold their peace, and if they cannot get heat, why let them shiver their life away; and, while they remain addicted to their delights, or rather corrupt appetites, I beg them to let me follow my own bent during the brief life accorded to us."[13]

But in the first two objections there lay hidden another, and most important question. Boccaccio's whole career had been placed under the aegis of 'feminine' muses. Both the form and the subject matter of his tales and romances had often, and avowedly, been conditioned by the needs, and directed to please the taste, of a feminine audience. Dante himself had already justified the use of the vernacular in literature addressed to women.[14] Nor was the appeal to a feminine audience a mere rhetorical convention. Indeed, at the base of courtly love lay the hopes and aspirations of women, who had been the center of inspiration and the intended audience of most of that literature. We have seen how Chrétien de Troyes seemed to have some misgivings about his woman-centered *Lancelot,* so that he took pains to warn his readers that plot and treatment had been dictated to him by Marie de Champagne, his patroness. Albert Thibaudet has stated, in dealing with the evolution of the novel and its close connection with the social emancipation of women, that "roman et démocratie vont de pair."[15] Indeed, the historians of this genre well know how close women have been to the novel as readers, critics, and authors. But these historians have never gone, to my knowledge, farther back than the seventeenth-century French novel in this regard. The problem is, as we are now ready to see, much older. The role of the modern novel, this most 'democratic' and women-oriented of all literary forms, was fulfilled in the Middle Ages

by the 'romances' and various forms of 'tales' as well. The anti-
feminist Voltaire once maliciously stated that "Les femmes
surtout donnent la vogue à ces ouvrages [namely, romantic
novels], qui les entretiennent de la seule chose qui les intéresse
[= love]," and the feminist Mme de Staël was soon to notice
that, "Avant que les femmes eussent créé des intérêts dans la
vie privée, les aventures particulières [typical subject matter of
eighteenth-century novels] captivaient peu la curiosité des
hommes."[16] Such statements could as well be applied, for all
they are worth, to Boccaccio's times, and particularly to his
works. In fact, when he changed his mind on the 'educative'
value of his fiction, he took pains to warn his good friend
Mainardo Cavalcanti to keep such books out of reach of the
honorable ladies in his household, as we shall shortly see. Similarly, in the seventeenth and eighteenth centuries, the literary
enemies of the novel were often conservative moralists of anti-
feminist sentiments, who were worried about the alleged corruption of tastes and mores brought about by the social tyranny
of women and the authors' catering to their whims. Such were,
undoubtedly, Boccaccio's critics, and we are therefore fully
entitled to give this Proem a high place in the centuries-old
querelle des femmes. Concurrently, from a more literary viewpoint, the critics of the novel, like those of the *Decameron* and
of much of earlier narrative, turned up their noses at these
Cinderellas of literature, popular but lowly, frivolous, un-
learned, and, last but not least, such that on them an author
could not even make a decent living.

In the succession of the main stories the Proem has a strategic
position.

> The tale of Alibec (III, 10), one of many examples of
> love at its nadir, is followed the next day with a state-
> ment of the inescapable physical law [the Proem, Boc-
> caccio's 'manifesto on the laws of nature'] in turn suc-
> ceeded by the story of Ghismunda, in which, with no
> decrease of physicality, love reaches its zenith. By
> launching immediately afterwards into parody of the
> *donna angelicata*, Boccaccio marks the confines of his
> domain. Spacious as that domain may be, it is an earthly

> one. . . . Boccaccio . . . draws the line at the *donna
> angelicata*. She dwells across the boundary, and his
> laughter stands guard between them.[17]

This interesting thematic sequence has been pointed out by
Mrs. L. G. Clubb as part of a bold interpretation of IV, 2,
which I find interesting, though ultimately overstated. The
tale in question (Frate Alberto) is, according to Mrs. Clubb,
an unusual and unprecedented parody of the *Dolce Stil Nuovo*
(what I have generically called 'Gothic love'), within the framework of Boccaccio's "insistence that man honor the demands
and admit the boundaries of his nature."[18] It is right, I believe,
to find that Boccaccio "denies the love that denies the flesh,
specifically the love expounded by poets of the *dolce stil
nuovo*." For these poets had transformed the essentially human
love of the Provençal into "*supra*-human *caritas*," into a *scala
d'amore*, a Platonic-like ladder of love reaching to heaven, and
this was deeply alien to Boccaccio's *Weltanschauung*. "Keenly
aware of the generous but distinct limits of humanity, Boccaccio parts company with his revered Dante at the point
where love is dehumanized." Even while Boccaccio was still
under the direct spell of his great master, his imitation of
Dante's sublime allegories was somehow contradictory and out
of focus. In the *Ameto*, the protagonist "is ennobled by the
teachings of these voluptuous abstractions," that is, the nymphs
embodying the theological and cardinal virtues, "but he nevertheless itches to get his hands on them." And the final reward
expected in the *Amorosa Visione* is "ultimate pleasure with the
enticing lady of his dream," whereas the stilnovists had made
"love a rational desire by desexualizing its object."[19] Mrs.
Clubb, equally à propos, remarks that Boccaccio missed the
point (though I do not know how "deliberately" he did so)
when, in his *Vita di Dante*, he "ignored the function of the
donna angelicata as an ideal and a spirit whose influence
reaches its full strength only after death."

Nevertheless, I cannot bring myself to accept the provoca-
tive suggestion that the novella of Frate Alberto seducing the
foolish bigot Lisetta in the garb of the angel Gabriel is an in-

tentional parody of the *donna angelicata* in the form of a *uomo angelicato*. Given Boccaccio's profound reverence for a school of poetry which he felt he could not truly understand, let alone the possibility of embracing its metaphysical and ethical tenets, I cannot believe that he would have dared to approach that subject with such a violent, uncompromising iconoclasm. Nor do I find enough artistic and substantial elements in the story itself to support that thesis. But I do feel that Mrs. Clubb has revealed a basically unconscious, yet enlightening coincidence, a distant background against which Boccaccio is *de facto* reacting through the unplanned, yet effective allusory overtones of this naughty novella. And above all, Mrs. Clubb's interpretation is significative of the sort of challenge the *Decameron* represents for any sensitive reader who happens to come to it from the experience of Dante and the *Dolce Stil Nuovo*, as Boccaccio's contemporaries did.

Later, in the Epilogue to the *Decameron*, the apologia was pursued further by rejecting the possible charge of licentiousness. This "licenzia," the author contends, is only on the surface, it is a matter of deceptive appearance. He has, indeed, told some "dishonest" story, but "con onesti vocaboli," which makes it such "che non si disdica ad alcuno." In any case, should some fair readers still feel offended, he has a strong argument for his defense: namely, the correspondence of form and content, a cornerstone of all true art: "Se alcuna cosa [disonesta] in alcuna n'è, le qualità delle novelle l'hanno richesta," which he firmly claims could not be told otherwise without destroying the unity of words and meanings, signs and references, expression and impression, form and content, thereby sinning against truth and reality. "Sarà conosciuto, se io quelle *della lor forma trar* non avessi voluto, altramenti raccontar non poterle."[20] Has he, after all, done anything that painters do not do all the time without anyone even thinking to censure them for it? They paint Adam male and Eve female, and quite safely drive nails through our Savior's hands and feet. They respect the truth of their stories, and so does he. Does he provide some possible cause for scandal? So do the Holy Scriptures to those who might read them with impure eyes and unclean minds. Others will consider such subject matter unworthy of a grave scholar as he is expected to be. But he has taken example from the sermons of good priests and monks, filled as they are with stories and jokes and gibes, that is, *exempla* as they call them, "il più oggi piene di motti e di ciance e di scede" (II, p. 669 23 —just as Dante had, in his turn, pointed out: *Paradiso* XXIX, 115). The only difference is that he, Boccaccio, does not pretend to correct the mores, but simply to 'chase the blues' from the delicate minds of his dear lady readers: not "rimorder delle loro colpe gli uomini;" only "cacciar la malinconia delle femine" (ibid.). And just in case he had been too successful in causing merriment and laughter, the remedy is near at hand—a few Jeremiads, easily available, will do: "Se troppo per questo ridessero, il lamento di Geremia, la passione del Salvatore e il ramarrichio della Maddalena ne le potrà agevolmente guerire." At last, *Johannes tranquillitatum* gracefully looses his patience, and rests his case with a sneering but humorous allusion to that last class of critics, those who cast reproach upon the satire of monks (rather, his having told the truth about them, "scrivo il ver de' frati"). Frankly, these critics do deserve forgiveness, for their cause is just. Friars are worthy persons, who avoid discomfort for the love of God, once in a while pour secret, intense blessings on a disconsolate woman, and keep it to themselves, too ("per ciò che i frati son buone persone e fuggono il disagio per l'amor di Dio, e macinano a raccolta e nol ridicono," p. 670 26). Were it not that they smell a little, they would indeed make perfectly delightful company ("e se non che di tutti un poco viene del caprino, troppo sarebbe più piacevole il piato loro").

This embroidery of idiomatic phraseology echoed from brilliant passages of the collection,[21] somehow parallels, in a minor key, the summary of all the basic themes of the book in the Ninth Day, as a coming together of all the *Leitmotivs* before the finale (as Branca has shown); and thus both the book and the self-defense come to a fitting close. The author seems to be warning his public: Do not presume that I have done what I have done unwittingly and unprepared to take the consequences. If you are pleased with what I have done, let me add that it is not a result of chance; it was so planned. If, however, you should have objections, please do not waste your time: I have myself anticipated them all and brushed them aside; I will not be moved to change my mind.

Rarely had such a determined and direct self-defense been seen against such criticism. A certain parallel exists in the *Roman de la Rose.* After defending his use of allegedly obscene terms (vv. 6928–7228), Jean de Meung again apologized for shocking some of his readers, then went on to profess that he addressed himself to women, and finally refused to take responsibility for the reactions of hypocrites if they considered themselves his target (vv. 15,243–15,302).[22]

Similarly Alan of Lille, one of Jean de Meung's masters, as the reader will recall, had accepted the principle of correspondence of style to subject matter: "Sometimes . . . since speech should be related to the matters of which we speak, deformity of expression ought to be molded to ugliness of subject." However he had refrained from applying it himself out of respect for his learned and refined audience: "But in the coming theme, in order that evil words may not offend the reader's hearing . . . I wish to give to these monstrous vices a cloak of well sounding phrases."[23] But the most befitting antecedent I can locate is in the poet who had taught so much to Abélard and Héloïse, the courtly poets, Capellanus, Jean de Meung, and to Boccaccio himself. In his *Remedia Amoris* (vv. 361–396) the facile Sulmonese poet countered the censure obviously caused by the earlier appearance of his *Ars Amatoria* ("nuper enim nostros quidam carpsere libellos"). We encounter a string of striking parallels between the respective apologias of Ovid and Boccaccio. Firstly, the censors have found the Sulmonese licentious ("nostra licentia") and shameless ("quorum censurā Musa proterva mea est"). But he does not care, as long as he is read and admired all over the city, especially by the faithful cohorts of Venus, for he knows that it is envy (*livor*) which moves his critics—and the bite of envy is apparently implied in the metaphor I quoted from Petrarch's defense of the *Decameron,* "canum dentibus lacessitum," as well as in Boccaccio's original word *morditori.* Envy, at any rate, attacks the great ("Summa petit livor, perflant altissima venti"; "Summa petunt dextra fulmina missa Iovis")—the same metaphors which appear at the beginning of the Proem, although Boccaccio professes to have kept away from the heights precisely to avoid the attacks of envy. Why have his critics not considered, Ovid asks, that his licence befits the genre ("ad numeros exige quidque suos")? He has followed the rules of the game, keeping true to the nature of his subject; the language is free because the life of Thais is his topic ("Thais in arte mea; lascivia libera nostra est. / Nihil mihi cum vitta; Thais in arte mea est; / Si meae materiae respondet Musa iocosae, / Vicimus, et falsi criminis acta rea est," vv. 385–388). The correspondence of form and content is the law invoked by both Ovid and Boccaccio in their defense. The elegy, whose argument is love, already claims him, Ovid adds, as its great master—and this is all he asks; Boccaccio, in turn, pleads only for the approval of his intended audience, the girls in love, who applaud his novellas, because they soothe their blues.

BEFORE AND AFTER THE MASTERPIECE

As to his assuring the critics that he would never have to retract, Boccaccio, we know, did not keep his word: he did change his mind. Nor is this too surprising: the more definite and radical one is in one's *prises de position,* the more likely one will be to shift even to an opposite position.[24] Contradiction is rare in the *Decameron,* but frequent in the life and work of its author. When the crisis came, touched off by the visit of one of the monks he had taken so lightly (Gioacchino Ciani, spring of 1362), it fell to his friend Petrarch to save his spirit from a final, complete turn-about. This fortunate intervention throws light on psychological differences in the two personalities that reflect on their respective literary and historical roles.

Petrarch's life was dominated by a basic conflict between

the influence of his medieval environment and his clear-headed striving toward the new culture of Humanism. He seems to suffer from this contrast and to be looking now ahead, now behind, reluctant and unable to make up his mind and renounce either of the two possible worlds. On the surface, Boccaccio appears to be the light-hearted, serene, unproblematic man who has definitively brushed aside the supernatural preoccupations and psychological complications of the Middle Ages, and is nonchalantly looking forward. A deeper acquaintance with both men reveals in Petrarch a less medieval, more 'modern' man than Boccaccio. Petrarch is the mature sage, constantly analyzing himself and discovering the two faces of his Adam, but he has this problematic process almost completely under control. Tradition, the past, is strong within him, but will never take his hand. His 'civic spirit' can never obliterate his longing for 'solitude,' but he will never break down under the stress. Balance, equilibrium, the rational weighing of pros and contras is the distinctive mark of his personality. Boccaccio, on the other hand, is the youthful, instinctive nature that impetuously embraces life and novelty with his whole heart and without either soul-searching premeditation or afterthoughts. He is a man of the Middle Ages in the ease with which he tends to radicalize and exaggerate. Far from being blind to the implications and consequences of his acts, he sees them quite clearly and takes time to put his hands forward and stake his claims, lest someone might think that he is bluffing or does not know what he is doing. We have just witnessed such an aggressive display of awareness. And yet, this awareness is overstated. Not falsely stated, but just overstated, hence it sounds (psychologically) slightly suspicious. In the middle of the fourteenth century, such a profession of naturalism jeeringly thrown in the face of the recognized authorities, the acknowledged teachers of values and standards, could be seriously carried to its extreme consequences only by a reformer's temper—a temper which was quite alien to Boccaccio's personality.

Petrarch was essentially the 'introvert' who *de facto* places himself at the center of the world, for in the end he was chiefly interested in his ego, and in others only inasmuch as they filled *his* environment and contributed to make *his* world. This is the nature of the true lyricist. Hence he exercised his introspection to the point where he came to realize Socrates' supreme teaching and to 'know himself.' Boccaccio had not enough of a genuine interest in himself, for he enjoyed and loved 'people' too much; not 'subjective' enough, he was too 'objective,' and too outward-bound. Life was not for him an inner drama, but a fascinating spectacle of playful characters, whose most serious achievement was *the show* itself. Even when speaking about himself he kept contributing to the show he was contemplating; he was simply becoming one of his own characters (as Billanovich has shown in reconstituting Boccaccio's life, and proving how fictional his statements about himself are).[25] These methodic 'lies' are shining proof of his being a born narrator. We can thus see Petrarch as the prototype of Italian lyricists (followed by Tasso, Foscolo, Leopardi, all so different, and yet all of one mold, the 'lyrical'), Boccaccio of Italian narrators (and if I am allowed to use the category of narrator somewhat metaphysically, I find Boccaccio's mold in Ariosto and Goldoni).

In the end, his 'classic' self-control enabled Petrarch to save his friend by persuading him that his religious crisis was based on rather superficial, though strong impressions without sufficient meditation in depth. Boccaccio understood, or at least sensed, the profound wisdom of his great friend, listened to his advice, and decided not to destroy the *Decameron,* nor to disperse his library, nor to give up literature. But he never was the same man again, and no longer wrote fiction. After the *Corbaccio* he had already turned exclusively to Latin, and had become a pure scholar, a 'humanist.' His long 'youth' had come to an end, and he could now feel completely mature.

The change had come upon him not abruptly, but gradually and somewhat unconsciously, and it had started, we must assume, soon after completion of the *Decameron* (1351?). But the crisis of 1362 dramatized it and brought all its elements to the fore. For his impetuous readiness to enjoy life as it comes and to heed the pagan warning *carpe diem,* in thoughtless, carefree nonchalance about the 'sin' that this entails, was threatened by an unexpected, hidden urge to stop suddenly and place everything under discussion, with the danger of a rash, ruinous decision. This psychology belongs to a kind that we can discover in a number of people at all times, and at times in collective attitudes of whole nations (such as the Russia of Dostoyevsky), but is particularly characteristic of the Middle Ages. Nevertheless the *Decameron,* with its own unity and its particular personality, and especially on account of its balanced, all-pervasive, well-formulated and consciously defended 'naturalism,' does not belong to the Middle Ages; it opens a new vision of the world. When Boccaccio, the man, is making merry, we may feel his mood can change; but in the *Decameron* 'nature' is a closed world, accomplished and perfect in itself—it does not need any help from the outside nor will it admit of any. It is a 'naturalistic' world, like that of L. B. Alberti, Poliziano, Ariosto, Rabelais.[26]

In his biography of Boccaccio, Filippo Villani commented on the author's change of heart as follows: "There remain several works wherein he goes somewhat astray by indulging in the liberties of a youthful and voluptuous disposition; but in growing older he himself preferred to let those works go unmentioned."[27] The humanists of the following century tacitly endorsed Boccaccio's and Petrarch's condemnation, which was first clearly announced in the former's Twelfth Eclogue (*Buccolicum Carmen* XII, of ca. 1355). There he had Calliope question him severely: "Have I not seen you some time ago singing a poem in the vulgar tongue, in the public places, to the applause of the uneducated populace?" To which the repentant author humbly replied: "It is so, I stand confessed. We do not always pursue the same goals. In my youth I cherished the vernacular letters."[28] This is usually considered a reference to the *Decameron,* and may well be a comprehensive indictment of his Italian work. This eclogue, together with the XIII

(*Laurea*), which praises the virtue of poetry above the material blessings of wealth, is a defense of poetry parallel to the celebrated Fourteenth Book of the *Genealogie Deorum Gentilium*, but of a higher poetry (symbolized in the title *Sappho*) than that which he confesses to have cultivated in his earlier career. It is the poetry of Humanism, withdrawn from the urgency of the present world into the seclusion of an austere life of study, as exemplified by Petrarch (here significantly named *Silvanus*, the one who haunts the wooded wilderness). This poetry also, like the Muses of the *Decameron*, scorns her numerous attackers, here, as in *Genealogie* XIV, identified with the false shepherds (theologians) and the false priests of mercenary culture (physicians and lawyers).[29] It may be worth noting that the apologetic allusion to his errors as 'juvenile' apparently conflicts with the reflection in the *Decameron*, IV, Proem, to the effect that "at his age it is not proper to pursue these things, namely, to talk about women or condescend to them"—with the witty rebuke that "the leek's head is white but the tail green" (pp. 450 6 and 456 33). The fact is that this idea of 'age' was more an index of maturity than a matter of years. Boccaccio refers to himself as 'youthful' in his late thirties because only now, in his early forties, he feels truly mature, having left all that 'nonsense' behind him. Besides, 'youth' was a standard excuse for such errors.

A detailed elaboration of the new, moralizing outlook is finally offered to us in the second letter to Mainardo Cavalcanti of 1373, where the ailing Boccaccio appears to seal the long story of his 'conversion.' Here, at short distance from his own disappearance from the world of the living, the author warns his friend:

> I cannot praise your having allowed the honorable ladies of your household to read my trifles, rather I beg you not to do so again. You know how much there is in those writings that offends honesty, how much stimulation from the unwelcome Venus, how much encouragement to vice even for the most tried character. Even though virtuous ladies may not be directly forced into dishonest actions by such things, the stimuli of lascivi-

ousness insensibly begin to enter their souls and sometimes affect the impure minds with the corruption of
foul concupiscence, which must be prevented by every
means. . . . Leave such trifles to the young beaux in the
retinue of passions, those who prize highly a reputation
for having stained the honesty of a host of ladies with
their forwardness. But in case you felt unconcerned
about the good name of your ladies, do at least spare
my honor. . . . My readers will think me a filthy pro-
curer, a lewd old man, an uncleanly being, loose and
ill-willed in his language and given to indiscretion on
others' misdeeds. I will not always find someone to
stand up and excuse me by saying:—He wrote this in
his youth, and under the iron rule of one much too
powerful [Cupid]—. . . . Although I am unworthy and
have once been even more so, I should hate to see my
name fouled by the verdict of such ladies.[30]

One of those willing to 'excuse' the *Decameron* as a juvenile
error was Petrarch: "the book you wrote, I take it, in your
youthful age"; "I thought the age could be your excuse."[31]

The *De Casibus Virorum Illustrium,* a sort of anti-*Decameron,* marks the transition from the imaginative freedom of
fiction (the *fabellae* of the *Decameron*) to the austere reality of
historiae morales (Petrarch also raised the question of *fabellae*
or *historiae* in his letter touching upon the *Decameron* and his
translation of the Griselda story: *Sen.* XVII, 3). This point is
deftly made by R. M. Ruggieri, who goes on to analyze the
compromises, uncertainties, and ambiguities which characterize
all of Boccaccio's career, as various critics have pointed out in
dealing with matters of content and style.[32]

The heart of the matter, then, is that within the framework
of Boccaccio's long and composite career the unequivocal,
coherent, and militant naturalism of the *Decameron* is only a
brief moment of happy equilibrium that was destined to be
soon overcome by the basic moralism and 'realism' which
became hallmarks of Renaissance Humanism.[33] The epithet
Johannes tranquillitatum given to our author by his protector
Acciaiuoli in Naples, and used by De Sanctis to emphasize his
'unmedievalism' in contrast to the dramatic spiritual disquiet-

ude of a Dante, will then have to be qualified to remain acceptable as an appropriate one. For there is at least one sense in
which Boccaccio could as well have been nicknamed *Johannes
inquietudinum*.[34] In the complexity and restlessness of his
changing and contradictory, even though ultimately 'superficial'
personality, he is eminently a figure of transition, between two
epochs and cultures.

And yet, the naturalistic lesson of the *Decameron* was the
direct ideal opening of the nonhumanistic Renaissance with its
antitranscendentalism, in which the dualism still persisting in
the medieval tradition of courtly love is vigorously brushed
aside and obliterated. Similarly, the moralism of the *De Casibus*
and of all the humanistic career of Boccaccio was not a return
to the Middle Ages, since the ethics now sought was not the
transcendental movement to supernatural motivation and justification, but the effort to understand the rules and patterns of
man's real behavior in his natural world.

Ultimately, it was Petrarch who was most responsible for
Boccaccio's literary and moral conversion, which he also prevented from degenerating into a violent religious crisis in 1362.
Boccaccio himself avowed Petrarch's original influence on his
conversion in Eclogue XV (ca. 1367), to be read with the help
of the allegorical exegesis of the *Epistola* XXIII to Fra Martino
(see below, pp. 123–124). In an early biographical fragment on
Petrarch, he claimed that the latter had been occasionally
troubled by concupiscence, but never let it conquer him completely.[35] Indeed Boccaccio saw in his master a teacher of
continence, and in the light of this his curious interpretation of
the *Canzoniere* sounds as interesting as it is biased. Laura
appeared to him as the symbol of poetic fame: "I take it that
this Laura must be interpreted allegorically as the poet's laurel,
with which he was later crowned."[36] Such an interpretation,
indeed not an original one but all the more striking coming
from such a reader, may belong to as early a period as 1341–
1342, surely no later than 1350.[37] But, gradually, that which was
Petrarch's authentic conception of love came to contribute to
the ending of Boccaccio's naturalism in favor of a spiritualistic

idealism, naturalistic only by comparison with that of Dante and even the *stilnovisti*. In other words, a previous 'materialism' retreated in the face of a humanistic idealism without returning to supernaturalism.

The two great literati first met in Florence in September of 1350, then again in Padua in the following year. A. F. Massèra first competently indicated the radical change that Boccaccio's Latin style underwent around 1350 under Petrarch's influence.[38] The medieval epistolary *dictator* with rhythmic *cursus* and Apuleian and Fulgentian vocabulary, often disarmingly rare and precious, gave way to the style of free harmonious junctures that the humanists methodically revived from the classics. For this reason, among others, I am inclined to assume that the *Decameron* was completed by 1350 and no later, since it seems difficult to believe that its style, so rich with medieval, *cursus*-like cadences (as Branca has shown), could have been so lovingly polished by an author while he was in the process of divesting himself of such patterns in his Latin writing.

Unique as the *Decameron* may seem for its perfect coherence as a statement of naturalism, it will be expedient to retrace part of our way and investigate briefly the parable of such a position in terms of its struggle against different tendencies of Boccaccio's spirit. We shall then be able to view his 'crisis' in the light of a partial rejection of his basic naturalism.

In the *Ameto* one noticed the lack of a harmonious and logical transition from the naturalness of Ameto's and the Nymphs' loves to the allegorical interpretation attached to them; we find it difficult to take at its face value the author's statement that he is *not* dealing with "that Venus, whom the foolish call goddess of their disorderly concupiscence, but that [other Venus] from which the true and just and sacred affections of love descend among the mortals."[39] The realism of Boccaccio's genuine attitude toward his characters may be covered and disguised by the conventions of medieval transcendence in the forms of *Dolce Stil Nuovo* and Platonic love, but the latter remain an unconvincing superimposition.

Our impression of Boccaccio's inability (in spite of his occasional intentions) to raise his goals from sensuality up to the high level of *Dolce Stil Nuovo* amorous spiritualism was confirmed by the *Amorosa Visione*, where the realistic sentiment of love contrasts with the effort of sublimation through the toil of allegory.[40] In this work we have the author's exceptional attempt to present a case of love in harmony with reason. In Capitolo XLVIII the two Ladies (the Guide and the Beloved) meet and discover their basic agreement, whereas the Guide had previously tried to keep the Dreamer (Boccaccio himself) away from all mundanity, including love and beauty, and in particular the Beloved. In fact, this latter is not a Platonic love in Dante's or other fashion, but a carnal one (see Capitoli XL and L). Hence the obvious and miserable failure, logical and aesthetic, of this poem, since it is supposed to represent the ideal journey from lowly worldliness to perfect purity through love, but it remains, on the contrary, thoroughly ambiguous in the persistence of the sensual desire. The Beloved had even forewarned the Dreamer not to obey his Guide if her instructions were hostile to their love—a transparent reminiscence of the struggle of Love and Nature against Reason in the *Roman de la Rose*.[41]

In the *Fiammetta* we have a forceful restatement of the irresistible force of love as instinct and passion; love has "laws just as any other god," and he can afford to "scorn and cancel the laws of the others, since he is the strongest and imposes his own." In fact, in the *Ninfale Fiesolano* Pruneo revenges the death of the two lovers by destroying the cruel customs established by the rival goddess, the chaste Diane; he scatters the nymphs or forces them to marry.[42] Accordingly, Africo's love is all tender passion issuing from the inextinguishable, unsophisticated desire of the senses, and yet, far from being a temporary and superficial whim, it wholly invests the simple, elementary destiny of the charming shepherd.

But immediately after the *Decameron*, under the apparently medieval surface of the misogynous *Corbaccio* we sense the change of mind brought about by "the disdain of the humanist

who, offended in his dignity, withdraws unto himself and rediscovers, in the midst of his books and in the cult of poetry,
a higher ideal of life, a narrower but more austere morality."[43]
We are, indeed, tempted to view the problem of the *Corbaccio*
from the standpoint of medieval psychology, in which philog-
yny and misogyny were the two dialectical extremes that often
and easily touched each other: the logic of the courtly worship
of the woman was inevitably coupled with the cursing of the
goddess whenever she appeared to behave beneath the faithful's expectations.[44] And yet we must not overlook a relevant
difference: Boccaccio had doubtless been a worshiper of
woman, but we are disinclined to assume that his expectations
were excessive, beyond the possibility of human fulfillment. In
his so rare psychological realism he had surely not placed the
object of his veneration on too high a pedestal, as the courtly
poets had—nor had he placed it too low. His abrupt change
of heart must then be attributed to some other reason than the
one which was customary for his and the preceding age.

At any rate, whatever its cause, the disengagement seems
final and complete. Love is now sternly defined as "a passion
that blinds the mind, sways the intellect, thickens, rather stifles
the memory, scatters the vital faculties . . . a death, the parent
of all vices . . . a state totally deprived of reason, orderliness
and stability, a vice of unhealthy minds, which erases all human
liberty."[45] Ironically, the analogy between women and devils
makes a new appearance in the *Corbaccio*, but the author is no
longer inclined to laugh about it: "Wherefor do you go looking
under the widows', or rather the devils' cloaks, you who could
enjoy the sublime companionship of the Muses whenever you
should wish for it?"[46] The behavior which in the *Decameron*
was deemed 'wise' is still considered so, but sarcastically. After
classifying the various types of serious wisdom, we read about
the "saviezza cianghellina," the wisdom of lady Cianghella,
who,

> after long and serious debate in the women's 'discreet'
> council, had her motion passed, whereby it was con-
> cluded that all those fearless and hearty women who

> know how to be as often and with as many men as their
> concupiscent appetite [*appetito concupiscibile*] de-
> mands, shall be called wise [*savie*], all the others, good-
> for-nothing [*decime o moccicose*].[47]

Totally absent from the *Decameron,* the sense of sin by
sensuality rings clearly in the language of passages such as the
following from the *Genealogie,* where the attributes of the
mystic Venus are explained through the application of Christian feelings to pagan forms, not without a curious lack of
historical perspective: "They say she is the guardian of roses,
because they turn red and sting, which is characteristic of lust;
we blush for the ugliness of the sin and we feel the sting of
remorse for our awareness of it."[48] This work acknowledges the
justice of banishing the immoral poets, as Plato wished, that is,
of the poets "criminum suasores," persuaders of lasciviousness,
like Ovid.[49] But hear how detachedly the author speaks of those
who delight in literature such as the *Decameron* at the same
time as they hypocritically condemn it:

> These zealots [the theologians and priests who make
> themselves prosecutors of 'immoral' poets] are given to
> flirting and wenching . . . and to write their amatory
> poems and letters resort to the help of instructors in
> such art. Hence they leaf the volumes of Catullus,
> Propertius, Ovid, whereby . . . their hearts are com-
> pletely seduced and possessed. . . . Indeed our critics
> are busy in truly momentous enterprises, since it is no
> trifle to serve Love, whose forces subjugated first Phoe-
> bus, then Hercules, the tamer of monsters![50]

The allegory of the Fifteenth Bucolic Eclogue is explained
as follows in the Latin Epistle XXIII to Fra Martino da Signa,
probably of 1374:

> The fifteenth Eclogue is titled *Phylostropos* because it
> treats the conversion from the lures of the love for
> things earthly to the love for things celestial; indeed
> the title comes from *phylos,* i.e., love, and *tropos,* i.e.,
> conversion. There are two interlocutors. . . . Phylostro-
> pos stands for my glorious teacher, Francis Petrarch,
> who oftentimes warned me to leave behind the pleas-

ures of the world and turn my mind to things eternal,
and thus changed my loves, though not perfectly, for
the better. Typhlus stands for myself, and for anyone
whose sight is blinded by the soot of the world, since
Greek *typhus* [sic; *typhlos*?] means 'blind.'[51]

This rather medieval phrasing of Petrarch's influence on him is,
however, slightly deceptive. In reality Boccaccio's new interests
were far less 'otherworldly' than these lines seem to imply. At
any rate, the passage here explained by the author is significant
as a rare admission of fault; in Eclogue XV (vv. 165–169)
Typhlus admitted to have given scandal and sinfully attacked
the clergy and the church: "Shall I go and visit the woods of
this elder from whom I remember having once stolen a young
cow, and whose laws and rites I trampled underfoot and with
unholy hands threw to the pigs of Dyones to be torn apart?"[52]

Nevertheless, even after his 'conversion' Boccaccio's world
remains ostensibly founded on natural arguments. Nature still
is the *"maestra delle cose* who cannot be rightfully blamed"
(*Corbaccio*, Bruscoli ed., p. 214), and God himself is introduced
debating with the author with human and natural arguments
at the beginning of the *Corbaccio*. In the *Genealogie* the respective dignity of different professions is stated in terms of
natural order, instead of the medieval hierarchical striving
toward the supreme and perfect goal. The study of letters is
thus justified, regardless of the relative worth of other disci-
plines. "Mother Nature, inexhaustible in her forces and perfect
in her mind, has produced mortals with different aptitudes
among themselves, so that Nature's foremost concern, the
preservation of mankind, could be fulfilled by the variety of
men's occupations." "Hence Nature in her discretion has made
one a carpenter, another a sailor, another yet a merchant." "Just
as Nature has divided the physical functions among the organs
for the benefit of our body, in order to give it being in diversity
like a melody from different tones, we necessarily had to be
born to different forms of activity for the preservation of mankind."[53] It is therefore against nature not to develop our inborn,
spontaneous calling:

Who will successfully dare to shift from that for which he was born to something else? [To surpass the forces of nature by our free will] is indeed a rare achievement, so great and almost invincible is the fateful force [*necessitas*] that urges us toward the form of activity for which we were born! Considering that we are born for different achievements, it will be quite satisfactory if we succeed in the full accomplishment of our calling, without wishing to achieve something else.

Indeed the reader feels a religious sense of nature's sanctity and irresistibility. It is too dangerous to attempt to go against its will, lest we should first miss our calling and then also fail in the new path: "There are those who tried this in vain: they missed the realization of their true being, without becoming what they wished to be."[54]

This is the guiding impulse and principle behind his own whole career—the irresistible call of the Muses, the natural path for him: "My soul did not tend toward poetry with all its power because of some newly made decision, but for the inner urging of its own most ancient disposition."[55] For this, he felt, he had been born, and this he pursued with spontaneity and determination (*sua sponte sumpsit ingenium*) with no outside help, rather against his father's obstinate resistance. These obstacles prevented him from becoming a truly great poet, which he trusts nature had made him to be, whereas he necessarily failed to become a merchant and a lawyer, as his father, against nature, wanted.[56]

The same basic idea was expressed in the Twelfth Eclogue: "We are born for different kinds of action, which if we follow with the best of our talents, we will easily be led to fruition of our goal."[57] And finally in the first letter of 1373 to Mainardo Cavalcanti, he will state his distrust of physicians despite his many ailments in the following terms: "I can find no remedies, neither in doctors nor in medicines, although I have no faith in them: I live *under the guide of nature and instinct*."[58] Which could have been his motto in the good old days.

EPILOGUE

Nature's Progress, or the Emancipation of the Negative

What hurts the soul
My soul adores,
No better than a beast
Upon all fours.
        W. B. Yeats, *The lady's first song*

From the vantage point of most of the naturalistic tradition which preceded him, the novelty of Boccaccio's position lay in his bold and unequivocal proclamation of the 'law of nature' as a new creed for everybody, in direct, explicit reply to the objections of official culture. Thus the religion of worldly love, inaugurated by the Provençals, erected to a formal code in the courtly milieu, subtly filtered through the intellectual experience of the Italian Sweet New Style, finally became an autonomous cult without institutionalized formalities and rituals outside a firm faith in its own abstract rightfulness, and later on contributed to the naturalism of the Renaissance. In this age man, at last completely left to himself, *homo sibi relictus,* found himself alone and naked before nature, without the support and the superstructure of the church, the court, or chivalry. At the same time, however, that this process was attaining to its fulfillment, we notice the practical disappearance of that complex of ideological and social motifs in which the particular medieval brand of naturalism had been embodied. Somehow it seems to thin itself out and all but vanish as though it had exhausted its function and outgrown its usefulness. Consequently, even in this aspect the Renaissance may appear to us as an island directly bridged to antiquity. Thus, ultimately, the medieval appeal to an irrational province of human experience, the naturalistic realm of 'absolute' eroticism, gave way to the basic, comprehensive rationalism of the Renaissance in this same sphere.

The Platonic view of passion as opposed to reason, its lawful master, of body and flesh as the servant of the mind, of nature in contrast with a supernature, the former only a first, inferior level of being with respect to the latter, prevailed in Humanism, although the supernatural of the humanist was no longer the medieval otherworld, but a higher level of human experience. Furthermore, all levels of reality were now measured by intellectual and rational values, and were seen as a harmonious totality, a cosmos.[1]

Petrarch, the "Prince of Humanism," still relied theoretically on a sharp distinction between body and soul that must lead to a downgrading of matter, and was thus essentially remote from that 'naturalism' which is based on a revaluation of matter and body as integral, nonseparable parts of reality. Generally speaking, we must acknowledge that Humanism saw man *within* nature but not *continuous* with nature inasmuch as man's characteristics keep him distinct from, and above the rest of the natural world. Consequently, the particular, limited 'naturalism' of the more typical literature of the Renaissance could not be satisfied with the mere fulfillment of natural goals, that is of instinctive desires that man has in common with lower forms.

Starting with P. P. Vergerio, whose ideas influenced Vittorino da Feltre, the first great practical educator among the humanists, humanistic education regularly insisted on controlling human passions and favoring only those movements which conform to reason.

Before Ficino gave a new, powerful impulse to the Neoplatonic mystique of love, the Quattrocento humanists, preoccupied as they were with their rationalistic and civic interests, had tended to dismiss love and all passions as negative experiences. As their authoritative spokesman we could take L. B. Alberti, who in his *Intercoenalis* "Amator" lists love and wrath as undesirable emotions, *perturbationes,* which disturb the ideal equilibrium of the soul.[2] And in his *Della Famiglia* the sexual instinct is seen as the enemy of our freedom: "The soul must never be a slave. It is a slave whenever it is greedy, miserly, illiberal . . . for, then, vices rule the soul . . . and forbid it to gain worthy praise and fame with the harmonious exercise of its free will."[3] Ficino and his followers assigned to the Earthly Venus an essential role in the scale of man's ascent to perfect beauty and love, but this role was inferior to that of the Heavenly Venus.[4]

The conception of love which prevailed in the Renaissance was a notably intellectualistic one in a Platonic vein. No matter how irrational love might be conceived to be in its genesis and in its development as a passion, its aims were constantly to be controlled by the rational intellect, if it was to be an acceptable and 'good' state of the soul. More important still, 'serious' and noble love was given a rational, ethically good, and intellectually directed goal. The romantic, truly irrationalistic glorification of love as pure sentiment—a natural force above reason and social conventions—which had attained to its poetic climax for the Middle Ages in the Tristan legend and was to reappear later at the onset of the Baroque age, has no recognizable place in the Renaissance.

For its exceptional position within the development of Humanism, a special treatment is due, however, to Lorenzo Valla's *De Voluptate* (*De Vero Bono*), that amazingly bold, originally challenging, and, in part, paradoxically ambiguous defense of Epicureanism, interpreted as hedonism and moral utilitarianism. The curiously 'modern' ring of this rhetorico-philosophical treatise derives chiefly from its thoroughly critical, iconoclastic attack on all that had been and still was officially sacred.[5] Valla condemns Stoicism for its lack of understanding toward nature, for its heroic morality based on the rejection of that which is the true motivation of human activity, 'pleasure.' And his polemic against the traditional insertion of Stoic axioms into Christian ethics is, ultimately, a sweeping indictment of the asceticism that dominated medieval Christianity.[6]

The interlocutors of the dialogue are Leonardo Bruni, later replaced by Catone Sacco in the second and third versions; Panormita, later Maffeo Vegio; and Niccolò Niccoli, later Antonio da Rho (Raudensis). Bruni-Catone (the Stoic) defends 'virtue' and 'honesty,' and is declared "nemico della natura e della voluttà," enemy of nature and of pleasure, which are in turn defended by Panormita-Vegio (the Epicurean). In drawing a conclusion from their debate Niccoli-Raudensis will denounce Stoicism as abstract and inhuman and attempt a reconciliation of Epicureanism and Christianity, which he regards as basically in agreement. Catone (to take the characters of the final draft) had begun the praise of Stoicism by imputing the rampant viciousness of man's behavior to a congenital fault of nature. We are naturally born bad. Vegio begins his confutation by an apologia of nature (and consequently of humanity). For him Epicureanism is philosophy according to nature, while Stoicism is contrary to nature. And in the final conclusion Raudensis will try to cleanse nature of all of Catone's charges (Book 3).

The 'Epicurean' 's oration ended with the definition of pleasure (*voluptas*) as harmony with nature. Hence every desire deserves satisfaction, adultery and the community of women are natural, virginity is unnatural, the tyranny of families and society on nuns is criminal. Since pleasure, of which love is made ("voluptas ipsa amor est" in the third version), knows no boundaries, Aristotle's principle of "virtus in medio," virtue as a middle point between extremes, is theoretically to be rejected. The excellence of our senses, specially sight, taste, and smell, is a sign of humanity, since they are not shared by animals in the same degree (a humanistic theme to which Montaigne will markedly react). In the polemic of Book 3 against intellectualistic morality one learns that nature, not reason, should be our teacher. Vegio argues that nature teaches us to follow the senses and the instincts, pursue pleasure as our final goal, accept sensuality, and fight chastity as well as all social and moral impediments. 'Honesty,' that is, virtue for its own sake and as its own reward is an empty word, at worst a misunderstanding or even hypocrisy. Consequently we are warned: ". . . do not let yourselves be fooled by the cunning of men who introduced a certain imaginary honesty; but rather follow and cherish the law of nature."[7] The Epicurean then defends free love, adultery, and, even if it should mean incest, the complete community of women according to "the law of Plato, or rather of nature" (p. 67). Furthermore, he explicitly contrasts the law of nature, "followed by many nations," with the civil law (quoting the *Lex Julia de adulteriis*). In terms worthy of Jean de Meung (the episode of Venus and Vulcan) and of Boccaccio (Madonna Filippa, VI, 7) he blames Menelaus for bringing about the Trojan war by refusing to share Helen with Paris: a truly liberal decision that would have meant no loss to anyone: "even if a thousand receive this beneficence, it will not deteriorate in itself" (p. 68)!

At last, the audience is surprised by an unqualified reproof of virginity even though it were maintained for the sake of religion (or, rather, "superstition"); for even courtesans are said to be more praiseworthy than virgin nuns: they serve society better (pp. 70–77)! The origin of such a discreditable custom as enforced virginity is attributed to the avarice of old parents who wanted to save the dowry. One of these forced virgins is introduced pleading in the forum of a "Platonic senate" against such an "unnatural" and "unhealthy" institution; and subsequently against the unjust inequality of the sexes. Priests and priestesses ought to marry. The speaker establishes the equivalence between the innate search for pleasure and the teaching

of nature, after Epicurus and Lucretius. To the gods themselves, in a way "one and the same thing with nature" (p. 78),
the poets, most worthy among mortals, have attributed such
qualities and customs that their existence is a fabric of flirta-
tion, incest, and adultery.[8] Indeed a good guide for us.

Later Raudensis, in a 'neo-Christian' context, seems to shun
the traditional dichotomy of body and mind: he refutes Plato's
and Aristotle's distinction of physical pleasures and spiritual
pleasures (see Aristotle's *Nicomachean Ethics*, X, 4 and 5):
"Every pleasure is felt not so much with the body as with the
mind, which rules the body [see Epicurus]: who can doubt
that physical pleasures are generated with the help of the
soul and the spiritual ones with the cooperation of the body?"[9]

The same need for a more harmonious balance between the
ideal and the material seems to inspire another, and most singular product of humanistic culture, namely that famed *Hypnerotomachia Poliphili* whose incunabulum edition has been
acclaimed as the most beautiful achievement of Renaissance
printing.[10] It is, indeed, in such nonconformist and exceptional
works as the *De Voluptate* and the *Poliphilus* that one must
look for the naturalistic undercurrent of the early Italian Renaissance—an undercurrent which carried in its bosom the seed
of new, radical developments, but which the Counter-Reformation later prevented from coming boldly and widely into the
open to bear its logical fruits.

The *Poliphilus* is a hermetic allegory couched in eccentrically
humanistic language and intemperately weighted with classical
erudition. It consists of a vision which counts among its an-
cestors Guillaume de Lorris, Dante, and the Boccaccio of the
Ameto and the *Amorosa Visione*. The young Poliphilus visits the
Kingdom of Art, and once confronted with the triple choice
of seeking God's glory, earthly glory, or pleasure, against the
advice of Reason decides to pursue the last, and consequently
does attain perfect happiness in the contemplation of the naked
Venus. We are thus presented with a story of sensual love,
wherein, to quote the competent conclusion of Vittorio Rossi,
"A new deity, Nature, succeeds the transcendental God [of the

Middle Ages]; a deity in which the human being finds its rest as in the necessary foundation and never-failing companion of all spiritual activity."[11]

In the sense explained above it is ambiguous to speak of naturalism in the Renaissance without clearly distinguishing its characteristics from those of medieval naturalism. The latter had been, basically, in opposition to the dominant idealistic rationalism. By the time of the Renaissance, however, the acquisition of the realm of nature is an accomplished fact and is understood as part of reason's widened domain. Precisely because so much is then taken for granted, we have doubts, at times, as to the real extent of such acceptance of 'nature.' Thinking of Erasmus, for instance, Huizinga has asked the legitimate question: "Did he share without reserve his friend Thomas More's intense and frank sense of the blessing of a life lived according to nature? Did the rich flowering of the Renaissance also find expression in him?"[12] But this question is destined to remain unanswered, for there is a serious gap in our knowledge of the mind of the Second Prince of Humanism. As Erasmus himself tells us, at the time of the *Encomium Morias* "we had a series of three declamations in mind: the praise of folly, of nature, and of grace, but the peevishness of certain people led me to renounce the idea."[13] And Huizinga comments on this fascinating suggestion:

> One asks oneself in vain what form this Praise of Nature may have had in Erasmus's mind. There must have been something daring about it; why should he otherwise have abandoned his intention because of the criticism to be expected? The Praise of Nature as the central panel of a triptych. . . . : we can vaguely divine the highest intellectual achievement of an Erasmus unknown to us. Folly, nature, and grace as a trinity of ascending potential; is it not as if we here have lost a most intimate credo of the Renaissance?[14]

In a philosophical sense, a naturalistic 'rehabilitation' of the world of matter did originate in the Renaissance. This took place with Telesio, Bruno, and Campanella, who, in opposition to Aristotle's dual view of nature as made of form and matter, strove to identify one moving force in the universe. Bruno and Campanella conceived this unitary element as a universal soul pervading the whole and every part of the cosmos. But to turn to the poets' intuition of the world, let us briefly consider the position of the greatest and purest poet of the Italian Renaissance in its maturity. One can safely state that Ariosto's poetic, freely re-created cosmos transcends nature, though it certainly moves in a sphere completely deprived of the supernatural in any religious sense. It presents us with a new world whose denizens have a nature of their own, a set of patterns of behavior, instincts, and a consistent code given to them by their 'creator,' the poet himself.

Yet, the powerful inroads made by the naturalistic spirit are immediately clear to any reader of the *Orlando Furioso*. Beneath and beyond the idealistic convention of a chivalric structure, the forces which move this human world are those of 'real' sentiments and affections. The fate of the main heroine, Angelica, celebrates the definitive refutation of all the courtly prejudices. Requested of her love by the cream of the chivalrous society, the most glorious paladins on earth, she turns them all down and will eventually stoop to ask mercy of Medoro, a humble soldier. It would seem that it is, above all, this intolerable absurdity (from the courtly viewpoint) that drives Orlando mad. What Orlando is unable to perceive, is the 'providential' value of that shocking mésalliance, the punishment of Angelica's ineffable pride.

As in real life, we are always introduced to situations in which we are apprehensively expecting reason to determine the outcome and have the best of a difficult crisis. Instead, unreason and the unexpected (*Fortuna*, 'chance') do prevail. But this unreason is not simply the want of reason, the inexplicable absurd, it is the emerging of other and deeper forces, freshly out of the inner psyche of the characters. Let us take, as an example, a crucial incident in the poem: namely, the 'multiple duels' of Canto XXVI. When the dreadful duels simultaneously involving Marfisa, Ruggiero, Rodomonte, and Mandricardo are interrupted by Doralice's riding off the field (so that both her lovers, Rodomonte and Mandricardo, are obliged to follow her), love is, by obvious implication, understood to be stronger than both the personal motives of the duels (briefly, chivalric 'honor') and the loyalty to the sovereign (for which they all would rather postpone their quarrels and go to the battle of Paris).[15]

Likewise Bradamante, the most serious feminine character in the poem, prefers to forego honor and even honesty rather than renounce her love for Ruggiero. She decides to break her word to marry the knight who can win her in duel, and likewise to break her faith to her family (who want her married to Leone) and to Charlemagne (who made himself warrant of her promise to accept the winner).[16] And her betrothed, Ruggiero, the alleged ancestor of the poet's patrons, had lightheartedly laid aside his vows of eternal fidelity and made ready to take advantage of the beautiful and helpless Angelica, thereby shamelessly yielding to the first temptation which came his way (end of Canto X).[17]

Ariosto may well be the poet of Cosmos and Harmony, provided we do not lose sight of the fact that the matter of his harmonious representation is the Chaos of the Irrational of which true life is made.[18]

But Ariosto makes his point in the most effortless manner, as if his stand could be taken for granted by the reader. It was only at the end of the Renaissance that, in the perturbed climate of the Counter-Reformation, what was obvious to previous generations became again a subject for earnest argument, to be eventually justified or rebuked. It was only then that the conscious representation of erotic passion as a natural force good in itself reappeared in a polemical context. Tasso announced it in the *Aminta,* but he guiltily shrouded it in the melancholic consciousness of its being an impossible dream, and later pronounced his self-criticism for having let this dream disrupt the 'regular unity' of his *Gerusalemme.*[19]

But after the deep crisis of the Reformation and Counter-Reformation, the times were ripe for a change, and such a change was witnessed in what we call the Baroque age. It is perhaps in Christopher Marlowe's *Hero and Leander* (1593) that one can indicate the emergence of a new attitude which seems to culminate in the *Lettres d'une Religieuse portugaise* (1669). Beside their psychological realism, one senses in such texts the presence of revolutionary phenomena, which make them comparable (but obviously not identical) only to the Tristan story, of all preceding literature: first, the expression of the contradictory character of psychic life, the life of emotion and sentiment; second, the positiveness of what had so far been constantly rated negatively, and to a degree continued to be so. On the plane of physical reality, from the Greeks to the Renaissance the Platonic notion of the Good being identical with the One, namely the immutable enjoying its perfect unity within itself, had been the highest and most prevalent expression of a deep theoretical distrust for those characteristics of the world of nature and history which Heracleitos had, quite atypically, attempted to rehabilitate. It was not until Galileo that variety and change ceased to be considered inherently ignoble—a profound mental revolution which was later paralleled by the birth of modern historicism in the study of human behavior and events. In the moral sphere, we witness the appearance of what we can call the intuition of the positiveness of the negative and of the irrational, "the prodigious power of the negative," to use Hegel's inspired phrase.[20] This new dialectical position is felt in the tone of approving acceptance of a tragic reality—tragic inasmuch as certain forces are found to be inescapably bound to conflict with others to which they are neither inferior nor ready to submit. Victims of the erotic passion are represented as heroes, they remain ultimately unvanquished by reason, rather tend to subjugate it and make it a tool for their ends (as the cynic, unwittingly hypocritical rhetoric of Leander's speeches brilliantly shows).[21] As to the tremendously popular letters attributed to Sister Alcoforado, if our memory is tempted to hark back to Héloïse's letters to Abélard, it will be fair to remind ourselves once again that the medieval public presumably was quite far from reacting to such letters in the way in which the readers of the Portuguese nun reacted. Abélard himself—

and not only because he was a philosopher, a teacher, and a monk—answered with the proper advice to let reason have the best of that embarrassing situation—which was not the likely solution in the mind of the Marquis de Chamilly, the seducer of the unfortunate nun.

The slow progress of the attitudes we are here describing is made immediately apparent if we but think that the most dramatic type of 'wicked hero' of the Baroque age, the Don Juans of Tirso de Molina (published in 1630) and Molière (1665) still were exemplary cases of the evil character of natural drives, as Faust had been in the Renaissance, on the more intellectual level of naturalistic curiosity (*Historia von D. Johann Fausten,* 1587; Marlowe's *Dr. Faustus* between 1588 and 1593). Both Don Juan and Faust were piously made to end in the hands of the devil. It is only with Lessing (17th *Literaturbrief*) and Goethe that the Faust theme underwent a decisive change toward the modern treatment, whereby the evil forces became dialectically allied to the noblest goals. Ch. D. Grabbe (*Don Juan und Faust,* 1829) united the two heroes in a treatment of the dualism of material and spiritual that was inspired by Byron's *Manfred.*[22]

The central importance of the doctrines of nature for the eighteenth-century Enlightenment is well known. It is particularly interesting, for our purpose, to analyze the influence of such doctrines on Rousseau, and his personal reaction to them in the *Nouvelle Héloïse* (1761), for the many hesitations, uncertainties, and compromises of the staunchest partisan of 'nature' at the very time when nature was most insistently deified will serve, I trust, as fitting counterpoint to the boldest naturalism we have witnessed in the Middle Ages.

In the sudden, dramatic proposal of elopement and consequent free union advanced by Saint-Preux to Héloïse (Part 1, Letter 26) is reflected Rousseau's practical attitude against marriage, whereby he was never formally, sacramentally wed to Thérèse Levasseur. Nevertheless in Part 3, Letter 18, a true treatise on social duties, the sacred nature of marriage is extolled.

When the rights of nature (and of the senses) triumph, this triumph means a defeat for society, with its principles of honor, reputation, innocence, "virtue." After yielding to passion, Julie will be devoured by remorse, because reason (allied to sentiment against the senses) insists that yielding to passion is criminal.[23] D. Mornet noted that in *Julie* for the first time in France remorse "cried" after a seduction.[24] In fact, the sentimental novel had only staged cases of love in which chastity triumphed, or married women who had sinned suffered more than they repented. Only Clarissa Harlowe had felt guilty and dishonored, even though she had been violated with the help of a narcotic. But in Rousseau's 'romanticism,' whereas society is often the villain, the 'natural' sensual instincts are finally overwhelmed and dominated by reason in the form of a superior, inner morality.

To understand more fully Rousseau's peculiar position one only has to turn to the key passage on *pudeur* in Letter 50 (Vol. II, pp. 171-172): "Le véritable amour est le plus chaste de tous les liens." "C'est lui . . . qui sait épurer nos penchants naturels, en les concentrant dans un seul objet" (and this object, thanks to its sublimation through love, loses its 'sex'). "Le coeur ne suit point les sens, il les guide." "La décence et l'honnêteté l'accompagnent [that is, le véritable amour] au sein de la volupté même, et lui seul sait tout accorder aux désirs sans rien ôter à la pudeur." "La débauche et l'amour ne sauroient loger ensemble." More than Platonic love, it is a Christian approach tinted with a good deal of puritanism that characterizes Rousseau's views. This sense of *pudeur* so effectively and originally stressed by Rousseau was central in most of love literature (and practical mores) of the Christian era. Ugo Foscolo, a most sensitive critic and a great poet of love in his own right, defined the impact of Petrarch's poetry by attributing to him the achievement of having refined pagan sensuality by veiling it with the Christian modesty, to the effect of turning a physical movement into a sublime spiritual affection.[25] And, of course, this was true as well, though less distinctively, of many an earlier poet. But it certainly did not apply to Boccaccio, whose naturalistic representation of love was characterized by the absence of this modesty. Yet Boccaccio's naturalism still remained different from pre-Christian, pagan eroticism—of which it lacked the rather unsophisticated, candid immediacy—while it could be regarded as a natural reaction to the excesses of Christian *pudeur*. Far from being so vigorously held up above everything else, what had been traditionally regarded as 'nature' is, instead, downgraded by Rousseau as the realm of sheer sensuality, animal and elementary, whereas the dramatic and spiritual value of the love relationship is seen in function of the constant tension between the rights of free election and the rights of social order (in this case, symbolically, the unequivocal parental opposition). Consequently, the true essence of Rousseau's 'naturalism' as well as of his view of love is the attempt to save both the instincts and all the socially conditioned virtues of innocence, respectability, decency, restraint, chastity, outward honesty, in a relationship guided and dominated, rather than by sheer reason, by *le coeur* and *le sentiment*.

The key word is, then, *pudeur,* a basic word in all romance languages which has, interestingly enough, no Germanic or English equivalent. With his remarkable formula Rousseau was far from defeating the erotic passion, for *pudeur* added to sensuality spiritualizes it by rendering it more challenging, more tantalizing, more disturbingly delightful. This is one aspect of the impact of civilization on human nature—an aspect to the development of which Christianity has contributed so much, and which no author has analyzed with greater efficacy than Rousseau. *Pudeur* keeps the outbursts of the senses (sharpened by long expectation or even self-denial) on a high, 'sublimated' level of control and decency at the same time that the more prevalent moments of purely intellectual, moral, and spiritual communion are 'spiced' by the admittedly everpresent but repressed desires of the senses. Rousseau's heroes could thus feel satisfied with both their *honnêteté* and their *volupté,* in a chaste sensuality that was, strictly, neither chaste nor sensual, nor even entirely immune from a touch of masochism in the intensity of its process. All this was extremely typical of the eighteenth-century *sensiblerie,* although the *philosophes* had repeatedly exalted the lack of *pudeur* in the natural, straight-forward customs of "savages."[26] Indeed, Rousseau's *philosophe* knows a subtler kind of pleasure: "Ainsi s'aiguise la volupté du sage: s'abstenir pour jouir c'est la philosophie; c'est l'épicuréisme de la raison" (Part 6, Letter 5, p. 216). This love, then, rather than eliminating sensuality, refines it in a new, subtle 'chastity,' burns it up in a balanced, peaceful state of 'sensual' sentimentality without sexual attachment (see Part 6, esp. Letters 6-8).[27]

The intransigent, somewhat 'masochistic' virtue of Rousseau's lovers appears ever more obvious in *Les amours de Milord Edouard Bomston* (in appendix to the *Nouvelle Héloïse*), where love is described as a pure movement of the heart, which develops independently from, and on an absolutely higher plane than the sexual interest, since it arises not from such interest, but from an encounter with virtue. Indeed, in spite of all the talk about nature, Rousseau's views tended irresistibly to the triumph of a pure sentiment, wherein a total elimination of sensuality could never be achieved, but was always before the mind as the ideal, theoretical goal. This may remind one of many a *stilnovista* attitude (see the 'woman angel'), more than of any phase of Platonic love, including the English Pre-Raphaelites. As the author said of himself in his Correspondence: "L'amour que je conçois, celui que j'ai pu sentir, s'enflamme à l'image illusoire de la perfection de l'objet aimé; et cette illusion même le porte à l'enthousiasme de la vertu, car cette idée entre toujours dans celle d'une femme parfaite."[28] And to the consolation offered by Saint-Preux after the seduction: "N'as-tu pas suivi les plus pures lois de la *nature*?" Julie replies: "Ce doux enchantement de vertu s'est évanoui." (Letter 32, p. 115). For one notable asset of Rousseau's is his insistence on the nonidentity of pleasure and happiness: "Nous avons recherché le plaisir et le bonheur a fui loin de nous" (ibid.).

The Christian dichotomy of body and soul, 'nature' and 'spirit,' returns in full bloom with Rousseau: the basic situation of the *Nouvelle Héloïse* is so typical in its substance, despite the originality of the formal presentation, that we can easily find parallels from the origins of the romance literary tradition. One could, for instance, recall the notorious adventures of Rigaut de Barbezieux, whose relationship with his beloved 'Better-than-a-Lady' (Mielhs-de-Domna) was described as follows: "Rigaut begged her to show mercy and grant him the favors of love, and the lady replied that she was willing to oblige him as long as her honor was preserved, and said that, if Rigaut loved her as much as he professed, he ought not to press for more in words or deeds than he was already getting from her."[29] But, in a manner most unlike Rousseau, such a lady will later be punished by Rigaut's taking leave of her, at the very moment when, in begging him to remain loyal to her, she belatedly pledges to grant him her once craved favors.[30] Provençal or not, there was a realistic (or 'natural') limit to Rigaut's sentimentalism.

Julie's methodic coquetry amounted to saying: I am disposed to go all the way with you, as is right, but I will put you to the test further, and ask you to prove your true love for me by loving without reward. The significant title chosen by Rousseau for his novel undoubtedly points to much more than a superficial relationship. We need but ponder a passage (Part 2, Letter 11, and esp. p. 298) where happiness is proclaimed to reside in absolute devotion without hope of fruition, despite all the world's and society's obstacles, and we shall realize how this is not only a 'return' to the medieval Héloïse, but to the purest, most idealistic, most abstract courtly love of troubadours and Platonists.[31]

The ultimate aim of Rousseau is a type of sublime, total love that will dominate all our behavior, to the extent of ennobling it in a virtuous transcendence of all egoistic interests. Its inspiration and operating medium would be a constant, unlimited tension of sacrifice that threatens to abolish the human and turn it into angelic perfection. At the conclusion of Rousseau's glorification of nature there is a puritanic denial of the traditional 'rights' of nature: "la force de l'âme qui produit toutes les vertus tient à la pureté qui les nourrit toutes" (Part 6, Letter 6, p. 221). We are here reminded of the praise of chastity in the *Émile*, a praise rare in the eighteenth century.[32]

Yet, we shall not be surprised by the masterful *coup de scène* when Saint-Preux, in a forceful and dramatical letter (Part 3, Letter 11), makes a profession of faith in all the basic points traditionally posited by the literature of naturalistic love. In opposition to Julie's solution of her terrible dilemma by acquiescing to her father's will, Saint-Preux will claim that love has a right to free choice which is superior to all duties toward family and society, that is: independent of the parents' will and interests, and independent of social status (notably nobility's privileges, the major obstacle to Saint-Preux' marriage). All previous *aménagements* of Saint-Preux, far from being a recognition of the justness of Julie's objections and scruples, were a sacrifice in the name of the beloved's happiness, or rather peace. "Quel que soit l'empire dont vous abusez, mes droits sont plus sacrés que les vôtres; la chaîne qui nous lie est la borne du pouvoir paternel, même devant les tribunaux humains, et quand vous osez réclamer la *nature* [cf. Julie's letter], c'est vous seule qui bravez ses lois" (Vol. III, p. 26). And he continues with an eloquent and unswerving condemnation of nobility and 'honor,' the formal obstacles to their union ("maximes gothiques"; "je me soucie fort peu de savoir en quoi consiste l'honneur d'un gentilhomme," ibid.).

All this is small wonder for us, for we have seen how the polemic against family tyranny and class prejudice was intimately tied to the evolution of 'natural love.' As for Rousseau's view on the triangle of nature, love, and reason, we read that, "Si l'amour ne règne pas, la raison choisira seule. . . . Si l'amour règne, la nature a déjà choisi. Telle est la loi sacrée de la nature . . . ," and to break it in the name of rank or social station is a crime to be paid for by inevitable and fatal disorders (Part 2, Letter 2, p. 253). All laws that hinder a free choice are unjust: "Ce chaste noeud de la nature n'est soumis ni au pouvoir souverain ni à l'autorité paternelle" (p. 250). The literature of France and England was full of marriages where love triumphed over social differences: suffice it to mention Richardson's *Pamela* (and see Montesquieu's and abbé Leblanc's remarks on England's mores respectively in *Esprit des lois,*

XXIII, 8 and *Lettres d'un Français,* 10, these latter of 1745);
Marivaux' *La Double Inconstance, Les Fausses Confidences,
Le Préjugé vaincu.* The polemic against the aristocratic prejudice is very important in the *Nouvelle Héloïse,* as the quarrel
between Milord Edouard Bomston and the heroine's father
shows (Part 1, Letter 62). Milord Edouard's arguments have a
common ring with the traditional ones found, for example, in
Boccaccio.

In a moment of weakness Julie herself gives up and endorses
Saint-Preux' views: "Nature, ô douce nature, reprends tous tes
droits! J'abjure les barbares vertus qui t'anéantissent. Les penchants que tu m'a donnés seront-ils plus trompeurs qu'une raison qui m'égara tant de fois?" (Part 3, Letter 15.) So nature is
momentarily placed above virtue *and* reason! She will nonetheless persist in her respect toward her father's will ("autorité
sacrée"), but "devoir, honneur, vertu, tout cela ne me dit plus
rien"; her father is an "esclave de sa parole et jaloux d'un vain
titre." This will determine a contradictory situation (deplored
but obediently and piously accepted, as always, by Saint-Preux)
whereby she will marry an abhorred man as an homage to her
father's will, and continue to love Saint-Preux (who will
chastely cohabitate with the married couple). Actually, the
denial and despair of the values of virtue was only a temporary
result of a tremendous emotional crisis from which the heroine
will recover (Part 3, Letter 18). And it is interesting to note that
she attributed those moments of moral despair to the influence
of the *philosophes!* Indeed, one senses in this crisis a dramatic
struggle against the naturalistic philosophy of all times.

Of course, Rousseau's conception of nature is at variance
with, and partly opposed to that of the Encyclopaedists. These
latter's intellectual naturalism, allied with Rousseau's sentimentality, bore its ripest fruit in *Paul et Virginie* (composed around
1785), whereby Bernardin de Saint-Pierre, as part of his *Etudes
de la Nature,* proposed to prove the thesis that a simple life in
a natural environment was best for man, whose ills can be
traced to the depravity of society.

The French rationalists of the Enlightenment (and Rousseau

even more so) conceived of the 'natural' man (that is, the pre-civilization man) as a being who is good and noble because he lives by his pure, innocent instincts, uncomplicated, hence uncontaminated by the artificial conventions of sophisticated society.[33] The heritage of such a myth lasted well into the Romantic and post-Romantic age. For an eloquent illustration of its persistence beyond any barriers of time and space we can turn to an eminent son of the French rationalists, Tolstoy, who in his pre-'conversion' work often contrasted the natural man to the civilized man, the latter basically corrupt even though more 'honest' and 'moral.' We are reminded, in this context, of such novels as *Two Hussars, The Cossacks,* and in *War and Peace,* the characters of Natasha, Nicholas Rostov, Platon Karatayev. Indeed, of *War and Peace* as a whole an authoritative critic has said that "The philosophy of the novel is the glorification of nature and life at the expense of the sophistication of reason and civilization. It is the surrender of the rationalist Tolstoy to the irrational forces of existence."[34]

Close to Rousseau's was Leopardi's early conception of nature and correlative critique of civilization and history. But the great poet from Recanati proceeded to divorce nature from reason, after the equation or rather confusion operated by the Enlightenment. For him nature is the beginning of our history, the age of the noble "illusions" which urged men to great and memorable deeds. Reason is a poor imitator of nature, an inferior substitute, and replaces the irrational, emotional, and instinctive drives toward glory, patriotism, liberty, and love with the prosaic bourgeois principles of utility. (See, for example, *Zibaldone,* I, 544.)[35] Thus Leopardi, in what amounts to the most methodic statement of 'Romantic naturalism,' gives us a sort of apotheosis of primitivism, a philosophy of vitalism: the *philosophes,* in their attempt to form a people "esattamente filosofico e ragionevole" ("exactly philosophical and rational") failed to perceive that "ragione e vita sono due cose incompatibili" ("reason and life are two incompatible things"), (*Zibaldone,* I, 358). The organization of man into society, and its development through history, amount to nothing more than

the progressive corruption of human nature, as Cain, the myth-
ical founder of cities, was the symbolical founder of society itself
(*Zibaldone*, I, 191 and *Inno ai Patriarchi*). One is here reminded of William Cowper's "God made the country, but man
made the town." See, in fact, *Paralipomeni della Batracomio-
machia*, chap. iv, stanza 11 ff.: "il cittadin fu pria della cittade,"
rather than "la città fu pria del cittadino," that is, social institutions are not the work of nature, but of man.

The 'enlightened' century's process of extension of reason's
domain begins with Vico and ends with Kant. Reason and traditional morality seemed too limited for the vast and manifold
activity of humanity. Vico was the first to face the manifestations of the psyche not only when it operates in the clear light
of ratiocination, but also when it is "perturbato e commosso,"
perturbed and agitated by the overwhelming forces of the
senses and the imagination, and yet still sublimely creative.

It is possible to interpret such pre-Romantic manifestations
as the Marquis de Sade's extreme naturalism as a logical conclusion of the enlightened *philosophes'* radical critique of the
ethics heretofore accepted as absolute.[36] In denying the metaphysical validity of the moral postulates the *philosophes* had
opposed to the artificial ends of civilized society the natural,
egoistic and sensual instincts of the individual, and de Sade
shamelessly inferred that nature alone, that is, the instincts
were sacred, and therefore entitled to be left entirely free to
develop to their full extent, monstrous as this might seem.[37]
Finally there came Kant to insert 'sentiment' into the general
forms of spiritual activity. In his wake Romanticism, by upholding the rights of sentiment above and, if necessary, against
reason, by emphasizing the free development of the individual
personality above and against religious, moral, and social conventions, carried decisively further the emancipation of what
had in classical times been the 'negative,' brought about the
complete breakdown of the Platonic, harmonious cosmos
erected by the Renaissance, and firmly established a dualism
based on the conflict of reason and passion as both positive,

though opposed, elements in the binomial nomenclature of our psyche.[38]

With 'Aristotelian' compassion Racine had long before put on the stage the tragic conflicts of his heroes as victims of passion. But the Romantic hero will no longer be ashamed of his passions; he will be proud of them, and the Romantic audiences, well removed from Aristotle's "pity," will side with him and, from the bottom of their hearts, envy him. Of course Romanticism was not essentially a naturalistic movement. One particular example will help us, I believe, to focus more sharply upon a distinction we should always keep in mind in such inquiries. Prosper Mérimée (1803–1870) frequently represented love as conducive to perjury and murder (see "parjure" and "assassin" in the stories *L'amour africain* and *Une femme est un diable*).[39] Typically Romantic as this position was, it derived from a classical tradition that had placed love outside and against society and morality. But whereas naturalism and naturalistic views of love must be basically positive, here we can only see the Romantic appreciation of the negative as such. Not happiness, but tragedy, crime, and destruction are the outcome of this Romantic love. Consequently, Mérimée was against both the marriage of convenience and the love match, since in neither could he see the factual possibility of true love. Romanticism made possible a more thorough and consistent pessimism than ever before.

The cult of the negative, that attitude of radical revolt and upturning of values which had registered P.-J. Proudhon's cry "Dieu, c'est le mal!" found its extreme systematic expression in the nineteenth-century nihilist movement—and demonic nihilism played a basic role in the extremist mental attitudes among both progressives and reactionaries in our own century, eventually becoming mystic worship of death, destruction, total negation in the fascist, nazi, falangista milieux (the fanatics of this last group used to shout such notorious slogans as "viva la muerte" and "abajo la inteligencia").

Meanwhile, Nietzsche had offered the most methodic proposal for the elimination of the sense of sin. His sage was beyond good and evil ("jenseits von Gut und Böse") because he had understood the positiveness of evil. Later Thomas Mann was to reveal how he derived the idea of Leverkühn's decisive adventure from the dramatic visit to the house of ill repute by the puritanic, hypersensitive young Nietzsche.[40] Likewise the young Leverkühn, the genius-hero of Mann's *Doktor Faustus* (1949), overcomes the traumatic shock of his accidental encounter with a prostitute by clear-mindedly, satanically determining to consummate and faithfully pursue that adventure. It will fatally undermine his health and at the same time influence his whole musical career.[41] The circle of the 'positiveness of the negative' seems to be closed at last, in perfect fulfillment. The medieval official view of nature as fundamentally evil has evolved into a situation whereby the irrational forces hidden in the lowest strata of the unconscious are deified into a mystic, superior source of ineffable, inescapable, holy vitality, to be joyfully accepted as our surest guide. Thomas Mann's identification of that position as the origin of the new, modern barbarism, embodied for his country in Naziism, is only a commentary on one extreme aspect of the general process I have summarily described. No matter how, in his deep wisdom and as a result of his moral equilibrium and intellectual common sense, Mann felt about his character's plight, he artistically represented in Leverkühn his view of a culture that had upheld the unbounded rights of nature and its forces, sensual, emotional, and mental, and gone as far as holding unconditionally to the doctrine of the absolute priority and superiority of the 'natural' versus the human conventions of morality, sociality, civilization, religion—briefly, nature versus culture. And the root—or the symbolic beginning—of it all was the deification of that sensuality which under the labels of concupiscence, lust, incontinence, intemperance, carnal desires had been for the medieval man the supreme vice, and had now become the obsessive primeval revelation of the divine in us through the sacred channels of the instinctive and the elemental. It had become the mystic sensualism, the naturalism, the immanentistic amoralism, the cult of force and of the irrational, the religion of total love that we have witnessed as an essential aspect in the art of Wagner and D'Annunzio. Freud contributed the scientist's point of view with a reduction of all life, sensation, emotion, thought, work, and faith to 'cupido,' thus founding the last of the great religions, the religion of sex, a form of extreme naturalism.

On the artistic level, this new religion found its high priest in D. H. Lawrence, who appeared at the beginning of our century as a new prophet with his systematic and radical attempt to eliminate any negativity and sense of sin from the sexual experience, in an obstinate rejection of all other love than the erotic—a true religion of sex as the only salvation for modern man.[42]

All that had traditionally made up the realm of evil and wrong thus found, piece by piece, its rehabilitation. Positivism had redeemed madness itself (and not only in the ambiguous, half-joking mood of Erasmus) by relating it to, possibly identifying it with, superior intellect. That which had heretofore meant the peak of wisdom, the zenith of human reason, 'genius,' started to be looked upon as a sublime abnormality, an exquisite sort of disease, and conversely the worst eccentricities were curiously and sympathetically investigated and relished as possible sparks of profound excellence. Men as different as Marx, Bismarck, and Sorel concurred in vindicating the claim of violence and destruction to a positive role as legitimate forces of history. Finally Freud opened the realm of the unspeakable and raised the mysterious, the subconscious, to an object of scientific analysis for a revelation of deep, truer forces and motives.

Under the disturbing impact of so many 'revelations' the human mind started to vacillate and methodically doubt the possibility of any judgment of value, any distinction between true and false, right and wrong, good and evil. Reason's reaction to save man from total mental collapse was not too late in coming. One eminent voice among others was that of Benedetto Croce, whose lifelong campaign to uphold the rights of civilization and reason against the invasions of the irrational and the new

naturalistic primitivism has been recently summed up by one
of his followers. Decadentism, Mario Sansone contends, was
the literary and moral triumph of all the forces vigorously opposed by Croce, who combated in it not the rightful recognition of such forces, but the intended defeat of the conscious
ones of classical reason.

> The enemy of such an attitude [namely, Croce's] to-
> ward reality . . . is not life, this fascinating mystery of
> endless creativeness, for this is itself the eternal com-
> ponent of reality . . . as the unformed that ceaselessly
> takes form . . . complex and 'deep' as its sources may be.
> The enemy is not the unconscious or the subconscious,
> the instinctive, the unknown, but rather the presump-
> tion to have the whole of reality consist of that alone,
> the presumption to abstract man and reason from the
> area of the real and lower them to the level of an im-
> mediate refraction of that obscure pulsation. Nothing
> that is human, nothing that is vital is extraneous to man,
> provided the merely 'human' or 'vital' does not presume
> to swallow and smother man in its gulf.[43]

 Notes

Notes for CHAPTER I

[1] Poetically, 'nature' had stood for that happy beginning of things which is also the end of their existence. Virgil expressed this myth of the Golden Age in a famous passage of his Fourth Eclogue: "Magnus ab integro saeclorum nascitur ordo. / Iam redit et virgo, redeunt Saturnia regna; / Iam nova progenies caelo dimittitur alto." "The great sequence of the ages starts afresh. Justice, the virgin, comes back to dwell with us, and the rule of Saturn is restored. The first-born of the new age is already on his way from high heaven down to earth." (Virgil, *The Pastoral Poems*, trans. E. V. Rieu [Harmondsworth, 1949], p. 41.) The classical view of history was that of a cycle (*magnus ordo*), consisting of a process that goes from a pure, 'natural' start to decay and corruption, until a reform, a rebirth (*restitutio*) brings about a new beginning, a new cycle. This classical concept of revival expressed in Virgil's inspired lines, was soon interpreted as an announcement of Christ's coming, and finally became with Dante a prophecy of political and spiritual renewal for his own time. *Renasci, regeneratio, nova vita, renovari, renovatio, reformari* were always felt as *restitutio, restauratio,* that is, a return to the origins. It was not until the eighteenth century that the process of history was first seen in a rectilinear way, as 'progress.' Thus for Voltaire the 'century' of Louis XIV was greater than the three great ages which preceded it.

The most authoritative and comprehensive analysis of the concept of nature is, in English, A. O. Lovejoy and G. Boas, *Primitivism and Related Ideas in Antiquity* (Baltimore, 1935): see especially Chap. III, "Genesis of the Conception of Nature as a Norm," and the appendix on "Some meanings of 'Nature'."

[2] The conflict between *physis* and *nomos* is unequivocally illustrated by the saying attributed to Democritus, "Injustice is the opposite to nature. For laws are an ill invention, and it befits the wise man not to obey the laws, but to live in freedom." H. Diels, *Die Fragmente der Vorsokratiker* (Berlin, 1951–1952⁶), II, 54, 2ff., cited in Lovejoy and Boas, op. cit., p. 452. Similarly, in Plato's *Protagoras*, 337D the Sophist Hippias states: "Law is the tyrant of mankind, and often compels us to

do many things which are against nature" (Jowett trans.), "ὁ δὲ νόμος, τύραννος ὢν τῶν ἀνθρώπων, πολλὰ παρὰ τὴν φύσιν βιάζεται." The concept of 'natural law' came about somewhat as a reaction to the attitude of the Sophists. In Aristotle (*Rhetoric* I, 1373b 2 and *Nicomachean Ethics* V, 10, 1737b) the term was still ambiguously and vaguely used as an extension of 'common' (κοινός) or 'universal' law, contrasted with 'particular' law (ἴδιος) and defined as being according to nature simply because men appear to concur in admitting such laws always and everywhere. This view, as embodied in Cicero's and the Roman jurists' *lex naturae*, was in the background of the seventeenth-century doctrine of *jus naturae* (cf. Lovejoy and Boas, pp. 190–191). But the broadest, and truly pregnant ancient definition of natural law occurs in Justinian's *Institutes* I, 2: "Jus naturale est quod natura omnia animalia docuit . . . non humani generis proprium, sed omnium animalium." A true touch of 'primitivism' and 'naturalism' in such a sophisticated context!

The debate between φύσις and νόμος or θέσις is reflected in Plato's much-discussed *Cratylus*, as well as in *Gorgias*, 482C, end (esp. 482 E–500A), and was of great importance for the development of the philological sciences, divided along the two main currents of the analogists and the anomalists according to the different approaches to the problem of the nature of language. A curious development in this domain eloquently shows the relativity of the concept of nature. Φύσις was the original basis of analogy, but the Alexandrian analogists became the supporters of νόμος (*regula*, 'rule') in grammar versus the θέσις (*usus*, 'usage') of the Stoic anomalists of Pergamum. Thus nature came to mean two opposite things, according to whether it was seen as the basis for the rational or for the irrational. Cf. G. Funaioli, "Lineamenti d'una storia della filologia . . . ," in *Studi di Letteratura Antica*, I (Bologna, 1946), 186 and 200.

In discussing ancient ideas on nature one must bear in mind, however, that the deepest change in the history of this concept and related emotions has occurred rather recently, and we must try to divest the term, hard as this may be, of a good part of its modern connotations. It is this difficulty that has caused Gerardus van der Leeuw, *Phänomenologie der Religion* (Tübingen, 1933), *Religion in Essence and Manifestation*, trans. J. E. Turner (London, 1938), p. 53, to deny the concept of nature before Rousseau and the Romanticists, its alleged 'creators.' "For neither the primitive nor the ancient world was there 'Nature,' conceived as a realm set over against man and his deeds; nor, again, were the individual objects of Nature in principle distinguished by primitive and ancient man from artificial things." ". . . it is neither Nature, nor natural phenomena as such, that are ever worshipped, but always the Power within or behind."

³ Cf. Lovejoy and Boas, op. cit., p. 186, where it is indicated

that the term suffers from notable vagueness in Aristotle's ethical us-
ages. Moreover, a potential danger is pointed out in the principle
whereby man ought to behave as a political being because he is *by
nature* a political animal, and all natural faculties *must* be employed in
order that nature's ends be accomplished. It would ensue that, for nature's purposes not to be frustrated, the use of no means of self-fulfill-
ment that is in our power may be left inoperative (p. 187).

⁴ One must, nevertheless, note that the separation of nature
and 'supernature' came rather as a by-product of Platonism, for in
Plato's actual views the spiritual and the material were both within
nature, provided nature were no longer understood in the unilateral
manner of the early physicists. He asserted (*Laws*, 891–892; Jowett,
401–402) that the physicists (the early philosophers) were wrong in
maintaining that the material elements, fire, water, earth, and air, are
nature, that is the primeval causes and principles of the existent. They
were wrong in that they put first what was last, since the soul is the
first element and cause, and matter comes last, and since the true meaning of nature is the first creative power, the soul or mind being this
natural creative power.

⁵ *Phaedo*, 80C–82D; *Republic*, X, 618A, 620; *Phaedrus*,
248C–249C; *Timaeus*, 41D–42D, 76D, 90B–E, 91D–92C.

⁶ "Foedis immundisque libidinibus immergitur? Sordidae
suis voluptate detinetur" . . . "Sola mens stabilis super/Monstra quae
patitur gemit." *Consolatio Philosophiae*, Book IV, Third Prose lines
62–64, Third Meter vv. 27–28.

On the impact of the Circe myth and its relationship to Platonism,
especially in Italy, cf. E. Hatzantonis, "Il potere metamorfico di Circe
quale motivo satirico etc.," *Italica*, XXXVII (1960), 257–267.

⁷ The air, in particular, was considered the realm of demons.
In St. Paul, Epistle to the Ephesians, II, 2, the devil is called "the prince
of the power of the air." Thomas Aquinas spoke of the power of demons
over the air, where they can produce storms of wind and rain (*Summa
Theologiae*, Prima, Quaestio LXIV, Art. 4 and Qu. CXII, Art. 2; Prima
Secundae, Qu. LXXX, Art. 2). Accordingly, in Dante's famous story of
Buonconte da Montefeltro's death, the devil, angry at being foiled in his
hope of obtaining Buonconte's soul, wreaks vengeance on his body by
making it disappear in a storm conjured up by the devil himself for
this end. Cf. *Divine Comedy*, Purgatorio V.

As an example of what I have called the 'ontological' view, which is
related to the classical, especially Aristotelian, tradition, see Thomas
Aquinas in his commentary on Aristotle's *De Anima:* "The continent are
those in whom deliberation gets the better of passion. Note that it is
according to nature that the higher appetite should sway the lower. . . .
Likewise [i.e., like in planetary motions], the lower appetite, retaining

something of its own proper movement, is also moved by another, and this naturally, following the impulse of the higher appetite and of rational deliberation. If the converse takes place and the higher is in fact moved by the lower, this is contrary to the natural order of things." Cf. Aristotle's *De Anima* in the version of William of Moerbeke and the Commentary of St. Thomas Aquinas, trans. K. Foster and S. Humphries (New Haven, 1951), p. 481, §844.

[8] *De Hominis Dignitate* etc., ed. E. Garin (Florence, 1942). I quote from M. M. McLaughlin's partial translation in *The Portable Renaissance Reader*, eds. J. B. Ross and M. M. McLaughlin (New York, 1953), p. 478. The denial of a fixed human nature was related to the implicit identification of nature and the natural with the nonrational forces of instincts and matter. But for the background of this position, cf. Thomas Aquinas, *Quaestiones Disputatae*, "De Veritate," Qu. 14, Art. 10: "Unde non poterat ei [sc. homini] una via naturalis determinari, sicut aliis animalibus; sed loco omnium, quae natura aliis animalibus providit, data est homini ratio, per quam et necessaria huius vitae sibi parare potest, et disponere se ad recipienda auxilia divinitus futurae vitae." Cf. S. Tomae Aquinatis *Quaestiones Disputatae*, ed. R. Spiazzi (Turin-Rome, 1949[8]), I, 301. Also cf. E. Cassirer *et al., The Renaissance Philosophy of Man* (Chicago, 1948), with trans. of Pico's treatise.

[9] P. O. Kristeller, "Humanism and Scholasticism in the Italian Renaissance," *Byzantion*, XVII (1944–1945), 346–374; id., *The Classics and Renaissance Thought* (Cambridge, Mass., 1955), esp. Chap. II. Other scholars have expressed variedly differing viewpoints.

On Platonism in the Middle Ages see R. Klibansky, *The Continuity of the Platonic Tradition during the Middle Ages: Outlines of a Corpus Platonicum Medii Aevi* (London, 1939 and 1950).

[10] H. Liebeschütz, *Medieval Humanism in the Life and Writings of John of Salisbury* (London, 1950). On the general question of medieval classicism and humanism as distinct from Renaissance humanism see J. E. Sandys, *A History of Classical Scholarship* (Cambridge, England, 1908–1921, 3 vols.); G. Highet, *The Classical Tradition* (Oxford, 1949); R. R. Bolgar, *The Classical Heritage and Its Beneficiaries* (Cambridge, England, 1954) and, more particularly, A. Scaglione, "The Humanist as Scholar and Politian's Conception of the *Grammaticus*," *Studies in the Renaissance*, VIII (1961), 49–70.

With specific reference to the history of iconography, the methodic disguisement of classical material in medieval figurative art is masterfully treated by Panofsky as the principle of 'disjuncion' between classical 'motifs' and classical 'themes,' and the consequent coupling of the former with Christian 'themes': cf. E. Panofsky, *Meaning in the Visual Arts* (Garden City, 1955), 40–54. Also cf. J. Seznec, *The Survival of the*

Pagan Gods: The Mythological Tradition and Its Place in Renaissance Humanism and Art, Bollingen Series, XXXVIII (New York, 1953).

[11] J. H. Randall, Jr., *The School of Padua and the Emergence of Modern Science* (Padua, 1961); Lynn White, Jr., "Natural Science and Naturalistic Art in the Middle Ages," *American Historical Review,* LII (1947), 421–435.

[12] Toffanin's theses are well known to students of Humanism, and are profusely expounded in a wealth of volumes and articles. For a clear and concise synthesis of his position on the question discussed above, see his review of F. Simone's "G. Fichet etc." in *La Rinascita,* II, 5 (1939), 108ff. For a fuller treatment see his *History of Humanism,* trans. E. Gianturco (New York, 1954), a translation of *Storia dell'Umanesimo* (Bologna, 1950). This position can be traced back to E. Renan, *Averroès et l'Averroisme, Essai historique* (Paris, 1852). ˗

[13] E. Auerbach, *Mimesis. The Representation of Reality in Western Literature,* trans. W. R. Trask (Princeton, 1953), p. 198. Original title *Mimesis. Dargestellte Wirklichkeit in der abendländischen Literatur* (Bern, 1946).

[14] Implicitly referring to the attempts of traditional criticism to link the spirit of the *Decameron* to the Renaissance, and of recent scholars (such as Branca) to revindicate it for the Middle Ages, G. Petronio concludes his latest contributions on this thorny question with a note of wise, relativistic caution: "The *Decameron* escapes a unilateral [*univoca*] and definite historical determination within one type of civilization; it rather shares in a dynamic evolution of institutions, it mirrors a moment of transition, which is difficult to construe in the context of criticism." Cf. "La posizione del *Decameron,*" in *La Rassegna della Letteratura Italiana,* VII, 2 (1957), 189–207.

In a general philosophical sense, however, the Renaissance can rightfully be considered the proper climate for a new, conscious naturalism inasmuch as in that epoch the monolithic view of reality typical of the Middle Ages, "according to which no branch of human activity could be considered independently of its relationship to life as a whole," finally broke down. Nature as man's field of action, and each of man's various activities could then be conceived in their respective "autonomy." It is in such terms that F. Chabod speaks of the "realism and individualism" of the Renaissance in his *Machiavelli and the Renaissance,* trans. D. Moore (London, 1958), pp. 174–185, esp. p. 184.

W. Dilthey's study on "the analysis of man and the intuition of nature from the Renaissance to the eighteenth century," *Weltanschauung und Analyse des Menschen seit Renaissance und Reformation* (Leipzig and Berlin, 1914) is now a classic.

Notes for *CHAPTER II*

[1] Cf., for example, *Poésies complètes du troubadour Marcabru*, ed. J. M. L. Déjeanne, Bibliothèque Méridionale, XII (Toulouse, 1909), p. 150.

[2] *Hildegardis causae et curae*, ed. P. Kaiser (Leipzig, 1903), 68-69. Along with this information, the reader will find a valuable, brief *aperçu* of social conditions during the Middle Ages in S. Painter, op. cit. in fn. 8 below, pp. 95ff.

[3] *Gargantua and Pantagruel*, I, LVII (trans. Th. Urquhart, available in several modern editions). In the original: "Car nous entreprenons tousjours choses defendues et convoitons ce que nous est denié."

[4] A. Roncaglia, in "Di una tradizione lirica pretrovatoresca in lingua volgare," *Cultura neolatina*, XI (1951), 213–249, makes reference to the studies of Ramón Menéndez Pidal and Dámaso Alonso on the Arabo-Iberic antecedents of the troubadours. The general thesis of Arabic influences on Provençal culture is aptly expounded in D. de Rougemont, *L'Amour et l'Occident*, II, 9.

For the historical, social, and cultural background of courtly literature, the most exhaustive and dependable study is now Reto R. Bezzola's *Les Origines et la Formation de la Littérature courtoise en Occident (500–1200)*, Bibliothèque de l'Ecole des Hautes Etudes, First Part *La Tradition Impériale de la fin de l'Antiquité au XIᵉ siècle* (Paris, 1944, 1958²), Second Part *La Société féodale et la Transformation de la Littérature de Cour* (Paris, 1960, 2 vols.), Third Part not yet published.

[5] "'I' mi son un, che quando / Amor mi spira, noto, e a quel modo / Ch'e' ditta dentro vo significando." Purgatorio XXIV, 52–54.

As to the *vexata quaestio* of the 'origins' and 'causes' of Provençal poetry, the romantic-positivistic theory of the popular origin was definitively expounded by Alfred Jeanroy in his *Les origines de la poésie lyrique en France au Moyen Age* (1889, 1904², 1925³); the Late-Latin origin by Antonio Viscardi in *Storia delle letterature d'oc e d'oïl* (Milan, 1955²) and *Le Origini* (Milan, 1939), last chapter. Both theories are summarized by Guido Errante in *Marcabru e le fonti sacre dell'antica lirica romanza* (Florence, 1948), first appendix.

[6] The impact of the Provençal cannot be overstated, and not only with regard to literary history. Cf. W. T. H. Jackson, *The Literature of the Middle Ages* (New York, 1960), p. 275: "European manners to this day reflect the attitude to Woman which was exalted in the lyric of Provence."

On the relationship between Provençal and Italian literature cf. Santorre Debenedetti, *Gli studi provenzali in Italia nel '500* (Turin, 1911); Vincenzo Crescini, ed., *Provenza e Italia*, I (Florence, 1930), which contains S. Debenedetti, "Tre secoli di studi provenzali (XVI-XVIII)," A. Parducci, "Dante e i Trovatori," N. Zingarelli, "Petrarca e i Trovatori"; A. Viscardi, "La poesia trobadorica e l'Italia" in A. Momigliano, ed., *Letterature Comparate,* in *Problemi ed Orientamenti.* . . , IV (Milan, 1948).

⁷ E. Lommatzsch, *Provenzalisches Liederbuch* (Berlin, 1917), pp. 198–200. For the correct understanding of this poem it is important to bear in mind the rapports of Peire with the Albigensian heresy. Cf. K. Vossler, "Peire Cardinal, ein Satiriker aus dem Zeitalter der Albigenserkriege," *Sitzungsberichte der K. Bayerischen Akademie der Wissenschaften,* philosophisch-philologische und historische Klasse (Munich, 1916), pp. 1–195; A. Jeanroy, *La poésie lyrique des Troubadours* (Paris, 1933), pp. 187–193.

The question of the extent to which it is legitimate to assume a literally erotic interest in the courtly lover is still *sub judice,* and will long remain so. In a vigorous, though brilliantly amateurish fashion D. de Rougemont has popularized the thesis of a mystic and symbolic interpretation of *courtoisie.* He has particularly emphasized the principle of chastity as the central concern of the troubadour. "That which this high 'rhetoric' exalts is extramarital love, because marriage means but the union of the bodies, whereas 'love,' i.e., the supreme Eros, is the thrust of the soul toward a superior union—*union lumineuse*—beyond any love possible in this life. This is why love presupposes chastity. *E d'amor mou castitaz,* love bears chastity, as the troubadour from Toulouse, Guilhem Montanhagol, sang." (*L'Amour et l'Occident,* II, 6, p. 58 of 1956 ed.) True, although such a generalization may do injustice to those of the troubadours who were not so squeamish as to the physical limitations of the *octroi* or *merci* they expected of their beloved. At any rate, even if we felt inclined to accept this spiritualized view (which is connected with the 'Catharist' thesis of Otto Rahn, *Kreuzzug gegen den Graal* [Freiburg im Breisgau], 1933, E. Wechssler, *Das Kulturproblem des Minnesangs* [Halle, 1909], and other more moderate students of the puritan cult of the Woman-Mother-and-Lover within the Albigensian circles), the fact would remain that, sublimated or not, the sensual element was present, even basic in the *courtois* experience. After all, the chastity of the troubadour was not a repression of sensuality, but, to the contrary, a heightening of it, an exasperation of its insatiable urge by the planned withholding of its temporary satisfaction. Thus Saint Paul's precept, "It is better to marry than to burn," was utterly perverted into its direct antithesis. The courtly lover is against marriage and is 'chaste' because he finds his incomparable gratification in the very ardor of an

inextinguishable burning. Both marriage and the extramarital consumma-
tion of the desire would put an end to true love by taking away the
'passion,' i.e., the suffering.

⁸ The treatise is variously dated between 1174 and 1186,
or at the beginning of the following century. Cf. the Latin editions by
E. Trojel, *Andreae Capellani regii Francorum de Amore libri tres* (Copenhagen, 1892), and by A. Pagès (same title, Castelló de la Plana, 1930),
and Andreas Capellanus, *The Art of Courtly Love*, trans. J. J. Parry
(New York, 1941). I shall quote from this translation, with a few modifications for the sake of better adherence to the original. References to
the original will be based on the Battaglia ed. cit. below (fn. 16), which
is of easier access than the preceding ones.

For the general background, see Edgar Prestage, ed., *Chivalry* (New
York, 1928) [A. T. P. Byles, "Medieval Courtesy Books and the Prose
Romances of Chivalry," pp. 183–205] and, for the historical institutions,
Gustave Cohen, *Histoire de la Chevalerie en France au Moyen Age*
(Paris, 1949). Sidney Painter, *French Chivalry. Chivalric Ideas and
Practices in Medieval France* (Baltimore, 1940) contains a good synthesis
of "Courtly Love" (Chap. IV, pp. 95–148) and a discussion of the clashes
and compromises between Church and Court (Chap. V, "Criticisms and
Compromises"). For a recent, comprehensive monograph on Andreas, cf.
Felix Schlösser, *Andreas Capellanus. Seine Minnelehre und das christ-
liche Weltbild um 1200* (Bonn, Rheinische Friedrich-Wilhelms-Univer-
sität, 1959).

⁹ The overt assumption of the sinful and adulterous nature
of courtly love is in Capellanus, *De Amore*, I, end of G or Seventh
Dialogue, where it is pointed out that even within wedlock, 'true' love
must theologically be adulterous, since all passionate intercourse is sinful: "Whatever solaces married people extend to each other beyond what
are inspired by the desire for offspring or the payment of the marriage
debt, cannot be free from sin. . . . The too ardent lover, as we are taught
by the apostolic law, is considered an adulterer with his own wife"
(Battaglia, p. 172). Which was, for the time, theologically correct. The
perfect life for the medieval Christian was to be found in chastity, but
the Church had recognized the value and sanctity of marriage. Yet the
secular view, as inspired by courtly culture and by traditional misogeny,
was basically irreverent toward the institution of marriage. Contrary to
St. Paul' warning, for the courtly poet burning is the best thrill of life.

It is interesting that Lorenzo Valla should interpret *Ars Amatoria*,
I, vv. 31–32, as implying the exclusion of "nuns and virgins who have
taken the holy vows" from the kind of women ("the married ones") Ovid
teaches how to seduce (*De Voluptate*, Book I, in Valla, *Scritti filosofici
e religiosi*, ed. and trans. G. Radetti [Florence, 1953], p. 70). We now
know, instead, that those garments allude to "noble, free-born ladies,"
hence courtesans, not married ladies, are the alleged object of the *Ars*.

The persistence, then, of this mistaken interpretation even among the later humanists may be taken as a confirmation of the medieval interpretation of the *Ars* as a forerunner of courtly love. Accordingly, nuns were excluded by Capellanus from the service of love, though clerics were not—cf. Book I, chaps. 7 and 8. Bartoli was among the first to indicate a fabliau which offers a comparison between cleric and knight in the service of the god of Love, who gives the palm to the former: cf. Adolfo Bartoli, *I precursori del B.* etc. (Florence, 1876), p. 20, fn. 5, where the tale *Ci commence de Florence et de Blancheflor* is placed in relationship with a goliardic song for the dispute on "Quis aptior sit ad amorem." (Quoted from E. Barbazan, ed., *Fabliaux et contes* . . . [Paris, 1808], IV, 354). Cf. C. Oulmont, ed., *Les débats du clerc et du chevalier* (Paris, 1911), where clercs are preferred to the inevitably rather blunt and uncouth knights for the polished manners they are able to show in the battles of love. See now W. T. H. Jackson, "Der Streit zwischen 'miles' und 'clericus,' "*Zeitschrift für deutsches Altertum und deutsche Literatur,* LXXXV (1954–55), 293–303. Furthermore, in view of the future popularity of nuns in the novella genre (*Decameron* not excluded) it is interesting to note that Boncompagno da Signa (cf. *infra,* fn. 15) was not so discriminating as Andreas. After admitting *clerici* to love's realm and dividing them summarily into *prelati* and *subditi,* he neatly refused to reject nuns (*monachas vel moniales,* p. 13).

[10] Cf. in particular, Erich Köhler, "Zur Diskussion der Adelsfrage bei den Trobadors," in H. R. Jauss (and D. Schaller), eds., *Medium Aevum Vivum: Festschrift für W. Bulst* (Heidelberg, 1960), 161–178, now in Köhler, *Trobadorlyrik und höfischer Roman. Aufsätze zur französischen und provenzalischen Literatur des Mittelalters* (Berlin, 1962).

[11] A. J. Denomy, in *Mediaeval Studies,* VI (1944), 175–260, VII (1945), 139–207, VIII (1946), 107–149, 300–301, and *The Heresy of Courtly Love* (New York, 1947). Father Denomy studies the problem of "Averroism" (*ante-* and *post-litteram*) in *fin amors,* courtly love, and the doctrines of Andreas; he then concludes that they were patently immoral from the vantage point of the Christian doctrine. True enough, medieval sexual ethics presented a certain degree of flexibility that sounds curiously casuistic to us: for an interesting case involving the vague borderline between the allowed and the sinful in sexual promiscuity, cf. H. Newstead, "The Blancheflor-Perceval Question Again," *Romance Philology,* VII, 2–3 (1953–1954), 171–175, where a confirmation of Father Denomy's conclusions is implied. The problem involved here, whether the night spent together by Perceval and Blancheflor in Chrétien's *Perceval* (vv. 1699–2975) was chaste or unchaste, has become a classic *locus* for Arthurian scholarly polemic. Cf. for a recent summary E. G. Ham, "The Blancheflor-Perceval Idyll and Arthurian Polemic," *Kentucky Foreign Language Quarterly,* VI (1959), 155–162.

[12] Lewis, *The Allegory of Love* (London, 1938²), pp. 33–34.

Lewis specifically refers to *De Amore*, I, chap. 5, p. 13, Trojel's ed., but I should add I, chaps. 3, 4, and 8: "[Love] adorns a man, so to speak, with the virtue of chastity, because he . . . can hardly think of embracing another woman. . . . For when he thinks deeply of his beloved the sight of any other woman seems to his mind rough and rude" (chap. 3). "An excess of passion [rather, of sensuality] is a bar to love. . . . Men of this kind lust after every woman they see; their love is like that of a shameless dog" (chap. 4). "The readiness to grant requests is, we say, the same thing in women as overvoluptuousness in men—a thing which all agree should be a total stranger in the court of Love. . . . The man who is so wanton that he cannot confine himself to the love of one woman deserves to be considered an impetuous ass" (chap. 8).

For a fine analysis of the equilibrium between the spiritual and the sensual in the poetry of the troubadours, cf. L. Spitzer, *L'Amour lointain de Jaufré Rudel et le sens de la poésie des troubadours*, University of North Carolina Studies in the Romance Languages and Literature, V (Chapel Hill, 1944).

[13] "Credo tamen in amore Deum graviter offendi non posse; nam quod natura cogente perficitur, facili potest expiatione mundari." *De Amore*, I, Dialogue H or Eighth (Battaglia, p. 188). In this Dialogue the case for courtly love is laid courageously in the open. The lover argues that one has to make up one's mind with clarity and firmness, and decide to serve God or the world, for "we cannot serve two masters." If we want to be God's servants, we must exclude worldliness, *courtoisie*, and love altogether, since even in marriage intercourse *for love* would be a form of adultery. If, instead, we wish to remain in the world, we must give up the prejudice of sin in love, for "it does not seem at all proper to class as a sin the thing from which the highest good in this life takes its origin and without which no man in the world could be considered worthy of praise."

[14] A. Pope, *The Universal Prayer*. These lines, to be traced to Guarini's *Pastor Fido*, were struck from the final version of the poem. Cf. N. J. Perella, "Amarilli's Dilemma: the *Pastor Fido* and Some English Authors," *Comparative Literature*, XII (1960), 358. Another reading (*offend 'gainst Nature's God*) is given here.

Milton had said: "God and Nature bid the same" (*Patrologia Latina*, VI, 176).

[15] J.-J. Rousseau, *La Nouvelle Héloïse*, ed. D. Mornet (Paris, 1925), Part 6, Letter 6, p. 221.

[16] Andreas's treatise was well known in Italy: the *Livre d'Enanchet* (between 1226 and 1252) imitated and partly translated it, and two Tuscan translations from the fourteenth century are extant in several manuscripts. Cf. Werner Fiebig, ed., "Das 'Livre d'Enanchet'" etc., *Berliner Beiträge zur romanischen Philologie*, eds. E. Gamillscheg and E. Winkler, VIII, 3–4 (Berlin, 1939), and Fiebig, "Das *Livre*

d'Enanchet. Zur Frage der Namensdeutung und zu seinen Quellen," *Zeitschrift für französische Sprache und Literatur,* LXX (1960), 182–198, where a new critical edition is also announced; 'Enanchet' is interpreted as a diminutive of Seneca, and the poem would have been composed, perhaps at Padua, by a student of the Bolognese school of Boncompagno. Andrea Capellano, *Trattato d'Amore (De Amore Libri Tres).* Testo latino del sec. XII con due traduzioni toscane inedite del sec. XIV, ed. by S. Battaglia (Rome, 1947). Cf. Pio Rajna, "Tre studi per la storia del libro di A. Cappellano," *Studj di Filologia Romanza,* V (1889), 193–272. It is assumed that Boccaccio was well acquainted with the treatise in the original or at least in these translations, even at the time of the *Filocolo,* his earliest work of importance. Cf. Battaglia's Introduction to ed. cit., and C. Grabher, Particolari influssi di A. Cappellano sul Boccaccio, *Annali delle Facoltà di Lettere, Filosofia e Magistero dell' Università di Cagliari,* Vol. XXI, Part II (University of Cagliari, 1953), pp. 67–88. Also cf. *infra,* Chap. III, fn. 31.

Boncompagno da Signa (d. ca. 1240), in his time the most celebrated Italian rhetorician, proceeded textually from Ovid in offering his *Rota Veneris* (shortly before 1215?) as a *De Amore* in minor key, or rather in the garb of an *ars dictaminis.* Boccaccio is thought to have known this interesting work.

[17] "Amor est passio quaedam innata . . . per quem universus regitur mundus, et sine ipso nihil boni aliquis operatur in orbe." (I, 1 and 6E, ed. Battaglia pp. 4 and 114.)

[18] Johan Huizinga, *The Waning of the Middle Ages* (New York, 'Doubleday Anchor Books,' n.d.), p. 40. This telling passage does not quite correspond to the original since, as is known, the English version is not a faithful translation, but an adaptation by F. Hopman under the author's direction. The Dutch original was of 1919 (1921[2]), the English version of 1924. Although Huizinga was specifically dealing with fifteenth-century Burgundy, this statement applies to courtly culture and ethics in general.

[19] Ovid's extraordinary influence on medieval literature of love (and other) is well known. Cf. W. Schrötter, *Ovid und die Troubadours* (Halle, 1908); E. K. Rand, *Ovid and His Influence* (Boston, 1925). The puzzle of Andreas's palinode has led some critics to question its seriousness (cf. H. Hatzfeld, review of Denomy, *The Heresy* . . . , *Symposium,* II [1948], 285–288), others to interpret the whole work as a Christian condemnation of *courtoisie* (D. W. Robertson, Jr., "The Doctrine of Charity in Medieval Literary Gardens," *Speculum,* XXVI [1951], 36–39, 40–43, and "The Subject of the *De Amore* of A. Capellanus," *Modern Philology,* L [1953], 145–161).

[20] A. Scaglione, "Chivalric and Idyllic Poetry in the Italian Renaissance," *Italica,* XXXIII (1956), 252–260, esp. p. 255.

The 'recantation' is no more than a weak palliative, a hasty concession to the prevailing code in the unconvincing conclusion of Boncompagno da Signa's *Rota Veneris.*

[21] Bartina Wind, "Eléments courtois dans Béroul et dans Thomas," *Romance Philology,* XIV, 1 (1960), 1–13. This statement, here given in my translation, appears on p. 8. In Gottfried von Strassburg, also, the *Minnetrank* seems to hand the lovers over "to the tyranny of the senses, and this tyranny is so powerful that it brushes from its path all considerations of honour and loyalty," according to W. T. H. Jackson in his chapter on Gottfried in R. S. Loomis, ed., *Arthurian Literature in the Middle Ages. A Collaborative History* (Oxford, 1959), p. 153. Also cf., in this volume, H. Newstead, "The Origin and Growth of the Tristan Legend," pp. 122–133; F. Whitehead, "The early Tristan Poems," pp. 134–144.

The Tristan myth, in the light of Provençal culture, is the central concern in the well-known inquiry of D. De Rougemont, *L'Amour et l'Occident (Love in the Western World).*

[22] Wind, p. 8.

[23] Wind, p. 11. Here the author concurs with Pierre Jonin, *Les personnages féminins dans les romans français de Tristan au XIIe siècle. Etude des influences contemporaines* in *Publication[s] des Annales de la Faculté des Lettres, Aix-en-Provence,* n. s., 22 (1958), p. 291. For Jonin the uncourtly elements in Thomas counterbalance the courtly ones. Among the former he recognizes the lack of choice in the enamourment (blind fatality of the philter), the absence of the "secret," of the lady's preëminence, of mundane pastimes, as well as the physiological approach to the nature of love, the rehabilitation of the husband through his elevation to the rank of rival, and Tristan's 'substitution' of marriage for love. On the other hand, a fundamental element within the courtly tradition, seen in a Christian *forma mentis* but extraneous to the epic *gestes* is the representation of the interior debate which illustrates the full force and danger of carnal concupiscence (the wedding night with Iseut aux Blanches Mains, p. 456). Jonin regards, instead, the *Folie Tristan* of Oxford as the veritable courtly version of the legend. But he also contends, against those who regard Béroul as essentially exempt from courtly influences, that such influences are in him broad and deep.

[24] Wind, p. 5. Reference is here made to Jonin, op. cit., p. 107.

[25] Wind, p. 7.

V. Bertolucci-Pizzorusso, in "La retorica nel *Tristano* di Thomas, *Studi mediolatini e volgari,* VI-VII (1959), 25–61, attempts to establish a rapport between Andreas and Thomas, and to indicate in the latter's poem a virtual theoretical treatise on love through an exemplary story.

[26] Text in *Prose di Romanzi,* ed. F. Arese (Turin, 1950). The complete text of *La Tavola Ritonda* was edited by F.-L. Polidori (Bologna, 1864–1865, 2 vols.). Cf. V. De Bartholomaeis, *Tristano. Gli epi-*

sodi principali della leggenda in versioni francesi, spagnole e italiane (Bologna, [1922]). Cf. also C. Segre and M. Marti, eds., *La Prosa del Duecento*, La Letteratura Italiana. Storia e Testi, III (Milan and Naples, 1959).

[27] Cf. the *Vida* of Guillem de Cabestaing in J. Boutière and A. H. Schutz, *Biographies des Troubadours* (Toulouse-Paris, 1950). And see *Decameron*, IV, 9. Boccaccio did not pick up the detail of the murderer's punishment, but recalled the honors paid to the dead ones by the populace moved to compassion.

[28] J. Bédier-P. Hazard (P. Martino), *Littérature Française* (Paris, 1948), I, 29. With particular regard to the *Lancelot*, cf. T. P. Cross and W. A. Nitze, *Lancelot and Guenevere: A Study of the Origins of Courtly Love* (Chicago, 1930). On the ethical tradition of *courtoisie* see, beside C. S. Lewis, op. cit., C. Muscatine, *Chaucer and the French Tradition* (Berkeley and Los Angeles, 1957).

[29] In the *Perceval* Chrétien seems finally to have condemned what we could agree to call the naturalistic side of *courtoisie,* by extolling a chaste hero (whether or not we are prepared to accept the suggestion that the adventure of Blancheflor is *amor purus;* cf. E. B. Ham, "The Blancheflor-Perceval Idyll and Arthurian Polemic") and implicitly condemning the Fisher King (Roi Pescheor = Roi Pecheor, cf. L. Olschki, "Il Castello del Re Pescatore e i suoi misteri nel *Conte del Graal* di Chrétien de Troyes," *Atti dell'Accademia Nazionale dei Lincei,* Ser. VIII, Vol. X, 3 [Rome, 1961], 101–159). For a fresh survey of Chrétien's work see J. Frappier, "Chrétien de Troyes," in R. S. Loomis, ed., *Arthurian Literature in the Middle Ages,* pp. 157–191.

[30] S. Painter, *French Chivalry,* p. 131. On the realistic background and content of the courtly romances in general, see Anthime Fourrier, *Le courant réaliste dans le roman courtois en France au Moyen-Age,* I (Paris, 1960).

[31] Garin, "Umanesimo e Rinascimento," in A. Momigliano, ed., *Questioni e Correnti di Storia Letteraria* (Milan, 1949), p. 366: ". . . quelle note indicate dal Burckhardt . . . individualismo, naturalismo, senso e gusto della vita mondana, senso della storia, eresia, libero pensiero, sensualità. . . . Ha scritto il Nordström . . . che basta la vicenda d'Abelardo a distruggere la posizione di Burckhardt, e il Gilson l'ha ripetuto . . . e ha sottolineato i motivi classicheggianti e sensuali di tanta lirica dell'età di mezzo, ed ha svelato tanto *naturalismo* medioevale."

[32] J. Michelet, *Histoire de France,* VII, *Renaissance* (Paris, 1855), "Introduction" (of 1842, with notes of 1855), note on p. cxxxv: "Cette ère (viz., la Renaissance) eût été certainement le douzième siècle si les choses eussent suivi leur cours naturel." (In other words, the twelfth century was a *Renaissance avortée.*) As to Abélard, he is considered "le point de départ de la philosophie moderne" (p. cxxxvi).

For the true meaning of Michelet's position on the historical relationship between medieval culture and the Renaissance, and the place of his ideas within the tradition of the Renaissance concept, cf. L. Febvre, "Comment Jules Michelet inventa la Renaissance," *Studi in onore di G. Luzzatto* (Milan, 1950), III, 1–11, and, in gentle though firm polemic with Febvre, F. Simone, *Il Rinascimento Francese* (Turin, 1961), esp. pp. 259–296.

By contrast, J. Huizinga considered Abélard a "pre-Gothic mind" and, noticing that he had been called "the troubadour among the schoolmen," suggested he should rather be called the "knight errant" of the school-men: cf. his *Men and Ideas* (New York: Meridian Books, 1959), "Abé-lard," p. 189.

[33] G. Gentile, *Il Pensiero italiano del Rinascimento*, "Il carattere dell'Umanesimo e del Rinascimento" (Florence, 1940³), pp. 17–18.

[34] *Epistola ad Abaelardum*, in Migne's *Patrologia Latina*, CLXXVIII, 371B–376B. This passage on col. 372B.

[35] Etienne Gilson, *Héloïse and Abélard* (Chicago, 1951); French original *Héloïse et Abélard* (Paris, 1938). Whenever Gilson cites the original texts, I shall use this English translation, with occasional modifications.

At the bottom of Abélard's ethics one senses the strong Christian tend-ency reflected as early as in the Gospel of St. Thomas: the basic scorn of the flesh expressed in adversity to, and blame of women. Cf. Jean Doresse, *Les Livres secrets des gnostiques d'Egypte* (Paris, 1958), II, *L'Evangile selon Thomas* (version du copte et notes de J. Doresse) (Paris, 1959). There is an Italian translation: *Il vangelo secondo Tom-maso . . .* di J. Doresse, trad. A. Romanò e M. Andreose (Milan, 1960) as well as an English one: J. D., *The Secret Books of the Egyptian Gnostics . . .* trans. P. Mairet (London, 1960).

To return to the comparison of autobiographies, apart from any pre-conceived notion it seems obvious that the individualism of Abélard has little in common with that of Cellini: whereas the former considers his individual story worth telling as a stern moral *exemplum* to warn others, Cellini has no other purpose than the 'aesthetic' one of letting the whole world see how interesting a man he is, with his virtues and his vices as well.

The insistence on medieval individualism reminds me of the nominal-istic faith in theoretical schemas which reportedly led Giuseppe Mazzini to a typical paradox. Beginning with the sound consideration that Chris-tianity had inaugurated the era of the individual, and syllogistically in-ferring that the Middle Ages, the Christian age *par excellence*, was there-fore the individualistic age *par excellence*, Mazzini concluded that the French Revolution, the triumph of the individualistic philosophy of the Enlightenment, was the last word of the Middle Ages, hence, we could add, the historical crowning of Christianity as a social and political experience. Cf. L. Salvatorelli, *Il pensiero politico italiano dal 1700 al 1870* (Turin, 1943³), p. 238.

³⁶ *Historia Calamitatum,* Chap. V. *Patrologia Latina,* CLXXVIII, 126B.

³⁷ *Ibid.,* Chap. VII. *Patrologia Latina,* CLXXVIII, 130B.

³⁸ Gilson, p. 36.

³⁹ *Historia Calamitatum,* Chap. VII. *Patrologia Latina,* CLXXVIII, 134A. Also cf. J. Monfrin's critical ed.: A., H.C. (Paris, 1959).

⁴⁰ Abélard's second letter. The Correspondence is available in many translations, of which the French one by Gréard is of particular importance: *Lettres complètes d'Abélard et d'Héloïse,* trans. Octave Gréard (Paris, 1870).

⁴¹ *Historia Calamitatum,* Chap. VIII, *Patrologia Latina,* CLXXVIII, 132B. See Gilson, pp. 98–99; Gréard, pp. 17–18.

⁴² Héloïse's first and second letters (*Ep. II* and *IV*): *Patrologia Latina,* CLXXVIII, 186B–C, 188A, 196A. Also Gréard, esp. pp. 78–79.

⁴³ *Patrologia Latina,* CLXXVIII, 1179D. Gilson, p. 188.

⁴⁴ *Epistola VI, Patrologia Latina,* CLXXVIII, 216D: "quisquis evangelicis praeceptis continentiae virtutem addiderit, monasticam perfectionem implebit." (Also *passim.*)

⁴⁵ Ibid., 215A.

⁴⁶ Gilson, p. 189, fn. 36.

⁴⁷ Ibid., p. 137.

⁴⁸ For the tradition leading to Boccaccio's Griselda cf. Marcus Landau, *Die Quellen des Dekameron* (Stuttgart, 1884²), pp. 156–160.

⁴⁹ See the latter part of fn. 9 *supra.* As to the piousness or piety of love's servants cf. *De Amore,* I, end of Dialogue C (Third). Battaglia p. 78; Parry: "He should not utter harmful or shameful or mocking words against God's clergy or monks or any person connected with a religious house, but should always and everywhere render them due honor. ... He ought to go to church frequently."

⁵⁰ "Discant populi tunc crescere divam / Cum neglecta jacet." F. M. Ennodius (473–521), *Epithalamium* in *Carmina,* I, IV, 84: ed. W. Hartel in *Corpus Scriptorum Ecclesiasticorum Latinorum,* VI (1882), 512f.

⁵¹ Cf. Lewis, op. cit., pp. 98–105.

⁵² The charming *Lai de l'oiselet* (early thirteenth century, with Oriental sources) contains an interesting example of reconciliation of the divine with the mundane virtues, the ecclesiastical with the courtly. The lay's moral lesson is chiefly directed against bourgeois greed for material possessions ("He who covets everything loses everything": "Cil qui tot convoite tot pert"). But the story confronts a type of greedy prop-

erty owner with a high lesson in moral and spiritual values, uttered by a
wondrous bird singing in the man's garden. The bird says: "You O
knights, clerics, and laymen, who suffer from love, and you pretty virgins,
who wish to enjoy the world, I tell you that you must first love God . . .
because God and Love agree together. God cherishes honor and courtoisie, and so does fine Love. God hates Pride and falsehood, and so does
Love. . . . God appreciates generosity and all good qualities. That which
in the eyes of God is avarice, is envy in the eyes of Love, likewise the
property owners are the greedy, the villainous are the wicked, the cruel
are the unpleasant. On the other hand, Love fosters wisdom, courtesy
and honor. If you will follow this law, you can have both God and the
world" ("Et se vos à ce vos tenés, Dieu et le siecle avoir poés"). See the
text in G. Paris, *Légendes du Moyen-Age* (Paris, 1903, 1912²), pp. 225–
291, with a study on the *Lai*.

[53] "Ut vitium fugiat, Naturam diligat, illud / Quod facinus
peperit damnans, quod prava voluntas / Edidit; amplectens quidquid
Natura creavit." Alanus, *Anticlaudianus*, VII, chap. v: *Patrologia Latina*,
CCX, 553.

Alan's conception of nature can be traced back to the pagan mother-
goddesses through the intermediary of the Madonna and Mater-Ecclesia.

[54] Cf. Lewis, pp. 105–109.

This is, then, a first stage in that fight against *courtoisie* which will
much later end in its final dissolution. The methodic appeal to nature as a
supreme teacher is, indeed, a reaction against medieval asceticism as
well as against the excesses of romantic love ('spiritual' or sensual as it
might be), inasmuch as they could both be felt as socially dangerous. As
D. Comparetti put it (*Vergil in the Middle Ages*, trans. E. F. M. Benecke
[London-New York, 1895], p. 325): "Human nature in the middle ages
had need of all its strength to combat these two powerful principles [i.e.,
"the ideal of the Saint" and "that of the Lady"], of which the one wished
to turn the world into a desert, where every man should be for himself
alone, while the other strove to make of it a lunatic asylum, from which
morality and common sense were to be alike rigorously banished." This
sort of naturalism, however, which is found in the School of Chartres,
presents a sort of alliance between nature and reason, and as such is to
be kept distinct from the 'radical' naturalism of a Jean de Meung or a
Boccaccio.

[55] This is attributed to Alan as his claim to originality by
G. R. de Lage, *Alain de Lille* (Montreal, 1951), p. 10. Also cf. J. Hui-
zinga, "Über die Verknüpfung des Poetischen mit dem Theologischen bei
Alanus de Insulis" (1932), in *Verzamelde Werken* (Haarlem, 1948–1953),
IV, 3–84, and E. R. Curtius, *European Literature and the Latin Middle
Ages* (New York, 1953), *passim*, and p. 123 on the representation of na-
ture. Still useful the old M. Baumgartner, *Die Philosophie des Alanus de
Insulis* (Münster, 1896).

[56] "Dicitur potentia rebus naturalibus indita, ex similibus procreans similia, unde alquis dicitur fieri secundum naturam." Alanus, *Distinctiones,* s.v. "Natura," in *Patrologia Latina,* CCX, 871. The *Anticlaudianus* and the *De Planctu* are also available in Th. Wright, *The Anglo-Latin Satirical Poets and Epigrammatists of the Twelfth Century* (London, 1872), Vol. II. The *De Planctu* is translated in Alain de Lille, *The Complaint of Nature,* trans. D. M. Moffat (New York, 1908).

[57] As to the precise quality of such aberrations, cf. R. H. Green, "Alan of Lille's *De Planctu Naturae,*" *Speculum,* XXXI, 4 (1956), 649–674: "*De Planctu Naturae* is not 'about' sodomy, or even 'about' the much more pervasive figural and narrative issue of adultery. Within the sum of all the figures of natural and unnatural love, extending as it does from the providential love of the Creator to the physical desires of men and women, these aberrations are simply among the usable manifestations of moral decay" (p. 673). I.e., Alan's targets are all 'unnatural' forms of passion, all 'vices.'

[58] ". . . sed si eius [Cupidinis] scintilla in flammam evaserit, vel ipsius fonticulus in torrentem excreverit, excrementi luxuries amputationis falcem expostulat, exuberationis tumor solatium medicamenti desiderat. . . ." *De Planctu,* Beginning of Fifth Prosa. Cf. *Patrologia Latina,* CCX, 456; Wright, p. 474. The translation in the text is Moffat's, op. cit., p. 49.

[59] *De Planctu, Patrologia Latina,* CCX, 443; Moffat, p. 26. Also cf. *Dictinctiones* (s.v. "Mundus"), in *Patrologia Latina,* CCX, 866. For the important implications of the first part of this passage, within the doctrine of macrocosm-microcosm, cf. Plato, *Timaeus* 36D and Aristotle, *De Caelo* II, 2, 285b–286b.

The idea of an analogy between cosmos and moral order (i.e., celestial motions and movements of the soul), an idea of Platonic origin, was common at Chartres: cf., for instances, Chalcidius' *Platonis Timaeus interprete Chalcidio cum eiusdem Commentario,* ed. J. Wrobel (Leipzig, 1876), esp. xcvff., pp. 166ff. For this and other aspects of the Chartres 'Platonism,' the chief theoretical work was Bernardus Sylvester's *De Mundi Universitate . . . sive Megacosmos et Microcosmos,* eds. C. S. Barach and J. Wrobel (Innsbruck, 1876).

For a recent summary of this tradition of the two cosmological movements cf. J. Freccero, "Dante's Pilgrim in a Gyre," *PMLA,* LXXVI (1961), 168–181, esp. 172–176.

[60] Lewis, op. cit., p. 197.

For a recent study on the *Roman* see A. M. F. Gunn, *The Mirror of Love: A Reinterpretation of 'The Romance of the Rose'* (Lubbock, Texas, 1952). For the formal aspect of the work see C. Muscatine, *Chaucer and the French Tradition,* esp. Chap. III. On 'naturalism' in the traditional or special senses, in the *Roman* and its time, see W. Goetz, "Die Entwicklung des Wirklichkeitssinnes vom 12. zum 14. Jahrhundert," *Archiv für*

Kulturgeschichte, XXVII (1937), 33–73; F. W. Müller, *Der Rosenroman und der lateinische Averroismus des 13. Jahrhunderts* (Frankfurt, 1947), pp. 14–15, 24–27.

[61] "Puis vendra Johans Chopinel . . . / [Qui] Me servira toute sa vie, / . . . E sera si trés sage on / Qu'il n'avra cure de Raison" etc. (vv. 10565–10583). I quote the text in E. Langlois' critical edition, Société des Anciens Textes Français (Paris, 1914–1924, 4 vols.).

[62] "Mais qu'eus ne puissent aperceivre / Que vous les baez a deceivre" (vv. 7420–7421).

[63] "Mout est fos qui tel chose esperne; / C'est la chandelle en la lanterne: / Qui mil en i alumerait, / Ja meins de feu n'i trouverait" (vv. 7409–7412). Cf. the speech of Madonna Filippa in the *Decameron* (VI, 7): "That which I have left, after giving myself to my husband, am I expected to throw it to the dogs?" ("devo io gettarlo ai cani?")

[64] The 'discours du Jaloux' has traditionally been interpreted in terms of the author's antifeminism and bourgeois realism. Such antifeminism had already aroused debate and occasional reaction in medieval and Renaissance times. The polemic waged by Christine de Pisan (1364–1430?) is the most eloquent intervention against this aspect of the *Roman.* Recently a rather unconvincing attempt has been made to discharge Jean de Meung of misogyny in the Jaloux episode, on the assumption of a 'theatrical' objectivity whereby the opinions expressed would be not those of the author but of his characters: cf. L. J. Friedman, " 'Jean de Meung,' antifeminism, and 'bourgeois realism,' " *Modern Philology,* LVII (1959), 13–23.

[65] Migne, *Patrologia Latina,* CCX, 454B.

[66] Translated from G. Paré, *Les idées et les lettres au XIII° siècle: Le Roman de la Rose* (Montreal, 1947), p. 284.

[67] Vv. 19701ff. The metaphorical use of this verb *arer* 'to plough' runs through the whole of this inspired exhortation by Genius. Cf. Lovejoy and Boas, *Primitivism and Related Ideas in Antiquity,* pp. 281–82, where Alan's *De Planctu* as well as the *Roman de la Rose* are said to derive their praise of *Venus Genetrix* and consequent denunciation of celibacy as contrary to life and nature from Seneca's *Phaedra,* 446–454 and 461–482.

> [68] Ja de sa fame n'iert amez
> Qui sires veaut estre clamez;
> Car il couvient amour mourir
> Quant amant veulent seignourir.
> Amour ne peut durer ne vivre
> S'el n'est en cueur franc e delivre.

(Amis à l'Amant, vv. 9437–9442).

Concerning the attitudes toward marriage in medieval French litera-

ture in general, cf. J. Coppin, *Amour et mariage dans la littérature française du Nord au Moyen Age* (Paris, 1961).

> [69] Pour ce, compainz, li ancien,
> Senz servitude e senz lien,
> Paisiblement, senz vilenie,
> S'entreportaient compaignie.

(Amis à l'Amant, vv. 9493–9496).

> [70] C. Muscatine, *Chaucer* etc., p. 76.
> [71] Mout fu fos quant faire l'osa,
> Car cil a mout po de saveir
> Qui seus cuide sa fame aveir . . .
> D'autre part, eus sont franches nees;
> Lei les a condicionees,
> Qui les oste de leur franchises,
> Ou Nature les avait mises;
> Car Nature n'est pas si sote
> Qu'ele face naistre Marote
> Tant seulement pour Robichon . . .
> Toutes pour touz e touz pour toutes,
> Chascune pour chascun comune,
> Et chascun comun a chascune. [vv. 13847ff.]

Lovejoy and Boas, in *Primitivism and Related Ideas in Antiquity*, p.
456, cite vv. 13875ff. of the *Roman de la Rose* as example of repercus-
sion of the classic motive whereby ethical changelessness (faithfulness) is
'against nature," since mutability is a physical characteristic of nature.
Hence the law of nature would be that of free love. Other witty, later
repercussions are to be found in some of John Donne's poems (not too
correctly indicated by the same authors, ibid.), namely "Confined love,"
"Elegie III" (Change), "The Progresse of the Soule" (First Song), vv.
191ff. At least a few lines from the second bear quoting *in extenso* in
the present context: "Foxes and goates, all beasts change when they
please, / Shall women, more hot, wily, wild than these, / Be bound to
one man, and did Nature then / Idly make them apter to'endure than
men?"

> [72] Si s'efforcent en toutes guises
> De retourner a leur franchises
> Les dames e les dameiseles. [vv. 13895–13897.]
> [73] Mais Nature ne peut mentir,
> Qui franchise li fait sentir;
> Car Horaces neïs raconte,
> Qui bien set que tel chose monte:
> Qui voudrait une fourche prendre
> Pour sei de Nature defendre,
> E la bouterait hors de sei,
> Revendrait ele, bien le sai.

> Toujourz Nature recourra,
> Ja pour abit ne demourra . . .
> Trop est fort chose que Nature,
> El passe neïs nourreture. [vv. 14017–14038.]

Cf. Horace, *Epistolae* I, 10, v. 24 ("Naturam expelles furca, / Tamen usque recurret"). As to the *abit* of v. 14026, cf. vv. 14009–14012.

[74] Jean de Meung's cynic judgment of the foolishness of the vengeful cuckold is echoed by Boccaccio in his retelling of the Venus-Mars-Vulcan triangle: cf. *Amorosa Visione,* Capitolo XIX, esp. 28–39 (". . . molto meglio cheti si stariéno . . .").

[75] "N'onc ne fui d'Amours a escole / Ou l'en leüst la theorique, / Mais je sai tout par la pratique: / Esperiment m'en ont fait sage, / Que j'ai hantez tout mon aage" (vv. 12802–12806). It is such passages that have made of Jean an exponent of the naturalistic spirit in the scientific, empirical sense as well.

[76] Cf. E. Faral's pertinent conclusion on the *Roman* in J. Bédier-P. Hazard (P. Martino), *Littérature Française* (Paris, 1948), I, 98: "Voilà l'idée profonde de Jean de Meung: l'amour est une force naturelle, rien de moins, mais rien de plus." As to Friend's advice and the Lover's adoption of the special strategy to appease Love, cf. esp. vv. 7307–7318, 10285–10306. Abstinence and False-Seeming work in concert in order to persuade Male Bouche to free Bel Accueil (esp. vv. 12097–12249), but they are ultimately condemned as an untrustworthy—or perhaps just unacknowledgeable—pair (vv. 19351–19368).

[77] "Fa che m'adori, ched i' son tu' deo; / Ed ogn'altra credenza metti a parte, / Né non creder né Luca né Matteo, / Né Marco né Giovanni . . ." (Son. 5). Cf. *Il Fiore e Il Detto d'Amore,* ed. E. G. Parodi (Florence, 1922). *Il Fiore* is also available, in Parodi's text, in *Poemetti del Duecento,* ed. G. Petronio (Turin, 1951), with bibliography. Facsimiles of the texts in *Il Fiore e il Detto d'Amore attribuiti a Dante Alighieri: testo del sec. XIII,* con Introduzione di Guido Mazzoni (Florence, 1923).

On the *Roman de la Rose* in Italy, from Brunetto Latini to the sixteenth century, see L. F. Benedetto, *Il "Roman de la Rose" e la letteratura italiana,* Beiheft 21 to *Zeitschrift für Romanische Philologie* (Halle a. S., 1910).

[78] "Dall'altra parte elle son franche nate; / La legge sì le tra' di lor franchezza, / Dove natura per sua nobilezza / Le mise quando prima fur criate. / Or l'ha la legge sì condizionate / Ed halle messe a sì gran distrezza, / Che ciascheduna volontier s'adrezza / Come tornar potesse a franchitate. / Vedi l'uccel del bosco . . ." (Son. 183).

[79] The *Epître* and the *Dit* are published in Christine de Pisan's *Oeuvres Poétiques,* ed. M. Roy, Société des Anciens Textes Français (Paris, 1886–1896), Vol. I. The documents of the *Querelle* are in C. F. Ward, "The Epistles on the Romance of the Rose and Other Docu-

ments in the Debate" (University of Chicago, unpublished doctoral dissertation, 1911), except Gerson's *Traité contre le Roman de la Rose,* which was edited by E. Langlois in *Romania,* XLV (1918–1919), 23–48.

[80] Simone, *Il Rinascimento Francese,* cit., esp. pp. 245–246.

[81] "Le Moyen Age," 2d part, in Bédier-Hazard, *Littérature Française,* pp. 76–80. Also J. Bédier, *Les Fabliaux* (Paris, 1925⁵), pp. 371–385. For a comprehensive edition, cf. *Recueil général et complet des fabliaux des 13e et 14e siècles,* eds. A. Montaiglon and G. Raynaud (Paris, 1872–1890, 6 vols.).

[82] However, cf., for instance, the fabliau "Uns evesques jadis estoit, / Qui moult volantiers s'acointoit / De dames et de demoiseles," in Th. Wright, *Anecdota Literaria* (London, 1844), pp. 68–73. Besides, the official sanctions against *jongleurs* and their alleged habit of irreverently referring to high authorities seem to me a relevant index of a state of affairs whereby this literature did contain more arrows than some critics are ready to admit. Cf., for instance, the *Ordonnance de Police* of 1395 (B. Bernhard, "Recherches sur la Corporation de Ménétriers ou Joueurs d'Instruments de la ville de Paris," in *Bibliothèque de l'École des Chartes* [Paris, 1841–1842, III, 404]): "Nous deffendons à tous dicteurs, faiseurs de dits et de chançons, et à tous autres menestriers . . . que il ne facent, dyent ne chantent en places ne ailleurs, aucuns ditz, rymes ne chançons qui facent mention du pape, du roy notre seigneur, de nos diz seigneurs de France, etc."

[83] Likewise, and more recently, for P. Nykrog, *Les Fabliaux, Etude d'histoire littéraire et de stylistique médiévale* (Copenhagen, 1957), the fabliaux were predominantly addressed to a courtly audience. Nykrog's thesis is confirmed but tempered by T. Rychner, *Contribution à l'étude des fabliaux: variantes, remaniements, dégradations. I. Observations. II. Textes* (Neuchâtel and Geneva, 1960). Also cf. A. Vàrvaro, "I *fabliaux* e la società," *Studi Mediolatini e Volgari,* VIII (1960), 275–299.

[84] Lucien Foulet has approximately dated the first fifteen 'Branches' of the *Roman* from 1174 to 1200, and Branche XVI at 1202, XVII at 1205. The episodes I refer to occur in Branche VII and XVII, respectively. For the social background and the audience of the *Renart* see an assessment similar to those of Faral and of Bédier for the fabliaux in L. Foulet, *Le Roman de Renard* (Paris, 1914), pp. 496–535. Also cf. E. Vidal's review of R. Bossuat, *Le Roman de Renard,* in *Romance Philology,* XIV, 1 (1960), 90–95. Texts in *Le Roman de Renart,* ed. M. Roques, Classiques Français du Moyen Âge (Paris, 1948–1960, 5 vols.).

[85] Lewis, p. 218.

[86] C. S. Lewis has also shown how, in England, Dante's *stilnovismo* acted, for instance, on an author like Thomas Usk, who in his reconciliation of earthly and celestial love (*The Testament of Love*) endowed his lady Margaryte with all the anagogical attributes of Beatrice

(op. cit., p. 225). Within the framework of his views on love, Spenser offered a paradigmatic conception of nature that belongs in the culture of the Renaissance, although it is made up of all the traditional motifs. Nature symbolizes God Himself as the "greatest of his shining ones," but only in opposition to the artificial, not to the spiritual or the civil values (ibid., pp. 324–333). Spenser had learned from Seneca that *nature* is good, *art* is bad, and in the *Faerie Queene* he expressed this distinction by the opposition between the Garden of Adonis and the Bower of Bliss. "Most commonly he understands Nature as Aristotle did—the 'nature' of anything being its unimpeded growth from within to perfection, neither checked by accident nor sophisticated by art. To this 'nature' his allegiance never falters" (p. 330). Book II is dominated by the theme of Life and Health, and "its subject is the defense of Health or Nature against various dangers" (p. 337), including the hypertrophies and diseases of natural desires, Mammon and Acrasia. Eros, Storge, Philia (Canto IX) are "three kinds of Love." "The Bower is the home not of vicious sexuality in particular, but of vicious Pleasure in general" (p. 339). In conclusion, "Courtly Love is in Spenser's view the chief opponent of Chastity. But Chastity for him means Britomart, married love" (p. 340). One can only add that, seen in this light, the ideal affinity between Alan of Lille's 'naturalism' and that of Spenser is obvious. An ideal bridge connects the two poets, the medieval Humanism of Chartres and that of the Renaissance. Also cf. W. H. Schofield, *Chivalry in English Literature* (Cambridge, Mass., 1925) and, for the last century of the Middle Ages, A. B. Ferguson, *The Indian Summer of English Chivalry. Studies in the Decline and Formation of Chivalric Idealism* (Durham, N.C., 1960 and London, 1960). For an interesting, original interpretation of some of these puzzling questions, see P. J. Alpers, "Narrative and Rhetoric in the *Faerie Queene*," *Studies in English Literature*, II, 1 (1962), 27–46: "Human love must involve the flesh and hence must involve desire and pain. Spenser's conception of chastity as marriage rather than virginity demands that he keep this point firmly in view" (p. 45, à propos of Amoret tortured by Busyrane, *F. Q.* III, xii). Robert Ellrodt, *Neoplatonism in the Poetry of Spenser* (Geneva, 1960), is to be used with caution, for he propends, perhaps uncritically, to divorce Spenser's cultural formation from contemporary, especially Italian, sources.

[87] Olivier de La Marche, *Le Triumphe des Dames*, ed. J. Kalbfleisch-Benas (Rostock, 1901). For the general problem, see R. L. Kilgour, *The Decline of Chivalry as Shown in the French Literature of the Late Middle Ages* (Cambridge, Mass., 1937), esp. pp. 108–194, on courtly love.

[88] Jean le Sénéschal, *Les Cent Ballades*, ed. G. Raynaud, Société des Anciens Textes Français (Paris, 1905).

[89] *Le Livre du Chevalier de la Tour Landry, pour l'enseigne-*

ment de ses filles, ed. A. de Montaiglon (Paris, 1854); *The Book of the Knight of La Tour Landry,* ed. and trans. G. S. Taylor (London, 1930). Specifically, the Chevalier's wide rejection of courtly love shows the resistance of the more conservative nobility.

[90] E. Deschamps, *Oeuvres,* eds. Q. de Saint-Hilaire and G. Raynaud, Société des Anciens Textes Français (Paris, 1878–1903), Vol. IX of the 11 vols. series.

[91] A. de La Sale, *Le Petit Jehan de Saintré,* eds. P. Champion and F. Desonay (Paris, 1926). See P. Toldo, *Contributo allo studio della novella francese del XV e XVI secolo* (Rome, 1895); A. Coville, *Recherches sur quelques écrivains du XIVe et du XVe siècle* (Paris, 1935), and *Le Petit Jehan de Saintré, Recherches complémentaires* (Paris, 1937).

[92] J. de Bueil, *Le Jouvencel,* eds. C. Favre and L. Lecestre (Paris, 1887–1889, 2 vols.). Concerning the contrast between courtly and 'realistic' elements in fifteenth-century French prose, seen from a stylistic vantage point, the student can now profitably consult Jens Rasmussen, *La prose narrative française du XVe siècle. Étude esthétique et stylistique* (Copenhagen, 1958).

Notes for CHAPTER III

[1] Pp. 322 and 326–327. I quote from B. Croce's edition (Bari, 1958⁶, 2 vols.) of the *Storia.* All quotations will be from Chap. IX in Vol. I. On the questions raised by De Sanctis' approach, cf. Petronio in Binni, op. cit. in fn. 4 below, p. 207.

[2] "Questo mondo superficiale, appunto perché vuoto di forze interne e spirituali, non ha serietà di mezzi e di scopo. Ciò che lo muove . . . è l'istinto o l'inclinazione naturale." *Storia,* p. 322. The statement, "L'arte è la sola serietà del B.," is on p. 344.

[3] *Storia,* p. 328.

[4] On the history of Boccaccio criticism cf. G. Petronio, "G. B.," in W. Binni, *I classici italiani nella storia della critica* (Florence, 1954), I, 169–228. For other surveys of Boccaccio scholarship and criticism, see A. Chiari, "La fortuna del B.," in A. Momigliano, ed., *Questioni e Correnti di Storia Letteraria* (Milan, 1949, 1952²), pp. 275–341, esp. 275–290 (history of criticism on the *Decameron*); V. Branca, "G. B.," in *Letteratura Italiana. I Maggiori* (Milan, 1956), pp. 185–244, esp. 233ff. See also the title in fn. 12 below.

Concerning the questions raised by the text of the *Decameron* and by its tradition and popularity, see V. Branca, "Per il testo del *Decameron:* I. La prima diffusione; II. Testimonianze della tradizione volgata," *Studi di Filologia Italiana,* VIII and XI (1950 and 1953), 29–143 and 163–

243, and "Copisti per passione, tradizione caratterizzante, tradizione di memoria," in *Studi e Problemi di Critica testuale* (Bologna, Commissione per i Testi di Lingua, 1961), 69–83.

[5] In this respect, cf. especially G. Berchet, *Lettera semiseria* (Lanciano, 1931), I, 134–135; C. Cantù, *Storia della letteratura italiana* (Florence, 1865, 1887²), pp. 88 ff., *Della Letteratura italiana* (Turin, 1860²), pp. 40–46, *Storia degli Italiani* (Turin, 1893⁴), III, 300–301, 318–324; Villemain, *Cours de littérature française* (Paris, 1882), II, 32–51. The Romantic critics (and to those already named one should add at least Foscolo and the Schlegels) tended to emphasize the negative function of B.'s work against the positiveness of the Middle Ages. They were, of course, far from insensitive to B.'s genius. Friedrich Schlegel, for one, was profoundly impressed with other aspects of B.'s works, for instance the classical grandeur of the analysis of love in the *Elegia di madonna Fiammetta*. Cf. F. Schlegel 1794–1802, *Seine prosaischen Jugendschriften,* ed. J. Minor (Vienna, 1882), II, 396–414, "Nachricht von den poetischen Werken des Johannes Boccaccio" (pp. 408ff. on the *Elegia*).

[6] *Heptaméron*, ed. B. Pifteau (Paris, 1937), I, 318.

[7] Petronio, cit., p. 210. In Italian literary parlance 'historical criticism' (*critica storica*) refers to the method of the positivistic school. Petronio justly stresses the anticlerical bias of post-De Sanctis scholarship, but he goes to the other extreme of refusing to read any anticlerical intentions into the stories of the *Decameron*. This rather curious, though partly understandable, reaction results in the denial of positions taken by the most sensitive critics today as well as in the past. Chiari has attacked the fallacy of this anti-Romantic reaction whereby Croce, Russo, Grabher (and others I discuss below) have attempted a somewhat captious defense of B.'s morality and even religiousness against the traditional accusations: cf. "Polemica sul B.," in Alberto Chiari, *Indagini e Letture,* 1st series (Florence, 1954), 35–87.

[8] Bartoli, *I precursori del B. e alcune delle sue fonti* (Florence, 1876). For the present state of our notions of B.'s 'sources,' cf. D. P. Rotunda, *Motif Index of the Italian Novella in Prose* (Bloomington, 1957), *passim*, and, beside Landau, *Die Quellen des Dekameron,* the old but still useful studies by A. C. Lee, *The Decameron, Its Sources and Analogues* (London, 1909) and Gustav Groeber, *Ueber die Quellen von Boccaccios Dekameron* (Strassburg, 1913).

[9] G. B., *Il Decameron, 49 novelle commentate da A. Momigliano* (Milan, 1924).

[10] Croce, *La novella di Andreuccio da Perugia* (Bari, 1911).

[11] Croce, "Il B. e Franco Sacchetti" (1930), now in *Poesia popolare e poesia d'arte* (Bari, 1933). Cf. Petronio in Binni, p. 217.

[12] V. Branca, *Linee di una Storia della Critica al 'Decameron'* (Milan–Genoa–Rome–Naples, 1939, p. 62), recalls that in an article

of 1930 (*Corriere della Sera*, May 7) Momigliano seemed to hint at the impossibility of solving this question for the *Decameron*, for, in Momigliano's words: "Artistic unity is only possible where there is a spiritual problem and a particular (ethical) attitude dominates the author's conscience: when this is lacking, the unity is dissolved, and the coherence of the parts is reduced to particular technical affinities." This characteristic impasse is, I feel, a symptom of the close relationship of aesthetic form and (broadly) ethical or intellectual content. But Momigliano's judgment seems to me excessively negative on the moral count, hence also on the aesthetic one. On my part, I would not hesitate to speak of an 'ethics of nature' in the *Decameron*.

Croce himself, the master of the quest for principles of artistic unity in individual works of art, saw the *Decameron*, as Branca again points out (ibid., p. 65), "above all as a work of poetry, which, while escaping judgments of ethical and practical character, cannot even be reduced to unilateral aesthetic definitions or critical formulas, precisely because it is, above all, a work of poetry." Here I see a precious test of Croce's general method in the light of some leading, sometimes unavowed principles which I have tried to assess in my "Croce's Definition of Literary Criticism," *Journal of Aesthetics and Art Criticism*, XVII, 4 (1959), 447–456.

[13] U. Bosco, *Il Decameron* (Rieti, 1929).

[14] G. Petronio, *Il Decameron* (Bari, 1935), and his essay in Binni, op. cit., p. 221.

[15] M. Bonfantini, "B. e il *Decamerone*," *Pegaso*, II, 7 (1930), 13–28.

[16] S. Battaglia, "Schemi lirici dell'arte del B.," *Archivum Romanicum*, XIX, 1 (1935), 61–78.

[17] Cf. the Introduction to B., *Il Decameron*, ed. N. Sapegno (Turin, 1956, 2 vols.), and Chap. VI on Boccaccio in Sapegno, *Il Trecento* (Milan, 1955²).

"In the *Teseida, Ameto, Fiammetta* we have attempts for compromise. True enough, in the three works there prevails, as already in the *Filocolo*, the general learned and academic tone, which stifles or withers the freshest touches of realism. . . . But in the *Ninfale Fiesolano*, as well as in the *Filostrato* the realistic and popular note dominates again." *Il Trecento*, p. 338.

Recently Ruggiero M. Ruggieri has studied some aspects of this struggle in his "Medioevo e umanesimo, materia e stile in G. B.," in *Studi in onore di A. Monteverdi*, II (Modena, 1959), 655–680.

[18] *Il Trecento*, p. 296.

The perhaps excessive, and somewhat ambiguous insistence of the critics (Bosco and Petronio, in particular) on the motif of 'intelligence' has logically bred some discontent. The most outspoken reaction can be found in S. B. Chandler, 'Man, Emotion, and the Intellect in the *Decamer-*

on," Philological Quarterly, XXXIX (1960), 400–412. Chandler attempts to revise the traditional formulae by opposing love and all emotion to intelligence as forces which circumscribe it and render it subservient within the circle of man's behavior. I feel inclined to sympathize with this plight, which shows the difficulties of the traditional approach inasmuch as it seems to do injustice to the role of the irrational in this masterpiece. Nevertheless I do not find that Professor Chandler has rendered a great service to a basically good cause, since his treatment is occasionally intemperate and hasty, and the point is, in the end, overstated.

[19] G. Di Pino, *La polemica del B.* (Florence, 1953), p. 220: "L'amore dei protagonisti del *Decameron* è sempre una denuncia di libertà: libertà contro le convenzioni di una società conservatrice e vendicativa; libertà contro ogni disumana accezione del 'peccato.'" See a discussion of this thesis in F. Tateo, "Il 'realismo' del *Decamerone* nella storia della critica," *Dialoghi,* VI (1958), 18–36. Tateo tempers the statement of B.'s engagement in social problems in the face of his 'humanistic' estrangement from the precise confines of historical moment and place into a poetically concrete, but ideal world of dreamed harmony and universal humanity.

[20] Boccaccio's own characterization of the novella could be seen in this light of 'realism': "Fabula est exemplaris seu demonstrativa sub figmento locutio," "potius hystorie quam fabule similis est," *Genealogie,* XIV, 9. But see, also, the conclusion of the following Chap. 10, where the author goes so far as subtly defending even the popular tales of ogres, fairies, and witches, which he seemed to give up in this Chap. 9. Cf. G. B., *Genealogie deorum gentilium libri,* ed. V. Romano, II (Bari, 1951; B., *Opere,* XI), 706, 707, 711.

[21] V. Branca, *Boccaccio Medievale* (Florence, 1956).

[22] G. B., *Decameron,* ed. M. Marti (Milan, Rizzoli, 1958), p. 24. Also in "Interpretazione del *Decameron," Convivium,* XXV (1957), 285.

For a review of the most recent scholarship on Boccaccio cf. A. E. Quaglio, "Studi sul Boccaccio," *Giornale Storico dell Letteratura Italiana,* CXXXVII (1960), 409–438. To this list I should like to add: D. Rastelli, *Letture boccaccesche,* in *Studia Ghisleriana,* II, 2 (Pavia, 1957), pp. 129–175. Also E. Sanguineti, "Rassegna boccacciana," *Lettere Italiane,* XII (1960), 76–100, and the competent and informed bibliographical analysis by Bernhard König, "Boccaccio vor dem *Decameron.* Ein Forschungsbericht," *Romanistisches Jahrbuch,* XI (1960, but 1961), 108–142.

[23] For this return to the theme of 'realism' the following are to be added to Tateo's art. in *Dialoghi,* cit. above, and to Branca's well-known studies: D. Rastelli, "Il disinteresse narrativo nel *Decameron,"*

Siculorum Gymnasium, X, 2 (1957), 167-185 (esp. p. 183 on the new application of the medieval *exemplaritas* to the novella); R. Montano, "Erich Auerbach e la scoperta del realismo in Dante e B.," *Convivium*, XXVI, 1 (1958), 16–26; D. Gagliardi, "Il 'realismo' nel *Decameron*," *Le parole e le idee*, I, 2–3 (1959), 72–79 (negative).

[24] J. Huizinga, "Renaissance and Realism," in *Men and Ideas*, op. cit., p. 291: "Examples of this ethical realism can be found, for example, in the ascetic literature of ancient India and of Christendom. The descriptions of the superficiality of physical beauty intended to arouse revulsion and disgust, the oft-repeated theme of the tracts *De contemptu mundi*, are frequently based on St. John Chrysostom. . . . Closely related to the penitential sermon and the ascetic tract in its end and its means is the satire. Its realism is also of the ethical sort. There is another close link between the satire and the folk tale, etc." But Huizinga eventually refused to recognize the validity of the concept of realism for the understanding of the Renaissance, while relating it rather to the spirit and forms of medieval art. See the Appendix in this volume. The essay quoted was first published in final draft in *Cultuurhistorische Verkenningen* (Haarlem, 1929).

For the *exemplum* in the early novella as compared with the *Decameron* cf. Aldo Borlenghi, "La struttura e il carattere della novella italiana dei primi secoli" (Milan, La Goliardica, 1958), (lithographed).

[25] I find an interesting and effective assessment of the coupling of spiritualism and antinaturalism inborn in Indian culture and, for the West, typical of the Middle Ages, in an Indian novel originally written in English, Kamala Markandaya's *A Silence of Desire* (New York, 1960), p. 223: "In this country [i.e., India] the body had long taken second place, forced into that position by a harshness of circumstance which it would hardly have weathered without the sustenance of the spirit; by a harshness of climate . . . ; and by the teachings of a religion, itself perhaps shaped by these, which sought to turn the eye inward and find there the core of being." Likewise, the Middle Ages experienced a decaying of material conditions from the classical times, which conditioned and partly justified the outburst of asceticism. The 'boom' and new sense of prosperity after the year 1000 A.D. triggered a widespread reëvaluation of the body and of the rights of nature.

Despite the now fashionable distrust of 'sweeping generalizations,' we are entitled to see a deep affinity between the 'dualism' of the medieval mind and that of the Baroque and the Romantic cultures, as opposed to the unitary thrust of the classical mind, the Renaissance, and the Enlightenment. This in the light, for our context, of the constitutional reliance of the former current on the duality of the meanings of reality parallel to the dualism which characterizes certain 'Manichaean' attitudes of medieval Christianity, while the latter strives to perceive in the best clarity the univocal, literal bond between phenomena and essences, and define it unequivocally. The medieval "polysemous" is rediscovered, for instance, by Thomas Browne in the seventeenth century: "This visible World is but a Picture of the invisible, wherein, as in a Pourtraict, things are not truely, but in equivocal shapes" (*Religio Medici*). And this 'allegorism,' which is ultimately an expression of utter disrespect for the autonomy and integrity of the natural, an act of *antinaturalistic* faith, is found again in Coleridge, who not by mere chance quoted this passage of Browne's in the epigraph to his Ballad of the *Ancient Mariner*, so that the same statement could reappear on the lips of *Moby Dick*'s Captain Ahab. Browne, Coleridge, Melville, like the mystics and Platonists of other times, see it as man's destiny constantly to fight nature to subdue it (as an evil and hostile force to be castigated and humanized), and to transcend it if it cannot be vanquished. Boccaccio, in this a typical man of the Renaissance (the Renaissance, say, of Politian, not that of Ficino), makes his peace with Mother Nature, and lives (or wants to live) happy with her. He does not feel unhappy with the world as he found it, and does not strive to get it to play by his rules.

For the succession Browne, Coleridge, Melville cf. Cesare Pavese, *La Letteratura americana e altri Saggi* (Turin, 1932, 1953²), now translated as "The Literary Whaler," *Sewanee Review*, LXVIII, 3 (1960), 407–418 (see p. 412). Concurrently, in this same issue of the *Sewanee Review* (a valuable anthology of Italian criticism on American literature) G. Melchiori speaks of "the plurality of levels of significance" which Hawthorne transferred from poetry to prose, like Melville, Thoreau, Emerson, Poe. This allegoristic intention, the creation of ambiguous symbols, the reading of everyday reality as "cipher," "emblem," "hieroglyph" has been in Hawthorne an instance of that tendency toward symbolism which Matthiessen and Feidelson, as Melchiori tells us, have recognized as a truly native element in American literature (chiefly, may I add, Romantic and post-Romantic), and traced back to "a constant moral concern due to its Puritan origins" (p. 509).

[26] V. Branca, *Boccaccio medievale*, p. 110, contends that "B. managed to renovate the themes of the fabliaux and of the moral *exempla* and to give them, at last, an appropriate style by resolutely bringing them into a historical context, out of their abstract and episodic condition." Consequently, the exemplary character of the novella was dissolved into pure 'allusion,' and this allusion is the true extent and the limit of whatever remained in B. of the medieval novella's *exemplaritas*. I shall conclude, on my part, that in B. *fabula docet*, still, but the teaching is now entirely—explicitly and even polemically in the Balducci story —turned inward, toward nature and man, whereas it had previously been turned outward, not simply toward the supernatural and God, but outside the story itself. There had been, in other words, a duality between

novella and moral, while now the two coincide. The exemplarity is now, for the first time, fully realized, intrinsically and immanently, as pure symbolism.

On some aspects of the traditional heritage in B., cf. E. de' Negri, "The legendary style of the *Decameron*," *Romanic Review*, XLIII, 3 (1952), 166–189. For a recent study of the novella in Romance literature see Walter Pabst, *Novellentheorie und Novellendichtung. Zur Geschichte ihrer Antinomie in den romanischen Literaturen*, Universität Hamburg, Abhandlungen aus dem Gebiet der Auslandskunde (Hamburg, 1953). For the classical background of romanesque and erotic narrative literature the old E. Rohde, *Der griechische Roman und seine Vorläufer* (Leipzig, 1914³), esp. the first chapter, is still fundamental.

[27] Bernardus, *De cura rei familiaris*, ed. J. R. Lumby, Early English Texts Society, XLII (London, 1870), 6. Cf. Chaucer's Wife of Bath's Prologue, "For trusteth wel; it is an impossible, / That any clerk wol speke good of wyves, / But if it be of hooly seintes lyves, / Ne of noon oother womman never the mo" (vv. 688–691). Here and hereafter I quote from Chaucer, *Complete Works*, ed. F. N. Robinson (Boston-Cambridge, 1957²).

[28] This coexistence of distinct attitudes, not uncommon in the Middle Ages, may at times appear to us as a case of split personality. Aside from the conclusion of Capellanus' treatise, belying all the courtly foundation after having extolled it, the English John Lydgate (1370?–1450?) offers one of the most telling cases of monastic mentality and courtly attitudes in the same person: he was a monk and a courtly poet consistently, but distinctly.

[29] "Centrifugal" is the term used by Petronio in an attempt to moderate the excessive radicalism of Branca's reduction of Boccaccio to the medieval culture that lies at the bottom of his formation. Petronio insists on the organic character of the *Decameron*'s prose as opposed to the "barbarica inorganicità [della prosa medioevale] . . . in un prevalere . . . delle forze centrifughe." See his "Curtius o la critica del luogo comune," *Società*, XIV, 4 (1958) esp. pp. 791ff. The term "segmentation" of medieval (Latin and Italian) style I derive from L. Malagoli's "L'espressione letteraria medio-latina e volgare" (Pisa, Liberia Goliardica, 1953), (lithographed). Also cf. his *Aspetti dell'espressione letteraria negli scrittori religiosi delle origini* (Pisa, 1953), and "Forme dello stile medio-latino e forme dello stile volgare," in *Studi letterari. Miscellanea in onore di E. Santini* (Palermo, 1956).

On the medieval *cursus*, see A. Ronconi, "Il 'cursus' medievale e il testo di Cicerone," *Studi Italiani di Filologia classica*, n.s., XI (1934), now in *Interpretazioni grammaticali* (Padua, 1958), 223–247. On B.'s style cf. especially A. Schiaffini, *Tradizione e poesia nella prosa d'arte italiana dalla latinità medievale a G. B.* (Rome, 1943²); E. G. Parodi, "La

cultura e lo stile del B." (1914), now in *Lingua e letteratura,* ed. G. Fo-
lena (Venice, 1956–1957), II, 470–479; L. Malagoli, "Timbro della prosa
e motivi dell'arte del B. nel *Filocolo,*" *Studi Mediolatini e Volgari,* VI–
VII (1959), 97–111.

On the other hand, M. Marti has done well to compare Dante's style
(taking the example of the beginning of the *Convivio*) with B.'s (Introduction to the *Decameron*), to conclude that the famous 'ciceronian' style
of the latter is really, on close examination, the result of the narrator's
abandoning himself to the flow of the narration, so that the subordinate
and incidental clauses derive from the analytic insistence on the rhythmic
surfacing of the images, whereas in Dante the syntactical amplitude is
the capacity logically to articulate a thought in its constituents. Cf. G. B.,
Decameron, ed. M. Marti, pp. 29–30.

No matter from what angle we look at his work, we can safely conclude that, starting from traditional elements, Boccaccio created something profoundly new. The novelty of his 'organic' approach extends to
the content as well as to the form, as can be confirmed by even a cur-
sory comparison with a somewhat similar work contemporaneous with
the *Decameron.* In his *Libro de buen amor* Juan Ruiz (Archipreste de
Hita, d. ca. 1350) presents mainly cases of *loco amor,* earthly love, but
eventually protests his love for the Virgin, unlike Boccaccio who defends
what in Ruiz's official viewpoint would have been *loco amor.*

[30] On the ideological background and meaning of the Italian
Sweet New Style cf. K. Vossler, *Die philosophischen Grundlagen zum
'süssen neuen Stil'* (Heidelberg, 1904).

[31] G. B., *Il Filocolo,* ed S. Battaglia (Bari, 1938; G. B.,
Opere, I), pp. 337ff., esp. 338 and 340.

C. Grabher, "Particolari influssi di A. Cappellano sul B.," *Annali delle
Facoltà di Lettere, Filosofia e Magistero dell'Università di Cagliari,* XXI
(Cagliari, 1953), Part II, pp. 67–88, mentions Capellanus' influence in
the *Filocolo,* especially on the "Questions of Love" of Book IV.

The *Filocolo* is a case in point as regards the current revaluation of
direct French influences on early Italian literature. It now seems to be
related to *Flore et Blancheflor* rather than to an Italian intermediary, the
Cantare di Fiorio e Biancofiore, since the latter is said to be dependent
on the very *Filocolo* of which it was considered the antecedent. Cf. A.
Monteverdi, "Un libro d'Ovidio e un passo del *Filocolo,*" in *Studia phi-
lologica et litteraria in honorem L. Spitzer* (Bern, 1958), 335–340. Both
Monteverdi's and Grabher's studies touch upon B.'s reliance on Ovid.

The irrationality and fatality of B.'s conception of love are assessed
with reference to the theological speculations on free will and *Fortuna*
(starting with Boethius' *De Consolatione Philosophiae*) in the study of
W. Pabst, *Venus als Heilige und Furie in Boccaccios Fiammetta Dich-
tung,* Schriften und Vorträge des Petrarca-Instituts Köln, XII (Krefeld,

1958), pp. 29ff. Venus is the global symbol of the half heavenly, half hellish, irresistible power which, through deceptive promises, throws its unlucky victims into an abyss of guilt and grief. Also see the concurrent judgments of Bernhard König, *Die Begegnung im Tempel, Abwandlungen eines literarischen Motivs in den Werken Boccaccios,* Hamburger Romanistische Studien (Hamburg, 1960), esp. pp. 18–19.

[32] The origin of love in the sight was emphatically stated in Iacopo da Lentini's famous sonnet *Amore è un desio che ven dal core,* part of the first literary polemic in Italy concerning the theory of love. Iacopo had to insist on this principle in order to counteract the romantic idealism that could be derived from the legend of Jaufré Rudel, who had fallen in love by mere hearsay. For the Sicilian poet, instead, 'true' love is a fierce, 'furious' passion which finds its origin in the sensorial representation of a real object through the eyes, is then received by the heart with marked pleasure and operated upon by the imagination.

A propos of the expression "virtù della luce degli occhi vostri" in the Proem to the Fourth Day of the *Decameron,* Branca indicates these other passages: *Caccia di Diana* XIII, 29, *Amorosa Visione* XV, 61f.; *Rime* IX, XI, XII, XIII, XV, XX, etc.; *Filostrato* I, 29f. Cf. G. B., *Decameron,* ed. V. Branca (Florence, 1951), Vol. I, p. 456, fn. 7. More broadly the same scholar (*B. medievale,* Chap. 5, first composed in 1944 and previously published as "Schemi letterari e schemi autobiografici nell'opera del B.," *La Bibliofilia,* XLIX [1947], 1–40) has shown how B.'s paradigmatic, pseudo-autobiographic love for Fiammetta follows in almost every detail the established literary and rhetorical models—classical, medieval, from the *Dolce Stil Nuovo,* and even popular literature—in addition to the dictates of medieval love treatises such as those of Capellanus and Boncompagno da Signa. These views are now confirmed and extended by König, *Die Begegnung im Tempel* (see esp. p. 67). The heroine's fateful encounter with Hippolytus at the Eleusian mysteries, in Euripides' *Phaedra,* could be considered the prototype for an episode representing the onset of a passion of uncontrollable violence, according to the pattern systematically adopted by B.

[33] On this question and the medical literature quoted below cf. B. Nardi, "L'amore e i medici medievali," in *Studi in onore di A. Monteverdi* (Modena, 1959), II, 517–42.

[34] Halyabbas: "Coitus quoque cum ea que non amatur cogitationem flectit ab amata et extenuat ac amatam removet." Arnaldus: "Quantum est ex arte, coitus praecipue, si cum iuvenibus et magis delectationi congruis exerceatur." Quoted by Nardi, pp. 529 and 535.

[35] "Nam quum sensit applicationem eius quod diligebat, evacuavit quod habebat in brevi tempore; et existimavimus mirabile esse et significavimus obedientiam naturae meditationibus. Amplius, quum non invenitur cura nisi regimen coniunctionis inter eos secundum modum

permissionis fidei et legis, fiat; et nos quidem iam vidimus, cui redita est salus, et virtus, et rediit ad carnem suam, quum iam pervenisset ad arefactionem et pertransisset ipsam, et tolerasset aegritudines pravas antiquas et febres longas propter debilitatem virtutis factam propter nimietatem [amoris] ilisci. . . . " Cf. Avicennae *Libri in re medica* (Venetiis, apud V. Valgrisium, 1564), p. 480 (Liber III, Fen. I, Tract. 4, Cap. 22). It is Cap. 23 (misprinted as 24) in the edition Avicennae *Canon Medicinae* (Venetiis, Junta, 1595), p. 494.

[36] J. E. Shaw, *G. Cavalcanti's Theory of Love* (Toronto, 1949), with the text and translation of the 'canzone.' See my review in *R.Ph.*, VII, 4 (1954), 289–393. For a more definitive critical text I quote from G. Cavalcanti, *Rime*, ed. G. Favati (Milan-Naples, 1957), pp. 214–216. This passage corresponds to vv. 39–41 (p. 215).

[37] Cf. especially stanzas 3 and 4 for the aspects here indicated: the key passages are "non razionale, ma che sente, dico. For di salute giudicar mantene, ché la 'ntenzione per ragione vale. . . . Segue spesso morte . . . . Non perché oppost'a naturale sia . . . Oltra misura di natura torna . . . . Poco soggiorna . . . . Ira . . . . Né cert' à mente gran saver, né poco."

[38] Nardi, p. 518.
The theme remained a commonplace throughout the Renaissance. Cf. Shakespeare, Sonnet 129:

> Past reason hunted; and no sooner had,
> Past reason hated, as a swallow'd bait,
> On purpose laid to make the taker mad:
> Mad in pursuit, and in possession so;
> Had, having, and in quest to have, extreme, . . .

Cf. W. G. Meader, *Courtship in Shakespeare. Its relation to the Tradition of Courtly Love* (New York, 1954), Index, s.v. 'Hereos.' Also, for Spain, Otis H. Green, *Courtly Love in Quevedo* (Boulder, Col., 1952), pp. 43ff. ("un muy enamorado suele estar fuera de sí," Quevedo). Mario Equicola in his well-known treatise *Libro di natura d'amore* of 1525 (Venice, 1531), fol. 27, quotes Avicenna as stating: "Amor esser una specie di pazzia."

[39] P. O. Kristeller, "A philosophical Treatise from Bologna dedicated to G. Cavalcanti: Magister Jacobus de Pistoria and his *Questio de Felicitate*," in *Medioevo e Rinascimento, Studi in onore di B. Nardi* (Florence, 1955), 427–63 (with text).

[40] "Iste enim passiones sunt nobis maxime connaturales, ad quas maxime inclinamur, ut patet in eodem septimo [Aristotelis Ethicorum libro], unde dicit de concupiscentia venereorum, cibi et potus quod coniuncta est nobis a iuventute nostra." " . . . Redditur improporcionatum organum fantasie et ymaginacionis, sine quo bene disposito non contingit intelligere." " . . . ut homo pervenire possit ad specula-

cionem summi intelligibilis oportet amovere et detruncare sive regulare in passionibus venereorum." Cf. *Questio de felicitate,* ed. cit. pp. 455–456.

[41] "Va', o uomo d'altura . . . e considera la viltà della sepoltura. Va', garzone altiero e sanza freno, quando t'allegri co' compagni e vai in brigata sanza temperanza e seguitando i voleri tuoi, e pon mente ai sepolcri pieni di bruttura e di puzzolente lordura. Va', o donna svaliata e leggiadra, quando ti diletti d'esser guatata, e giovati d'esser pregiata e tenuta bella; sguarda nelle fosse de' cimiteri le carni verminose e fracide. Va', donzella vezzosa, che studi in . . . essere dagli amanti amata, ed ispécchiati ne' monumenti, pieni d'abbominevoli fracidumi." *Trattato dell'umiltà,* Chap. IV. Quoted in L. Di Francia, *La Novellistica* (Milan, 1924), I, chap. 2, p. 107. This sermon, that was delivered in the very church where the *brigata* of the *Decameron* gathered and decided to set forth on their pleasant holiday, was later incorporated in the *Specchio di Vera Penitenza.* For the compete text, in the absence of a critical edition, see the inadequate and incorrect I. Passavanti, *Lo Specchio della Vera Penitenza,* ed. F.-L. Polidori (Florence, 1856, 1863²), p. 253.

[42] See del Garbo's advice against the plague, in Di Francia, cit., p. 109: "Il più sicuro rimedio è fuggire di quel luogo ove allora sia la detta pistolenza, e andare al luogo ove l'aria sia sana. . . . Ora è da vedere del modo del prendere letizia e piacer in questo tal tempo di pistolenza, e nell'animo e nella mente tua. E sappi che una delle più perfette cose in questo caso, è con ordine prendere allegrezza; nella quale si osservi questo ordine, cioè prima *non pensare della morte,* ovvero passione d'alcuno, ovvero di cosa t'abbia a contristare, ovvero a dolere; ma i pensieri sieno sopra cose dilettevoli e piacevoli. L'usanze sieno con persone liete e gioconde, e fuggasi ogni maninconia; e l'usanza sia con non molta gente nella casa . . . ; e in giardini a tempo loro, ove sieno erbe odorifere, e come sono vite e salci. . . . E usare canzone e giullerie, e altre novelle piacevole, sanza fatica di corpo, e tutte cose dilettevoli che confortino altrui." Cf. *Decameron*'s Introduction, ed. Branca, Vol. I, pp. 16–17 20, where is given the very advice that the *brigata* will adopt.

[43] *I Libri della Famiglia,* II, in L. B. Alberti, *Opere Volgari,* I, *I Libri della Famiglia, Cena Familiaris, Villa,* ed. C. Grayson (Bari, 1960), p. 122: "A me certo pare stultissimo consiglio non amare più la vita certa di molti sani che la sanità dubbia d'uno infermo." And see this whole, detailed passage, which reminded V. Rossi of Ariosto's "Ché sarebbe pensier non troppo accorto, / Perder duo vivi per salvar un morto." (*Orlando Furioso,* XVIII, 189.) Cf. V. Rossi, *Il Quattrocento* (Milan, 1956⁶), p. 144.

[44] On the psychological significance of gardens, landscapes, *loci amoeni* in the Middle Ages one can consult, among others, F. Crisp, *Medieval Gardens* (London, 1924); H. R. Patch, *The Other World, according to descriptions in medieval literature* (Cambridge, 1950), *passim;*

E. R. Curtius, *European Literature and the Latin Middle Ages,* trans. W. R. Trask (New York, 1953), pp. 185, 193ff.

[45] U. Bosco, *Il Decameron,* p. 61.

[46] C. Grabher, "Particolari influssi di Andrea Cappelllano sul B.," pp. 84ff.

[47] In this context, it may be of some interest to recall a medieval precedent of Margutte's boasts in the fabliau *Le Credo au Ribaut* (E. Barbazan and Méon, eds., *Fabliaux et Contes* . . . [Paris, 1808], IV, 445).

[48] Cf. Barbazan-Méon, I, 212; III, 96; Le Grand d'Aussy, *Fabliaux* (Paris, 1781), I, 273. A similar situation obtains in a fabliau where Hyppocrates is the victim. Cf. Le Grand d'Aussy, I, 232ff.; J. Bédier, *Les Fabliaux* (Paris, 1925⁵), 446–447. See D. Comparetti's comments in *Virgilio nel Medioevo,* ed. G. Pasquali (Florence, 1946), II, 109ff. or Id., *Vergil in the Middle Ages,* trans. E. F. M. Benecke (London-New York, 1895), pp. 327ff.

[49] "la natura, che nel mondo dantesco è il peccato, qui è la legge, ed ha contro di sé . . . la società come si trova ordinata in quel complesso di leggi, di consuetudini che si chiamano 'l'onore.'" *Storia della Letteratura italiana,* ed. cit., pp. 326–327.

[50] *Storia,* p. 334.

[51] Lucretius had elegantly spoken of nobility being superseded by riches to the extent that the very ones who possessed the true ingredients of nobility (beauty and strength), once supremely appreciated, now bowed to the new aristocracy of wealth: "Posterius res inventast aurumque repertum, / Quod facile et validis et pulchris dempsit honorem; / Divitioris enim sectam plerumque secuntur / Quam lubet et fortes et pulchro corpore creti." *De Rerum Natura,* V, vv. 1113–1116.

The traditional Stoic theme of Juvenal's Eighth Satire, *Stemmata quid faciunt?,* is articulated into a three-pronged critique of nobility: Personal worth is a man's true coat of arms; History shows patricians to have been morally and intellectually inferior to the plebs; The claim of noble ancestry is but a prejudice, since one can always find a robber or a shepherd at the origin of a noble house.

This 'democratic' tradition was vigorously reborn in courtly literature and it is, in my opinion, also against this medieval background that we must view even such typically humanistic developments as the *Disputatio de Nobilitate* attributed to Buonaccorso da Montemagno the Younger (shortly before 1429). Cf. H. Baron, *The Crisis of the Early Italian Renaissance* (Princeton, 1955), pp. 365–366 and 623–627. The humanistic spirit of this important 'debate,' where a virtuous plebeian is preferred by a noble girl to an inept nobleman, is masterfully identified by Baron in the sociopolitical context and in the classical model (Sallust), but one cannot afford to ignore the medieval background of such discussions, which Baron does not indicate. Also cf. Chap. XI of the *Trac-*

tatus de Perfecto Amore attributed to Egidio Romano (edited with introduction and Italian translation by G. Bruni, Rome, 1951). The same opposition of plebeian and nobleman in love is also found in B.'s *Elegia di Madonna Fiammetta*, eds. A. Schiaffini and F. Ageno (Paris, 1954), pp. 18 and 124.

[52] "E domna non pot ren valer / Per riquessa ni per poder / Se jois d'amor no la spira." K. Bartsch, *Chrestomathie Provençale* (Elberfeld, 1875³), p. 46.

Useful observations on the development of Italian ideas on courtliness and nobility can be found in A. Vallone, *La Cortesia dai Provenzali a Dante* (Palermo, 1950), and *Cortesia e Nobiltà nel Rinascimento* (Asti, 1955), esp. pp. 33–50 for B.'s time.

In particular, the philological study by Maria Corti, "Le fonti del *Fiore di virtù* e la teoria della 'nobiltà' nel Duecento," *Giornale Storico della Letteratura Italiana*, CXXXVI (1959), 1–82, contains many erudite references (esp. pp. 63–82 for Dante's *Convivio*).

[53] "Sotto legge plebea correggendo la mobile pompa de' grandi e le vicine città, gloriosa si vive, presta a maggior cose; se l'ardente invidia e rapace avarizia con la intollerabile superbia, che in lei regnano, non la impediscono, come si teme." Cf. *Ameto*, in G. B., *L'Ameto, Lettere, Il Corbaccio*, ed. N. Bruscoli (Bari, 1940; G. B., *Opere*, V), p. 137.

[54] "Conosciamo lei essere tanto gentile o più, quanto se d'imperiale progenie nata fosse, se riguardiamo con debito stile che cosa gentilezza sia, la quale troveremo ch'è solo virtù d'animo." Cf. G. B., *Il Filocolo*, ed. S. Battaglia (Bari, 1938), p. 77. In a recent study of the work, the *Filocolo* as a whole is said to "represent a theme that B. was to treat with predilection and consummate art in later works such as the *Ninfale Fiesolano* and several tales of the *Decameron:* the natural or instinctive love that attracts two young people of the opposite sex and the persistence of their love against the obstacles erected by an unsympathetic law or by class-conscious relatives concerned with preserving the distinctions created by social and economic position." Cf. N. J. Perella, "The World of B.'s *Filocolo*," *PMLA*, LXXVI, 4 (1961), 330–339.

[55] Queste schifate ed abbiatele a vili,
    Ché bestie son, non son donne gentili.
    Perfetta donna ha più fermo disire
    D'esserne amata, e d'amar si diletta.
Cf. *Filostrato* VIII, 31–32. Critical edition in G. B., *Il Filostrato e il Ninfale Fiesolano*, ed. V. Pernicone (Bari, 1937; G. B., *Opere*, II). The translation is from G. B., *Il Filostrato*, trans. Hubertis Cummings (Princeton, 1924).

[56] Cf. V. Branca, *B. medievale*, cit., pp. 154–155. The relevant passages from the *De Amore* are on pp. 40–80 (Dialogues B and C) of the Battaglia edition.

[57] "Uom di nazione assai umile ma per virtù e per costumi

nobile." G. Boccaccio, *Decameron*, ed. Vittore Branca (Florence, Le Monnier, 1951, 1960², 2 vols.). Cf. Vol. I, pp. 462–463. I shall quote the *Decameron* from this second Branca edition, which offers the most reliable text, for the time being the closest to a truly critical edition, and the richest commentary available. G. Petronio's ed. (Turin, 1950), particularly open as it is to linguistic and stylistic considerations, will be helpful to a better understanding of the precise implications of my quotations. Of recognized philological importance is also the ed. by Ch. S. Singleton (Bari, 1952).

In translating from the *Decameron* I shall freely follow the "faithful" translation of J. M. Rigg (*The Decameron of G. B.* [London, 1906], 2 vols., also available in other editions), frequently modifying it to make it more truly faithful and less artificially archaic—since the now inveterate habit of translating old Italian authors into Elizabethan or pseudo-Elizabethan English does not take account of the different rhythm of evolution in the two languages. The language of Dante, Petrarch, and Boccaccio is remarkably closer to present-day Italian than Francis Bacon's is to present-day English.

[58] "Che io con uom di bassa condizione mi son posta: in che non ti accorgi che non il mio peccato ma quello della fortuna riprendi, la quale assai sovente li non degni ad alto leva, abbasso lasciando i dignissimi" (p. 470).

[59] " . . . noi d'una massa di carne tutti la carne avere, e da uno medesimo Creatore tutte l'anime con iguali forze, con iguali potenzie, con iguali virtù create" (p. 470). Capitolo XXXIII of the *Amorosa Visione* contained a polemic passage against nobility given by Fortune in favor of true nobility founded on virtue, and independent of Fortune. And lines 1–12 of Capitolo XXI attacked those parents who foolishly attempt to hinder the irresistible progress of love in their offspring. A lengthy discussion on true nobility is found in a letter to Francesco Nelli of 1363: cf. G. B., *Opere Latine Minori*, ed. A. F. Massèra (Bari, 1928; B., *Opere*, IX), pp. 172–173. B. argues against Niccolò Acciaiuoli's wish to have been born noble. Nobility originated from physical violence, and even this justification ceased to hold with the degenerate progeny of the 'heroes,' etc. Similarly, in the later *Corbaccio* we find: "He who pursued virtue was called noble, the others who, instead, pursued vice, ignoble. Hence nobility first came into the world from virtue." ("Colui che la virtù seguitò, fu detto gentile; e gli altri per contrario, seguendo i vizi, furono non gentili reputati: dunque da virtù venne prima gentilezza nel mondo.") But present-day aristocracy has degenerated: "The life of those [noblemen] who now live is such, that being dead would be far better." Cf. *L'Ameto, Lettere, Il Corbaccio*, pp. 255–256.

[60] "Le due ministre del mondo [natura e fortuna] spesso le

lor cose più care nascondono sotto l'ombra dell'arti reputate più vili, acciò che di quelle alle necessità traendole, più chiaro appaia il loro splendore." (VI, 2; Vol. II, p. 133.)

Cisti was introduced as follows: "Il qual Cisti, d'altissimo animo fornito, la Fortuna fece fornaio." A similar remark at the beginning of VI, 5 (Forese e Giotto). Elsewhere the injustice of having noble souls born in lowly social station or vice versa, or the cases of valiant men thrown into lowly conditions by misfortune, are called "peccato della fortuna," a sin of Fortune (cf. V, 7; Vol. II, p. 80).

[61] "Anche nelle povere case piovono dal cielo de' divini spiriti, come nelle reali di quegli che sarien più degni di guardar porci che d'avere sopra uomini signoria" (II, p. 659).

Griselda's tale, soon to be honored by Petrarch's translation and Chaucer's reëlaboration, was destined to enjoy a long success in Italy and, perhaps even more, abroad. Of particular interest is the story of its popularity in France, which is retold by E. Golenistcheff-Koutouzoff, *L'Histoire de Griselidis en France au XIVe et au XVe siècle* (Paris 1933) and by F. Simone, who has carried it on through the sixteenth century in his *Il Rinascimento Francese*, pp. 161–168. This for the literary image of feminine heroism in conjugal patience. The reality of it has had a much longer story, as we all know. One modern Griselda, for example, is portrayed in André Maurois' *Adrienne: The Life of the Marquise de La Fayette* (New York, 1961).

[62] "Scioccamente, sì come ancora oggi fanno tutto 'l dì i mercatanti, pensò di volere ingentilire per moglie" (II, p. 261 4).

[63] In V, 8 (Nastagio degli Onesti) no sympathy is shown to the lady so severely punished in the 'Purgatory of the Cruel Lovers' where hounds chase her and tear her apart, for she had perhaps been made insensitive to the suitor's great love by the foolish pride of her more noble blood: "tanto cruda e dura e salvatica . . . forse per la sua singular bellezza o per la sua nobiltà sì altiera e disdegnosa divenuta." Cf. my fn. 55.

[64] "Amor può troppo più che né voi né io possiamo." This 'profession of faith' is forcefully restated in X, 8 by Tito amidst the ordeal of his passion for Sofronia, his best friend's fiancée: "Le leggi d'amore sono di maggior potenzia che alcune altre: elle rompono, non che quelle della amistà, ma le divine" (II, p. 594). In Guiscardo's words L. Russo sees "an implied polemic against the rules of medieval asceticism": cf. G. B., *Il Decameron, Venticinque novelle scelte e ventisette postille critiche*, ed. L. Russo (Florence, 1939), p. 118. In his turn Tancred, "a coherent incarnation of a lack of coherence," is a paradigmatic character in his lack of that 'art of life,' *savoir vivre* which B. celebrates in his positive heroes, as G. Getto has revealed: cf. his *Vita di forme e forme di vita nel Decameron* (Turin, 1958), p. 115.

On the relative inadequacy of B.'s style to respond to the seriousness of intention and the tragic tone of this novella (especially at the end) and others, cf. E. Auerbach, *Mimesis,* pp. 216–231. For original views on the general problem of *sermo humilis* and sublime or tragic style cf., also, by the same author, *Literatursprache und Publikum in der lateinischen Spätantike und im Mittelalter* (Bern, 1958). See, however, Branca's objections to Auerbach in *B. medievale,* p. 28 fn. 25.

B. can be said to be stylistically pre-Dante inasmuch as he is still, in a typically medieval way, incapable of rising above the *sermo humilis* to a stylistic level which would be more than the medieval texture of high rhetoric, ornate pomp of rather mechanical devices—and he is also incapable of the biblical sublime, which Dante had achieved within the *sermo humilis* of his "comedy." Thus there is room, in B., for noble elegy (as in Lisabetta's case), not for tragedy—hence the failure of Ghismunda's rhetorical finale. Cf. also G. Di Pino, op. cit., "Intonazione media della scrittura," pp. 244-252.

[65] "Poi che attempati sono, d'essere stati giovani ricordar non si vogliono" (p. 264).

[66] "Currado . . . se io seco fui meno che onestamente, secondo la oppinion de' meccanici, quel peccato commisi il qual sempre seco tiene la giovanezza congiunto, . . . e il quale, se i vecchi si volessero ricordare d'essere stati giovani e gli altrui difetti colli loro misurare . . . non saria grave come tu e molti altri fanno" (p. 208).

[67] "Così si turbano come se contra natura un grandissimo e scellerato male fosse stato commesso." (Masetto di Lamporecchio's story; p. 318.)

[68] "Credono troppo bene che la zappa e la vanga e le grosse vivande e i disagi tolgano del tutto a' lavoratori della terra i concupiscibili appetiti e rendan loro d'intelletto e d'avvedimento grossissimi" (pp. 318–319).

[69] "Infra molte bianche colombe aggiugne più di bellezza un nero corvo che non farebbe un candido cigno," IX, 10. (II, p. 515.)

Similarly, the courteous competition in sublime magnanimity between Ruggiero and Leone in Ariosto's *Orlando Furioso* (Cantos XLV-XLVI) shows a certain affinity with the stories of *Decameron* X. Ariosto reveals there his aptitude for the medium style, rather than for the cases of sublime morality that were then popular, but came out somewhat 'forced' in his pages, as B. did in his. The reader finds unexplained certain exceptional heights and depths of love and generosity (see, for instance, *O. F.,* XLVI, 41). Cf. the end of preceding fn. 64.

[70] A. Scaglione, "Shahryar, Giocondo, Kote·rviky. Three versions of the motif of the faithless woman," *Oriens,* XI (1958), 151–161. The reader will find here comparative examples of misogynistic stories and parallels between Oriental and Western literatures in the novella genre.

[71] "Credendosi con quelle medesime opere sodisfare alla moglie che egli faceva agli studi . . . cercò d'avere bella e giovane donna per moglie, dove e l'uno e l'altro, se così avesse saputo consigliar sé come altrui faceva, doveva fuggire" (p. 295).

[72] "Con lui s'accontò e fece in poca d'ora una gran dimestichezza e amistà" (p. 298).

[73] "Conoscendo la sua follia d'aver moglie giovane tolta essendo spossato" (p. 304).

[74] "Del mio onore . . . fossonne stati [teneri] i parenti miei quando mi diedero a voi!" (p. 303).

[75] Petronio, ed. cit., p. 292, fn. 20.

[76] "E di pari consentimento tutte le donne dissono che Dioneo diceva vero e che Bernabò era stato una bestia" (p. 306). "S'imaginano che le donne a casa rimase si tengano le mani a cintola" (p. 294).

[77] "Sono . . . di carne, e . . . giovane; e per l'una cosa e per l'altra piena di concupiscible disidèro" (p. 469).

[78] *Essais*, III, v, 1000 of Thibaudet's Pléiade edition (Paris, 1950).

[79] *Essais*, III, v, 989 ed. cit. The 1588 edition added the further clarification, "ayant tant de pieces à mettre en communication on les achemine à y employer toujours la dernière puisque c'est tout d'un pris." Montaigne, with his distinctive psychological and historical foresight, concluded by the advice: "Il leur faut un peu lácher les resnes. . . . On alanguit le desir de la compaignie en luy donnant quelque liberté" (ibid.).

In the manners of Italy (and Spain), Montaigne praised the roundabout ways of wooing and winning which he picturesquely described as those of the one "qui desiroit le gosier allongé comme le col d'une grüe pour gouster plus longtemps ce qu'il avalloit," by contrast with "l'impétuosité françoise" ("nous faisons nostre charge extreme la premiere"), (III, v, 985–986). Montaigne had forgotten, as the good Frenchman that he was, to look back on his own French tradition, where he would have found plenty of that 'long-necked' love he missed in his country for the present. But by his time no cultivated Frenchman any longer read French Gothic romances, while he found the closest thing to it in Dante and even Petrarch. Notwithstanding, in Italy Gothic love, as all Gothic spirit, never really took root, and Dante's example remained rather exceptional and isolated. Whenever it found imitators, this occurred without profound inspiration. The 'immanent' love prevailed for good starting with Petrarch and Boccaccio. Besides, the social sensitivity that had veined at least part of French romantic literature (e.g., in Chrétien with his defense of marriage) was lacking in Italian love literature. Dante's own Beatrice is a figure without social connections, and the *dames* who had been loving wives, housewives, and mothers in Chrétien, will be nothing more than the knights' companions in Pulci, Boiardo, Ariosto, and Tasso (with some not too relevant exceptions).

[80] "Non a guisa di plebeio ma di signore . . . sopra gli omeri de' più nobili cittadini con grandissimo onore fu portato alla sepoltura" (IV, 6, p. 530).

[81] As a confirmation of some of these remarks, cf. G. Petronio, "La posizione del *Decameron*," *La Rassegna della Letteratura Italiana*, LXI, 2 (1957), 189–207.

[82] "Alcuni . . . più che l'altre genti si credon sapere, e sanno meno; . . . contra la natura delle cose [= nature, Lat. *natura rerum*] presummono d'opporre il senno loro; della quale presunzione già grandissimi mali sono avvenuti e alcun bene non se ne vide giammai" (p. 539).

[83] "E per ciò che tra l'altre naturali cose quella che meno riceve consiglio o operazione in contrario è amore, la cui natura è tale che più tosto per se medesimo consumar si può che per avvedimento alcuno tor via" (p. 539).

[84] Cf. Di Pino, *La polemica del B.*, p. 233 (conclusion on Martuccio's story): "L'avventura d'amore significa sempre, nella invenzione del B., l'imporsi della volontà degli affetti sopra un ordine costituito."

[85] Chaucer, "The Knight's Tale," vv. 1155–1171. (Robinson's ed. [1957²], p. 28). The vigorous and, to us, most pertinent thought contained in the lines "Thyn is affeccioun of hoolynesse, / And myn is love, as to a creature" found an equally effective, though indirect, echo in the lines attributed to the amorist poet Thomas Carew:

> I will not saint my Coelia, for she
> More glorious is in her humanity
>
> . . . .
> . . . . for she may sin
> Beyond hope of repentance; and therein
> Appear the odds; that maugre flesh and blood,
> Beauty, temptation, Devil, she is good.

[86] Capellanus, *De Amore*, I, 3: "Love causes a rough and uncouth man (*horridus et incultus*) to be distinguished for his handsomeness." S. Painter (op. cit., p. 113) quotes a relevant passage by the minstrel Aimeric de Pégulhan (Anglade, *Anthologie des Troubadours*, p. 140) which he so translates: "It [love] makes a vile creature into a distinguished man, a fool into a man of agreeable conversation, a miser into a spendthrift, and it transforms a rascal into a man of honor. By it insane men become sages, the gauche become polished and the haughty are changed into gentle and humble men." Similarly Guilhem de Cabestanh: "For the ladies always make valiant the most cowardly and the wickedest felons"; and more generically Pons de Chapteuil: "The most

valiant counts, dukes, and barons were more *preux* because of her"
(ibid.).

The theme of Cimon was first foreshadowed in the *Caccia di Diana,*
where the humanizing and civilizing power of womanhood on man was
celebrated in an upturning of the Circe motif. Instead of men being
turned into beasts by sensuality, here beasts are turned into eager, hand-
some youths by love. When Diane is rejected by her former followers,
the huntresses, Venus, invoked by them, appears and promises the maidens to satisfy their vows. Whereupon "Ciascuna fiera che v'era infiam-
mata, / Mutata in forma d'uom, di quelli ardori / Usciva giovinetto gaio
e bello" (XVII, 39–41). "E vidimi alla bella donna offerto, / E di cervio
mutato in creatura / Umana e razionale esser per certo" (XVIII, 10–12).
"Che, donandomi a lei, uom ritornai / Di brutta belva, a uomo d'intelletto"
(XVIII, 23–24). (For a rapport with the *Vita Nuova* and *Ameto* cf. Di
Pino, *La Polemica del B.,* pp. 58f.). The same motif recurs in *Amorosa
Visione,* Capitolo XXIII, vv. 16–18: "Armor, de' savi grazïosa luce, / Tu
se' colui che ingentilisci i cori, / Tu se' colui che in noi valore induce."
Also cf. the Hymn to Love, ibid., XLII, vv. 61–84, esp. 73–75; and,
above all, the main story of *Ameto,* with derivations from Ovid (Poly-
phemus and Galatea), *Met.,* XIII, 759ff. and 790ff. Cf. J. Gower, *Confessio Amantis,* IV, 2300, a paean in praise of Love: "it maketh curteis
of the vilein." And in Ariosto's *Mad Roland* that magnificent villain-
hero, Rodomonte, suddenly turns exquisitely humane at the sight of the
unfortunate and beautiful Isabella; his tragic love for her will make of
him a sublimely devoted knight. No specific source has been uncovered
for Cimon's story, in spite of numerous but vague hellenistic suggestions:
cf. E. Rohde, *Der griechische Roman und seine Vorläufer* (Leipzig,
1914³), pp. 538f. Branca (*Decameron,* ed. cit., II, 5, n. 1), aptly recalls
an important passage of *Genealogie* IX, 4, which could be rendered as
follows: "Thanks to this passion, as some authors maintain, youngsters
otherwise intolerably uncouth begin to strive toward virtue and illus-
trious enterprise, give themselves to gay social activities, groom themselves with splendid care, delight in song and dance, turn liberal."
Branca makes allusion to the extraordinary success of this story, from
Béroalde to Hans Sachs and Rubens.

[87] II, p. 17 *56. Virtù* is here used in a classical sense. For
the meaning of this word in B., see the beginning of the following chapter.

[88] "E ciascun lietamente con la sua visse lungamente con-
tento nella sua terra" (II, p. 20 *71).*

[89] "Ciascun si dée meritamente dilettare di quelle cose alle
quali egli vede i guiderdoni secondo le affezioni seguitare; e per ciò che
amare merita più tosto diletto che afflizione . . ." (II, p. 21 3).

[90] To the debated, and often biased, question as to whether the Renaissance really was immoral, or rather amoral, one could reply that it undoubtedly was an epoch of relatively low moral awareness at least inasmuch as it generally lacked the sense of sin. Even in Ficino and his Neoplatonist followers, who in a way seemed to return to the medieval concern for the transcendental and its mystic apprehension, the sense of sin was replaced by a thoroughly humanistic perception of the superior Harmony of all Being, with no realization that true religiousness takes its roots in, and thrives in the clash of irreducible contradiction and conflict. Cf. E. Gothein, "Die Weltanschauung der Renaissance," *Jahrbuch des Freien deutschen Hochstifts zu Frankfurt* (Frankfurt am Main, 1904), 94–131, esp. p. 126. Of course, this is not to imply that B., in this respect, belongs to the Renaissance. To the contrary, one cannot say that his lack of the sense of sin was due to a need for 'harmony.'

Notes for CHAPTER IV

[1] "Love, which exempts no loved one from loving in return": Dante, *Inferno*, V, 103. This passage has been linked to the sect of the "Fedeli d'Amore" ("Love's Faithful"), of which Dante would have been a member according to L. Valli, *Il linguaggio segreto di Dante* (Rome, 1928), pp. 434–435. Cf. B., *Filocolo*, p. 331: "E' non può essere ch'ella non vi ami, perciò che amore mai non perdonò l'amare a nullo amato." The general code upheld by Tedaldo is essentially the traditional one of courtly love.

[2] "L'usare la dimestichezza d'uno uomo una donna è peccato naturale" (III, 7, p. 391 45); "da malvagità di mente procede" (ibid.). Also cf. "da amor costretti . . . questo peccato, se peccato dir si dee quel che per amor fanno i giovani, hanno fatto" (V, 6; II, p. 70).

Moreover, for B. to resist the instincts of the flesh is well-nigh 'impossible': the 'nun of the breeches' "conchiudendo venne impossibile essere il potersi dagli stimoli della carne difendere" (IX, 2; II, p. 460). How B. must have felt about the theological view on sins of love of this and more serious kinds can be gathered from VII, 10 (Meuccio e Tingoccio), where the man who has been in Purgatory assures the other: "Va', sciocco, non dubitare; ché di qua non si tiene ragione alcuna delle comari!" Some critics may tend to go too far in discarding any ideological basis in such jibes for the sake of focusing the reader's attention on the mere aesthetic effect by which the author was guided.

[3] A. Graf, "Corso sul Boccaccio" University of Turin, Academic Year 1901–1902 (Turin, Bertero, 1902), (lithographed), p. 258; quoted by Bosco (see following fn.).

⁴ U. Bosco, *Il Decameron*, Chap. VI. As to the tradition within which one must view the particular argumentation and purpose of Tedaldo's 'sermon,' see *e.g.*, the firmness of the lover in rejecting religious objections raised by the beloved—who is no less than a nun—in Boncompagno da Signa, *Rota Veneris*, pp. 21–22.

⁵ Sometimes such terms are only used ironically; cf. IV, 10: the wife of Maestro Mazzeo della Montagna "sì come savia e di grande animo, per potere quel di casa risparmiare," decides to find a lover. For an interesting interpretation of *saviezza* in a rationalistic direction, see G. Petronio, *Il Decamerone* (Bari, 1935), Chap. II ("Spregiudicatezza e Saviezza'). Also see H. Baron, "Secularization of Wisdom and Political Humanism in the Renaissance," *Journal of the History of Ideas*, XXI (1960), 131–150, à propos of Eugene F. Rice, Jr., *The Renaissance Idea of Wisdom* (Cambridge, Harvard University Press, 1958).

⁶ In a typically humanistic context, and in Aristotelian language, L. B. Alberti gave of virtue a seemingly naturalistic definition: virtue is perfection of being, full realization of one's nature, entelechy; "non è virtù altro se none in sé perfetta e ben produtta natura" (and to say nature is almost to say God: "natura, cioè Iddio"). Cf. *I Libri della Famiglia*, in L. B. Alberti, *Opere volgari*, ed. C. Grayson, I, 63. The moral phraseology in Medieval and Renaissance Romance literatures (with references to B.) has been recently studied from a stylistic standpoint by Richard Glasser, *Studien über die Bildung einer moralischen Phraseologie im Romanischen* in *Analecta Romanica*, Beiheft 3 to *Romanische Forschungen*, ed. F. Schalk (Frankfurt am Main, 1956).

⁷ "Noi non ci nascemmo per vivere come bruti, ma per seguire virtù." *Il Filocolo*, ed. Battaglia, p. 268.

⁸ "Quantunque appo coloro che discreti erano e alla cui notizia pervenne io ne fossi lodato e da molto più reputato" (p. 3; Proem to the *Decameron*).

⁹ Of course, the term can also have the more limited, and current meaning of the necessary circumspection and practical sense to carry through a difficult matter with success, as in III, 4: frate Puccio's wife has learned how good don Felice's fare is, and settles down to carry on her affair with him wisely and discreetly: "sì s'avvezzò a' cibi del monaco, che, essendo dal marito lungamente stata tenuta in dieta . . . modo trovò di cibarsi in altra parte con lui, e con discrezione lungamente ne prese il suo piacere" (p. 356 32). In this case the word adds another touch of humor to the humorous situation.

¹⁰ Cf. I, 1 (Parry's trans.)

¹¹ The term referred to arrogance, in particular: cf. "Li baron tencent par grant desmesurance" in the twelfth-century *Raoul*. Dante related it specifically to economic wealth as greed and conspicu-

ous consumption: cf. "La gente nova e' subiti guadagni / Orgoglio e dismisura han generata" (*Inferno*, XVI, 73–74), but implicitly saw it as a negation of "cortesia e valor" (ibid., v. 67). The concept of virtue as a happy medium between extremes is rather pagan than Christian. The Delphic dictum Μηδὲν ἄγαν, *nihil nimis*, 'nothing to excess' was famous in antiquity; and the moralists spoke of ἀκολασία, 'immoderateness,' as opposed to σοφροσύνη, wisdom. This classic view will reappear in the Renaissance in humanistic and classical contexts. In *Della Famiglia*, IV, for instance, L. B. Alberti will counsel a string of practical, bourgeois, "unheroic" virtues (seek just revenge, but with measure, win but without damaging yourself, fight for liberty but do not lose your life for it). Even more typical is his search for the rules of good life on the economic plane, in a difficult and subtly defined equilibrium between avarice and prodigality. Cf. the *Intercoenalis* "Parsimonia," where the advice is the following: Be not spendthrifts, as if today were your last day ("ac si essent propediem morituri"), nor misers as if you were to live forever ("ac si aeternam cum superis vitam depacti essent"; cf. L. B. A., *Opera inedita et pauca separatim impressa*, ed. G. Mancini [Florence, 1890], p. 156), but spend freely yet wisely, i.e., be parsimonious, *frugi, massai,* in your desires even more than in your possessions. Cf. also the *Intercoenales* "Gallus," "Vaticinium," and the beautiful "Paupertas," where the medieval economico-ethical ideas are resolutely swept aside. The same, fundamental love for measure and harmony framed in good bourgeois common sense is revealed by Alberti in his treatment of human emotions: to love one's wife is healthy and good, but in the *Intercoenalis* "Defunctus" Neophronius makes a nuisance of himself by his tearful attachment to his dead wife, lovely as she may have been (O shades of Petrarch!). He is decidedly mad, as mad or hypocrites are those who exceed in outward manifestation of all passions, including grief for the disappearance of the loved ones.

[12] "Questo non monta niente; là dov'io onestamente viva né mi rimorda d'alcuna cosa la coscienza, parli chi vuole in contrario" (p. 37 *84*).

[13] Dante's horror for Semiramis who "made whatever was pleasing, legitimate in her laws" ("libito fè licito in sua legge"), will become admiration for the law of nature in Tasso's ideal though only idyllic and dream-like world: "If it is pleasing, it is allowed" ("s'ei piace ei lice"). Cf. *A Translation of the 'Orpheus' of A. Poliziano and the 'Aminta' of T. Tasso . . . by L. E. Lord* (Oxford, 1931), p. 129. The law of Semiramis was curiously attributed to Jupiter in the *Roman de la Rose* (vv. 20465–20481): "Communement abandonna / Que chacun en son bon droit fist / Tout ce que délectable vist, / Car délict ainsi qu'il pensoit / Est la meilleure chose qui soit / . . . Exemple de vivre fesoit / A son corps ce qui luy plaisoit."

[14] Occasionally we encounter a curious, picturesque juxta-

position of bigotry and license, as in the old woman ("santa Verdiana") of V, 10, who is described as a half-saint and a *baciapile biascica preghiere,* but is introduced in the act of comforting the discontented wife of a sodomite by seconding her fancy to take a lover, for it is truly sinful for any young woman to waste her time and forsake the sacred right to have her fun. She even offers to help her as a procuress with the added safeguard of her effective *paternostri.* There is apparently no awareness of the contrast, no intentional mockery of 'holy' hypocrisy. True enough, such a character was traditional (cf. *Roman de la Rose*).

[15] In the Introduction to the Sixth Day, from the hilarious bickering of two servants comes out the 'factual' statement that young girls do not waste their time waiting for their fathers' and brothers' so frequently delayed decisions to give them a husband, and that most of them have had their experience before entering the marital bed.

[16] *Essais,* III, 5, ed. cit., p. 963.

[17] "La donna racconsolata, veggendo il marito non esser turbato di questo fatto, e considerando che la figliuola aveva avuta la buona notte ed erasi ben riposata e aveva l'usignuolo preso, si tacque" (II, p. 50).

[18] "Tu non ci tornerai mai infino a tanto che io di questa cosa, in presenza de' parenti tuoi e de' vicini, te n'avrò fatto quello onore che ti si conviene" (II, p. 228).

[19] "Promise di mai più non esser geloso: e oltre a ciò le die' licenza che ogni suo piacer facesse ma sì saviamente, che egli non se ne avvedesse" (II, p. 231).

The story derives from Petrus Alphonsus' (fl. 1100) *Disciplina Clericalis* (12th tale, "Exemplum de puteo"), a collection of tales from the Arabic. See the ed. by A. Hilka and W. Soederhjelm (Helsinki, 1911), and cf. Di Francia, *La Novellistica,* pp. 146–147, or, better, A. Chiari, *Indagini e Letture,* 2d series (Florence, 1954), "Tofano e Ghita," pp. 80–101.

[20] In the source of the novella, the twelfth-century Latin poem *Comoedia Lydiae* attributed to Mathieu de Vendôme, we find the same three tests, but they are motivated by Lydia's need to convince Pyrrhus that she can deceive her husband without danger to her lover. Cf. E. Faral, "Le fabliau latin au Moyen Age," *Romania,* L (1924), 321–385, esp. 351–362 and G. Cohen, *La comédie latine en France au XII* siècle* (Paris, 1931) (text at end of Vol. I).

[21] "Del pero tagliato che colpa avuto non avea si doleano" (II, p. 287).

[22] "Quantunque rigido e costante fieramente, anzi crudele, riputassero lo scolare" (II, p. 389).

[23] The jest as a fine art, approved and cherished as a triumph of human ingenuity even when exercised in a vacuum, without any aim other than self-expression, is a notorious asset in Renaissance literature, especially in Italy. Cf. Chap. III, pp. 65–67 of the present book.

[24] "Non mi pare che agramente sia da riprendere . . . chi fa beffa alcuna a colui che la va cercando o che la si guadagna" (beginning of VIII, 9).

[25] "Con più *moderata* operazion vendicò; per la quale potrete comprendere che assai dee bastare a ciascuno, se *quale asino dà in parete tal riceve*, senza volere, soprabbondando oltre la *convenevolezza* della vendetta, ingiuriare" (II, pp. 389–390).

[26] "Uno che se l'andò cercando, estimando che quegli che gliele fecero non da biasimare ma da commendar sieno" (II, p. 396).

[27] Geri's famous story is the third of Anton Francesco Grazzini's first *Cena*, and in the same collection a splendid example of a wanton trick is the tenth of the third *Cena* (Lorenzo il Magnifico and Manente). See these stories in *Novelle del Cinquecento*, ed. C. Salinari (Turin, 1955), Vol. I.

Concerning the influence of B.'s novella cf. A. Chiari, *Indagini e Letture*, 2d series, "Imitazioni e deviazioni della novella di tipo boccaccesco," pp. 102–185.

[28] Cf., for instance, Bernhard König, *Die Begegnung im Tempel, Abwandlungen eines literarischen Motivs in den Werken Boccaccios*, Hamburger Romanistische Studien, R. A., XLV (Hamburg, 1960), 69 (with reference to the encounter in a church, frequent in B.'s early works): "Die religiöse Weihe enthüllt sich als Trug, die Liebe kommt nicht von Gott und führt nicht zu ihm, sondern in Tod (Troiolo) und Verzweiflung (Fiammetta)."

[29] Sapegno, *Il Trecento*, p. 307. On Chaucer's reëlaboration, cf. C. S. Lewis, "What Chaucer really did to *Il Filostrato*," *Essays and Studies of the English Association*, XVII (1931), 56–75. Also the bold and inspired essay by A. Renoir, "Criseyde's Two Half Lovers," *Orbis Litterarum*, XV (1962), 239–255. Lewis shows (brilliantly though a bit tendentiously) the contrast between the 'medieval' *Troilus and Criseyde* and the 'Renaissance' *Filostrato* (cf. also his *Allegory of Love*, 175–197). His analysis is more convincing on Chaucer than on Boccaccio. At any rate, Chaucer's *Troilus* is, in all the marvel of its supple and complex psychologism, a true 'study in the nature of love' taken as a natural phenomenon, although from the courtly viewpoint, and analyzed in order to understand it, not to judge the virtues and sins of the characters. Furthermore, courtly prejudices are transcended in the name of natural psychological pressures (Criseyde's betrayal breaks the laws of courtly love to obey those of nature). Nevertheless, I am compelled to add, Chaucer remains within the boundaries of the courtly world even when playing the rights of nature against its code, whereas B., at least in the *Decameron*, leaves that code behind in the name of a new ethics that admits of no opposition. For the background of Boiardo's Tisbina story, cf. L. Di Francia, *La Novellistica*, I, 560–563.

[30] It is interesting to note that even in one case where he followed a preëxisting model, B. tended to tone down the explicit insistence on women's congenital, treacherous unreliability; we can compare the treatment of Criseida's yielding to Diomedes in the *Filostrato* with that of Briseis' in the *Roman de Troie* by Benoît de Sainte-Maure. For an early comparison, see Bartoli, *I precursori*, pp. 65–71.

[31] "La donna, che di gran cuore era, sì come generalmente esser soglion quelle che innamorate son da dovero" (VI, 7; II, pp. 158–159).

[32] Cf. especially, for a recent and brilliantly polemical discussion of this question, König, *Die Begegnung im Tempel*. König radically denies the genuinely autobiographic nature of any of B.'s works.

[33] Petronio mentions naturalism without accepting it as the unifying center of the work (op. cit., pp. 39–40).

[34] *Il Decamerone*, p. 48.

[35] Cf. C. Grabher's rather hasty "Particolari influssi di A. Cappellano sul B."

[36] Pp. 140–150 in Trojel's ed.

[37] V. Branca in his Boccaccio bibliography (*Linee di una storia della critica al 'Decameron'* [Milan, 1939], p. 55 fn. 2) gives a summary of A. Wesselofsky, *Boccaccio, iero sreda i sverniki* (Petersburg, 1893), with reference to some apparently biased allusions to Capellanus.

[38] V. Branca, *B. medievale*, pp. 154–155. The relevant historical and critical details are given in my fn. 51 of Chap. III.

[39] Grabher, "Particolari influssi . . . ," pp. 69–88.

[40] W. A. Neilson, "The Purgatory of Cruel Beauties," *Romania*, XXIX (1900), 85–93, and L. Di Francia's rejection of the *Lai du Trot* as a source in *La Novellistica*, pp. 156–157. Cf. also C. S. Lewis, *The Allegory of Love*, p. 37. The tale, needless to say, was made more popular than ever by B.'s treatment, and with his typical interpretation. Ariosto's story of Lidia, e.g. (*Orlando Furioso*, XXXIV, octaves 4–43), develops this theme, namely that hell awaits ladies who reject their true lovers, with particular reminiscences from Dante and the *Girone il Cortese* (the King of Northumberland's daughter).

[41] "In quendam nos amoenum valde locum et delectabilem via silvestris direxit. Erat quidem locus herbosus et nemoris undique vallatus arboribus" (p. 106, Battaglia ed.).

[42] B.'s women are real, natural human beings, to be loved by "love as for a creature," not by "affectioun for holynesse," as the Provençal ladies so often were. As regards the specific term I have used, A. Viscardi, *Storia delle letterature d'oc e d'oïl* (Milan, 1955²) in dealing with Guillaume de Poitiers points out the singular and significant use of *midons* in Guillaume and Bernart de Ventadorn among others, in lieu of

the customary *ma domna*. Also cf., on the feudal patterns in Provençal poetry, S. Pellegrini, "Intorno al vassallaggio d'amore nei primi trovatori," *Cultura neolatina,* IV-V (1944–45), 21–36.

[43] A minor, though striking example of love's virtuous effects is in IV, 10, the story of the lover stolen by thieves in a chest. The lady has wanted a lover, chooses a rascal, but tries to rehabilitate him by giving him money and advice to change his life for the sake of his love.

[44] The courtly adversity to marriage left deep and durable traces in French culture, whereas it never really took root in Italy, except as a reflection of the intellectual's need for total personal independence (especially in the non-civic type of Humanism initiated by Petrarch). As a curious symptom of an almost unconscious persistence of misogamy in France, cf. the typical blunder in the French translation of Petrarch's Latin version of Boccaccio's Griselda story, where Petrarch's "sepe filii dissimilimi sunt parentum," given by the marquis as an objection to the excessive faith in marriage with a noblewoman, becomes "car souvent avient, chose est clere, / Ques l'enfant ne ressemble au pere," where one immediately grasps the sting of malicious ambiguity. Cf. G. Raynaud de Lage, 'Sur l'attribution de l'*Estoire de Griseldis,*" *Romania,* LXXIX (1958), 267–271.

[45] "Il prevalere dell'amore sulla castità non significa il trionfo del senso. E' il trionfo di un principio attivo e drammatico contro la tiepidezza e la rinuncia." "Il nobile amore è ardimento e dramma, tragedia anche, ma sempre operazione che innalza." Cf. Di Pino, *La polemica del B.,* "Venere e Diana." The quotes are from pp. 77 and 78 respectively.

Notes for CHAPTER V

[1] "Librum ipsum canum dentibus lacessitum tuo tamen baculo egregie tuaque voce defensum." Cf. Branca, *B. medievale,* p. 214. When Petrarch wrote this (1373) B. would no longer have subscribed to the "Proemio," and Petrarch himself had recanted his love in *Canzoniere,* 1. Cf. Petronio in Binni, op. cit., opening remarks on changes in early Latin Humanism.

As an example of the literary impact of B.'s self-defense on later authors, Straparola closely though poorly imitated it in the defense of his own work at the beginning of the Second Book of his *Piacevoli Notti* (1553).

Other aspects of this Proem than those concerning us here have been sensitively analyzed in the recent study of Guido Di Pino, *La Polemica del B.,* pp. 209–220. Di Pino sees in B.'s disdainful, bitterly resentful independence of character as manifested in the Proem, a reflection of

Dante's moral attitudes (pp. 218–219). Also cf. the detailed analysis in Walter Pabst, *Novellentheorie und Novellendichtung,* "Boccaccios Protest," pp. 27–41, and, for the general questions of B.'s poetics, F. Tateo, "Poesia e favola nella poetica del B.," *Filologia romanza,* V (1958), 267–342 and '*Retorica*' e '*Poetica*' *fra Medioevo e Rinascimento* (Bari, Adriatica Ed., 1960).

² Sérarpie der Nersessian, ed., *L'Illustration du Roman de Barlaam et Joasaf* (Paris, 1937). The text is in *Patrologia Graeca,* XCVI, 857–1240 and in *Patrologia Latina,* LXXIII, 443–604 (Latin text from the sixteenth century). The Latin version of the twelfth century from the Greek original of John of Damascus (d. 749) or Euthymius (abbot of Mt. Athos, d. 1028), is in Br. Mus. Additional MS. 17, 299. For a recent, rather superficial analysis of the text (esp. the Apologues), cf. W. F. Bolton, "Parable, allegory, and romance in the legend of Barlaam and Josaphat," *Traditio,* XIV (1958), 359–366. The text of the Provençal "Roman spirituel de Barlaam et Josaphat" is in R. Lavaud and R. Nelli, eds. and transs., *Les Troubadours* (Paris, 1960).

³ For a summary list of medieval versions of the story of the women-devils, cf. L. Di Francia, *Novellistica,* I, 15–16; D. P. Rotunda, *Motif-Index of the Italian Novella in Prose* (Bloomington, 1942), p. 197 (T 371) and S. Thompson, *Motif-Index of Folk-Literature* (Bloomington and Copenhagen, 1955–1958²), V, 382 (T 371). The motif may derive from the *Ramayana.*

⁴ Montaigne had claimed that "La fréquence de cet accident an doibt meshuy avoir moderé l'aigreur: le voylà tantost passé en coustume" (*Essays,* III, 5, ed. cit., p. 973), which, however, was still a long way from affirming *tout court,* even ironically: "cocuage est un bien," as La Fontaine did. Even earlier, in Ariosto's *Orlando Furioso* Rinaldo had 'wisely' refused to drink from the cup that revealed the faithfulness, or the lack thereof, of the drinker's wife (Canto XLII, end–XLIII, beginning). Whether or not one should consider such matters important, he preferred his peace to indiscreet knowledge. (This motif of the cup or horn of faithfulness also had a long history, dating at least as far back as Robert Biket's *Lai du Cor,* of the end of the twelfth century.)

⁵ This, when transposed from literary history to art history, seems to me a major objection to that part of the Woelfflin-Weise thesis that consisted of a rather indiscriminate use of the label 'naturalistic.' The Woelfflin-Weise theory is discussed in my Appendix.

⁶ Mimesis, "Frate Alberto," pp. 197–199, esp. 198 in Trask's trans. (New York, 1957).
Cf. Oscar Büdel, "B. ed Auerbach: A proposito di una interpretazione recente," *Romanische Forschungen,* LXXIII (1961), 151–159.

⁷ "Son più belle che gli agnoli dipinti che voi m'avete più volte mostrati."

[8] The reference to the Florentine Balducci as part of the 'modernization' of the anecdote in order to add credibility, fits into a pattern which runs through B.'s whole narrative, if we are to accept König's interpretation of the "proemi" to the *Teseida* and *Filostrato*. Cf. König, *Die Begegnung im Tempel*, esp. pp. 55–59 ("Autobiographie und Exordialtopik").

[9] Di Francia (*Novellistica*, p. 16) found the change from 'devils' to 'goslings' disappointing and unwitty. It may have been so in the sermons of Pierre de Limoges or Odo of Cheriton (from whose *Parabolae* or *Narrationes* B. probably got his text), but not in B.'s version, where it has its own function and flavor. *Diavoli* in this context would have been more blunt and too directly, polemically reminiscent of religious condemnation.

[10] Likewise, the tales of lust in monks and nuns had more than a role of attack on the clergy or sheer fun at their expense. They implicitly tended to prove the truth of the principle stated in the Proem. The medieval ascetic had not been unaware that the temptation is made fiercer by inhibition. But he had also believed that conventual seclusion would guarantee the suppression of desire by removing the occasion to fulfill it. B. apparently wanted to show the futility of this illusion, as prohibition, solitude, and consequent introversion increase the temptation until it becomes unbearable. (Abélard and Héloïse had discussed the problem, and Abélard had shown his naïve intransigence in the rigorous solutions he imposed on the Paraclete. Cf. *Epistola* VIII, and see p. 27 of this book.) B., therefore, rejects the idea of monasticism, and treats its sponsors as hypocrites (as Jean de Meung had called bigots *Papelards*— and *Papelardie* meant hypocritical prudery leaning on religious prejudice —cf. *Roman de la Rose*, vv. 11524 and 11963).

[11] "Compiacere a quelle cose alle quali Guido Cavalcanti e Dante Alighieri già vecchi, e messer Cino da Pistoia vecchissimo onor si tennono" (p. 457 33).

[12] As to the association of Muses with femininity, L. Russo, *Letture critiche del Decameron* (Bari, 1956), pp. 1–8, contends that the women to whom B. addressed himself as his audience are the very symbol of the Muses, and extends this personal interpretation to point out how with B. art thus ceases to have a mystic purpose and object and at last takes a purely human direction. This would be a sign of the *laicizzazione* and *mondanizzazione* of art and poetry. But I rather tend to accept this equation women-Muses only in the sense that B. and his predecessors had deified femininity and conversely humanized art and the deity itself. ("Deas fecit amor," as Father Porée said in paraphrasing Statius's "Deos fecit timor": *Mémoires de Trévoux*, June 1736).

[13] "Per che tacciansi i morditori, e se essi riscaldar non si possono, assiderati si vivano, e ne' lor diletti, anzi appetiti corrotti stan-

dosi, me nel mio, questa brieve vita che posta n'è, lascino stare" (pp. 459–460). An example of what B. meant by unnatural pleasures can be found in ser Cepparello's story (I, 1). Cepparello is portrayed as a totally bad man, loaded with all possible vices; one of these was that he did not care for women, another that he cared a lot "del contrario": "Delle femine era così vago come sono i cani de' bastoni, del contrario più che alcun altro tristo uomo si dilettava" (p. 50 *14*). In the context of B.'s work and tastes, this not unusual viewpoint acquires a particularly significant tone. Similarly, Pietro di Vinciolo's articulate wife contrasts her sins with those of her invert husband as follows: "Such pleasures [to be pursued with men] would be commendable for me, whereas they are strongly objectionable in his case: it is but the laws that I shall offend, while he offends both laws and nature" ("il qual diletto fia a me laudevole, dove biasimevole è forte a lui: io offenderò le leggi sole, dove egli offende le leggi e la natura." V, 10; II, p. 108 *13*).

[14] Starting as early as the *Filocolo*, and then regularly through the *Decameron*, the author had used the device of addressing his work to ladies or dedicating it to one particular lady (his beloved "Fiammetta"), or even of justifying it as a service to a lady who had commissioned it (*Filocolo*). For this reason, allegedly, his works were written in the vernacular—"del tuo volgar parlare ti sia scusa il ricevuto comandamento, che il tuo principio palesa" (*Filocolo*, ed. Battaglia, p. 565). And this well fitted into a literary tradition as a rhetorical topos, part of the technique of the *exordium*. Cf. Dante, *Vita Nuova*, ed. M. Barbi, Società Dantesca Italiana, Edizione Nazionale delle Opere di Dante, I (Florence, 1932), XXV, 6: "E lo primo che cominciò a dire sì come poeta volgare, si mosse però che volle fare intendere le sue parole a donna, a la quale era malagevole d'intendere li versi latini." Cf. König, op. cit., pp. 59–60.

On the role of women in B. and in the Italian and French novella, within the respective views on love, cf. E. Auerbach, *Zur Technik der Frührenaissancenovelle in Italien und Frankreich* (Heidelberg, 1921), Chap. II.

[15] A. Thibaudet, *Réflexions sur le Roman* (Paris, 1938), p. 157.

[16] Voltaire, *Œuvres complètes,* ed. L. Moland (Paris, 1879), XXV, 182; Mme de Staël, *De la littérature considérée dans ses rapports avec les institutions sociales* (1800), First Part, Chap. IX. I am indebted to Professor Georges May of Yale University for these quotations. Boileau's deprecatory remarks against the influence of women on literature are too well-known to need quoting (*X*e *Satire*).

[17] L. G. Clubb, "B. and the Boundaries of Love,' *Italica,* XXXVII, 3 (1960), 188–196. See p. 195.

[18] Article cited, p. 188.

[19] This and the preceding quotations from art. cit., p. 191.

But the last was a quote from Maurice Valency, *In Praise of Love. An Introduction to the Love-Poetry of the Renaissance* (New York, 1958), p. 227.

[20] II, p. 665 4. There is a parallel between *Raison's* defense of appropriate terms against the charge of obscenity in Jean de Meung (vv. 6928–7228, Langlois ed., and esp. around v. 7143: *Bourses, harneis, riens, piches, pines, putes, coilles,* etc.) and the *Decameron's* Epilogue ("foro e caviglia e mortaio e pestello e salsiccia e mortadello" etc.). B., however, appears to exclude such terms from "le scuole de' filosofanti," which is precisely the context of *Raison's* speech.

[21] E.g., VI, 10 39: "molti de' nostri frati . . . trovai assai, li quali tutti il disagio andavan per l'amor di Dio schifando"; VIII, 2 23: "noi facciamo vie miglior lavoria; e sai perché? perché noi maciniamo a raccolta."

[22] The 'naturalistic' language here defended, i.e., the principle of referring to impolite things by their proper names, is particularly the language of the Duenna, but this defense was first occasioned by Reason's direct and shocking reference to the "coilles" of Saturn (v. 5537). Indeed, it is Reason herself who, as God's coadjutrix, has given proper names to the things that make up God's creation.

[23] *Complaint of Nature,* trans. Moffat, p. 42.

C. Muscatine, *Chaucer and the French Tradition,* p. 79, relates a passage of the *Canterbury Tales* (General Prologue, 731–742: "The wordes moote be cosyn to the dede") to Jean de Meung (vv. 15159–15194), but it also reminds one closely of some elements of the *Decameron's* Epilogue. On the general question of B.'s influence in English literature cf. H. G. Wright, *B. in England from Chaucer to Tennyson* (London, 1957).

[24] B. was an emotional, impulsive man. Always frank and outspoken, he was inclined to vent his objections with a firmness more apparent than real, and with a generous bluntness that could even border on violence, without caution or afterthought. An enlightening example of this immoderate rashness even in private matters is the acidly wrathful, intemperately sarcastic, and, in the end, partly unwarranted letter of 1353 to Petrarch (*Ut huic epistole*) protesting against his acceptance of a tyrant's (Giovanni Visconti) hospitality. We find equally disproportionate the attacks against Niccolò Acciaiuoli and Francesco Nelli in the profuse letter of 1363 to Nelli, denouncing the undeserved treatment received at Naples as Acciaiuoli's guest. Cf. *Epistolae* IX and XII in G. B., *Opere Latine Minori,* ed. A. F. Massèra (Bari, 1928; G. B., *Opere,* IX), pp. 136 and 147.

[25] G. Billanovich, *Restauri boccacceschi* (Rome, 1947), esp. Chaps. II and IV. On the influence on Petrarch upon B. see, by the same author, *Suggestioni di cultura e d'arte tra il Petrarca e il B.* (Naples, 1946), pp. 4–20, "I primi incontri tra il Petrarca e il B."; *Prime ricerche*

dantesche (Rome, 1947), pp. 21–86, "La leggenda dantesca del B.";
Petrarca letterato, I, *Lo scrittoio del Petrarca* (Rome, 1947), pp. 59–294,
"Il più grande discepolo." R. M. Ruggieri, in "Dante, Petrarca, B. e il
romanzo epico-cavalleresco," *Lettere Italiane*, VIII (1956), 385–402, has
carefully traced the change in B.'s literary tastes and attitudes concerning the popular genres of the French and Italian Middle Ages, not without the powerful influence of the discriminating and puristic Petrarch.

 [26] The change that has attracted our attention concerns pri-
marily the 'official' face of the author, his writings. It should nevertheless
be borne in mind that a certain duality of attitudes must have characterized his behavior until the breaking of the crisis. This is the problem on
which Henri Peyre has recently commented in connection with an imitator of B., Marguerite of Navarre, and in the wake of the important
study by Lucien Febvre: *Autour de l'Heptaméron. Amour sacré, amour
profane* (Paris, 1944). After having considered "the contradiction between the substance and the tone of these tales [of the *Heptaméron*]
directed against monks and seeming to delight in sexual immorality and
even in violence, and, on the other hand, the refined and profoundly
religious personality of their author," Professor Peyre goes on to paraphrase the results of Febvre's study as follows: "The apparent incompatibilities in the Queen of Navarre's character are incompatibilities only for
us, moderns, who will admit contradictions as the successive phases of an
evolution but view them as evidence of hypocrisy, or of mental un-
balance, if they occur simultaneously in the same complex soul." H.
Peyre, "Religion and Literary Scholarship in France," *PMLA* LXXVII, 4
(1962), 345–363 (cit. p. 348). Indeed, B.'s everyday religious practices
may well have been, even at the time of the *Decameron*, more or less
mechanically entertained as they were by another, though more systematically "ondoyant et divers" character, Montaigne, who "went to
mass regularly, visited shrines like a good pilgrim during his travels,
believed in miraculous cures, prayed dutifully, "while a modern reader,
Sainte-Beuve, could interpret his work as that of a mocker of religion"
(ibid., p. 349).

[27] A. Solerti, ed., *Le Vite di Dante, Petrarca e B. scritte fino
al secolo XVII* (Milan, 1904), p. 675: "Exstant et quamplura . . . in quibus lascivientis iuventutis ingenio paulo liberius evagatur, quae cum
senuisset, ipse putavit silentio transigenda." Villani, however, goes on to
record the continuing popularity of the condemned works. As to the official reactions among the humanists, cf. Petronio in Binni, pp. 173–174.

[28] "Non ego te vidi pridem volgare canentem / In triviis
carmen, misero plaudente popello? / [Aristeus] Vidisti, fateor. Non
omnibus omnia semper / Sunt animo. Puero carmen vulgare placebat"
(vv. 48–51).

On the other hand, this sort of remorse, brought about by accusations

of a similar order, reappeared on other occasions later on in B.'s career.
Cf. the sonnets CXXII–CXXV of 1374 or 1375 in G. B., *Le Rime,*
L'Amorosa Visione, La Caccia di Diana, ed. V. Branca (Bari, 1939; G. B.,
Opere, VI), pp. 72–73, where the author seems to repent for having 'prostituted the Muses' by revealing the mysteries of the *Divine Comedy* to
the populace.

For a philological study of the tradition and popularity of these minor
works (*Caccia, Carmina, Rime*) see V. Branca, *Tradizione delle opere di*
G. B., I: *Un primo elenco di codici e tre studi* (Rome, 1958).

[29] Ecloga XII, vv. 157f. and *Genealogie,* XIV, *passim.*

[30] "Quod inclitas mulieres tuas domesticas nugas meas legere
permiseris non laudo, quin imo queso per fidem tuam ne feceris. Nosti
quot ibi sint minus decentia et adversantia honestati, quot veneris infauste aculei, quot in scelus impellentia etiam si sint ferrea pectora, a
quibus etsi non ad incestuosum actum illustres impellantur femine . . .
subeunt tamen passu tacitu estus illecebres et impudicas animas obscena
concupiscentie tabe nonnunquam inficiunt irritantque, quod omnino ne
contingat agendum est. . . . Sine illas iuvenibus passionum sectatoribus,
quibus loco magni muneris est vulgo arbitrari quod multas infecerint
petulantia sua pudicitias matronarum. Et si decori dominarum tuarum
parcere non vis, parce saltem honori meo . . . Existimabunt enim legentes
me spurcidum lenonem, incestuosum senem, impurum hominem, turpiloquum maledicum et alienorum scelerum avidum relatorem. Non enim
ubique est qui in excusationem meam consurgens dicat:—Iuvenis scripsit
et maioris coactus imperio— . . . et quamquam minus honestus sim et
longe minus iamdudum fuerim, non facile vellem iudicio talium mulierum
mea fedaretur fama vel nomen." G. B., *Opere Latine Minori,* ed. cit., p.
211.

[31] Petrarch, *Seniles,* XVII, 3. Cf. F. Petrarca, *Lettere Senili,*
Italian trans. G. Fracassetti (Florence, 1892), II, 542. The original text
of the *Seniles* is not yet available in a modern ed.; scholars must still
refer to the sixteenth-century collective eds., especially *Librorum F.*
Petrarche impressorum annotatio (Venice, 1501).

Petrarch pensively condemned the moral fall implied in his infatuation
for a mortal woman (*exhorbitatio mea*) in the *Secretum* and in the opening poem of his *Canzoniere,* but upheld the value of his love (later in the
Secretum) in a dialectical context that exalts the goodness of natural
experience and passion, while at the same time the author still struggles
under the medieval diffidence thereof.

[32] R. M. Ruggieri, "Medioevo e umanesimo, materia e stile
in G. B.," *Studi in onore di A. Monteverdi,* II (Modena, 1959), esp. p.
678.

[33] G. Billanovich, *Suggestioni di cultura e d'arte tra il*
Petrarca e il B., p. 78: ". . . difficile, fugace equilibrio entro il corso di
uno sviluppo mutevole di tendenze composite e opposte."

[34] The picturesque expression could be colloquially rendered as 'Take-it-easy John,' or 'Easy-going John.' Sapegno translates "G. dei suoi comodi." Cf. De Sanctis, *Storia*, ed. cit., p. 313: "L'uomo del B. è, al contrario, assiso, in ozio idillico, con gli occhi vòlti alla madre terra, alla quale domanda e dalla quale ottiene l'appagamento."

[35] *De vita et moribus domini F. Petracchi de Florentia*, in G. B., *Opere Latine Minori*, p. 243. For the dating of this interesting writing, cf. G. Billanovich, *Petrarca letterato*, I, *Lo scrittoio del Petrarca*, cit., p. 74, where the date of 1341–1342 is proposed as against the previous conjectures. Hauvette, Gaspary, V. Rossi, Massèra had proposed 1348 or 1349, Foresti 1350 or after: cf. B., *Opere Latine Minori*, p. 367.

[36] "Laurettam illam allegorice pro laurea corona quam postmodum est adeptus, accipiendam existimo" (ibid.). If we are to accept Billanovich's dating (see preceding fn.), these were the years of B.'s activity in creating the Fiammetta myth. So it is interesting to note that he was then inclined to disbelieve the "reality' of Petrarch's relationship with Laura, while he was himself, supposedly, engaged in giving shape to his own mental and fictitious feminine ideal. On Fiammetta as a fiction see, beside the basic works of Billanovich and Branca, B. König's op. cit. But the Sonnets CII and CXXVI, of apparently serious, religious inspiration, present a problem. There B. places the allegedly nonexistent Fiammetta in heaven with Beatrice and Laura after death, and wishes to join Dante and Petrarch there, in order to enjoy her sight again. Cf. *Rime* in G. B., *Opere*, VI, or better G. B., *Rime, Caccia di Diana*, ed. V. Branca, Collana di Testi e Documenti (Padua, 1958).

[37] See fn. 35 above. In a way, Petrarch himself was at the origin of this misunderstanding by his insisting, in the *Rime* as well as in the *Secretum*, on the ideal—or rather, 'nominalistic'—relationship between his lady and the laurel. But the movement was an inverse one: whereas, for B., Petrarch seemed to love Laura as a symbol of the *laurea*, Petrarch claims to have loved the *laurea* because it reminded him of Laura. Cf. *Secretum*, III, in F. P., *Prose*, eds. Martellotti, Ricci, Carrara, Bianchi (Milan-Naples, 1955), p. 158: "[Augustine:] Quam ob causam tanto opere sive cesaream sive poeticam lauream, quod illa hoc nomine vocaretur, adamasti."

[38] G. B., *Opere Latine Minori*, pp. 311–312.

[39] G. B., *L'Ameto, Lettere, Il Corbaccio*, ed. N. Bruscoli (Bari, 1940), pp. 141–142.

[40] Sapegno, *Il Trecento*, pp. 332–343.

[41] G. B., *Le Rime, L'Amorosa Visione, La Caccia di Diana*, ed. cit., p. 259. (*Amorosa Visione*, Capitolo XLVI, vv. 73–75.) For this work there is a more recent, critical edition outside the Laterza series of B.'s *Opere*, namely: G. B., *L'Amorosa Visione*, ed. V. Branca, Autori classici e documenti di lingua pubblicati dall'Accademia della Crusca (Florence, 1944).

[42] Carducci, as Sapengo recalls (*Il Trecento*, p. 342), rightly saw in this "the parable of the Renaissance on the ruins of the institutions of asceticism." I paraphrase some of Sapegno's masterly judgments on the *Fiammetta* and the *Ninfale*.

[43] Sapegno, op. cit., p. 373. For recent studies of this puzzling work see G. I. Lopriore, "Osservazioni sul *Corbaccio*," *La Rassegna della Letteratura Italiana*, 3–4 (1956), 483–489; J. Bourciez, "L'énigme du *Corbaccio*," *Revue des Langues Romanes*, LXXII (1957–58), 330–337.

Despite all the bitterness and violence, then, the *Corbaccio* somehow does look forward, whereas a comparable misogynous book such as the *Quinze joies de mariage*, of about half a century later, still is essentially medieval, since there the traditional distrust of women is not enlightened by the implicit affirmation of a nobler and higher pursuit. In and by itself, the misogynous stream seemed to run counter to naturalist inspiration. In his last book, for instance, Capellanus had typically withdrawn from his onslaughts on the female character "lest we be thought in some way to accuse nature" (Parry's trans., p. 198). And the alliance of misogyny with the *esprit gaulois* expressed in the satire of woman, marriage, and love (and the church) was a realistic (not naturalistic, and not immune from an ascetic tinge) trait of much of French medieval literature. Henri Chamard demonstrated the persistence of this spirit late into the Renaissance, in the works of Clément Marot, Rabelais, Ronsard, Pelletier du Mans, du Bellay. Cf. his *Les Origines de la poésie française de la Renaissance* (Paris, 1920), pp. 44–54 and *Histoire de la Pléiade* (Paris, 1939–40, 4 vols.), I, Chap. 1. Within the literature criticizing religious institutions, however, the naturalistic spirit emerges in the defense of marriage against celibacy, as in Guillaume Saignet, *Tractatus in quo natura lamentat contra celibatum presbyterorum* (1418), in the University Library of Basle, MS. A, VII, 37. Cf. A. Coville, *La vie intellectuelle dans les domaines d'Anjou-Provence de 1380 à 1435* (Paris, 1941), Chap. 7.

The simple fact that the same motif (like the criticism of women) should be considered to have different and even opposite meanings in different authors or contexts ought, of course, to surprise no one. The famous motif *ubi sunt?* (remember Villon's *Mais où sont les neiges d'antan?*), for example, is considered medieval by Huizinga when he finds it in fifteenth-century French or Burgundian literature, whereas nobody has judged Poggio Bracciolini at all medieval or any less of a humanist for using it in his *De varietate fortunae*. Franco Simone has objected to this as unfair (cf. his *Il Rinascimento Francese*, p. 245, fn. 1 and, with regard to the popularity of the mystery plays in the two countries, p. 80). But it seems to me that the main question here lies in the distinction between the ends of the invocation of such imagery. The rose motif, and the parallel one of the *ubi sunt?*, were used in a medieval spirit for an ascetic condemnation of the transitory, in a Renaissance spirit as an exhortation to enjoy the fleeting instant like Politian's roses, "ere their perfume pass away" (*carpe diem*). Cf. Mariantonia Liborio, "Contributi alla storia dell' *Ubi sunt*," *Cultura Neolatina*, XX (1960), 141–209, with rich bibliography.

B.'s late *Vita di Dante* ("Compendio," ed. E. Rostagno [Bologna, 1899], §§ 4–10) shows the author's final development in postulating the philosopher-poet's withdrawal from society, public offices, marriage, family, and even love. Such disengagement, similar to the Stoico-Christian medieval position, is typical of Humanism before the period of 'civic' Humanism around 1400. On the important question of B.'s attitude toward Dante see, now, Aldo Rossi, "Dante nella prospettiva del B.", *Studi Danteschi*, XXXVII (1960), 63–139. Also Giorgio Padoan, *L'ultima opera di G. B.: le "Esposizioni sopra il Dante"* (Padua, 1959). In commenting on a change which renders the author of the *Decameron* all but unrecognizable here, Padoan (p. 83) points up a passage (*Comento*, II, 142) where Dante's line *Amor ch'a nullo amato amar perdona* provoques B.'s following protest: "This, with all due reverence to the Poet, does not occur in this kind of love, but does occur in honest love (*amore onesto*)."

⁴⁴ The highly unstable and contradictory character of the medieval man's attitudes toward women is somehow a reflection of the fact that, while she was legally and practically at the mercy of men, the medieval woman could also dictate her point of view to the men who surrounded her, at least as the center of the romantic and literary life of the court. On the theoretical status of women in the society of the time see B. Jarrett, *Social Theories of the Middle Ages* (Boston, 1926), esp. pp. 70–73.

⁴⁵ "Una passione accecatrice dell'animo, disviatrice dello 'ngegno, ingrossatrice, anzi privatrice della memoria, dissipatrice delle terrene facultà . . . morte, genitrice de' vizi . . . cosa senza ragione e senza ordine e senza stabilità alcuna, vizio delle menti non sane, e sommergitrice della umana libertà." *Corbaccio*, p. 209 in G. B., *L'Ameto, Lettere, Il Corbaccio*, ed. cit. This passage echoes and expands Fiammetta's judgment on love in *Filocolo*, IV, pp. 338 and 340.

⁴⁶ *Corbaccio*, ed. cit., p. 223.

⁴⁷ Ibid., p. 235.

⁴⁸ "Nam turpitudine sceleris erubescimus et conscientia peccati vexamur aculeo." Book III, Chap. 23. Cf. G. B., *Genealogie Deorum Gentilium Libri*, ed. V. Romano (Bari, 1951, 2 vols.), Vol. I, p. 152 (G. B., *Opere*, X–XI).

⁴⁹ Ibid., Vol. II, p. 724 (Book XIV, Chap. 14); p. 725 (XIV, 15); p. 743 (XIV, 19).

⁵⁰ Ibid., Vol. II, pp. 729–730 (XIV, 16).

⁵¹ *Epistola* XXIII, in G. B., *Opere Latine Minori*, ed. cit., p. 220.

⁵² *Opere Latine Minori*, p. 79. The elder Theoschyros, for

whose pardon he humbly begs later (v. 200), represents the Lord or perhaps the Pope. Dyones (= Dione, Diona), as a symbolic name for Venus,
stands for earthly love (mythologically she was Venus's mother, sometimes Venus herself). The name is connected with the *Decameron*'s
Dioneo, the storyteller in whom some interpreters have seen a relative
self-portrait of the author. In *Epistola* II of 1339, to Petrarch, B. confesses to have been made "a Dyona spurcissimum dyoneum" (*Opere*, IX,
p. 113), and in *Ameto* Dioneo is a son of Bacchus and Ceres (*Opere*, V,
p. 77).

[53] *Genealogie*, ed. cit., XV, 10, pp. 775–776. Again the translation is mine, but Books XIV and XV are available in Osgood's translation: cf. Ch. G. Osgood, *B. on Poetry* (Princeton, 1930), pp. 130–131.

[54] "Quod dum iam dudum frustra temptarent aliqui, id
perdidere, quod erant, nec id potuerunt effici, quod querebant" (*Genealogie*, p. 776).

[55] "Nec ex novo sumpto consilio in poesim animus totis
tendebat pedibus, quin imo a vetustissima dispositione ibat impulsus"
(ibid., p. 776).

[56] Ibid., p. 777.

[57] "Nascimur in varios actus, quos optima virtus / Si sequi-
tur, facili ducetur ad ultima cursu" (vv. 190–91. cf. *Opere*, IX, p. 61).

[58] "Vivo natura et appetitu ducibus." Cf. *Opere*, IX, p. 206.
Later (p. 207) he states that he had refused to call a doctor during an
attack "for to that day I had been wont to let nature cure all accidents."
Skepticism toward medicine (and law) or, more accurately, distrust of
physicians and lawyers, is a well-known feature of much of the humanistic tradition. The comic theatre inherited these attitudes and carried
them on in the context of a polemical upholding of the ways of nature,
which both physicians and lawyers were felt to hinder or adulterate by
harmful complications. Molière and Goldoni are the outstanding witnesses of the vitality of this tradition; Molière was indeed convinced
that "la nature d'elle-même, quand nous la laissons faire, se tire douce-
ment du désordre où elle est tombée."

Notes for EPILOGUE

[1] The classical dualism entailed by this reaction of the
'higher faculties' against the 'lower ones' is clearly visible in the popular
acceptance of Petrarch's final 'condemnation' of his passion for Laura
as attested in the Renaissance commentaries (*Sposizioni*) on the *Canzoniere*. Cf. B. Weinberg, "The *Sposizione* of Petrarch in the early Cinquecento," *Romance Philology*, XIII, 4 (1960), 374–386. The final attitude of the poet was taken for granted as a formal recantation on philosophical or moral grounds, i.e., as the triumph of the rational part of

the soul over the sensitive appetites or as a lesson, *documento*, about the need not to fall prey to the snares of the world and of the senses. The moral interpretation is clearest and most pervasive in the most popular of the Cinquecento commentaries, Alessandro Vellutello's *Esposizione* (1525). In other words, the basic dualism (admiration for great and profound passions—pity and condemnation thereof) that had characterized both the ancient and the medieval psychological attitudes toward love poetry, continued through the Renaissance. Boccaccio himself paid homage to this general mood by condemning his *Decameron*.

The stress laid on the rational faculties as being the peculiar, distinctive traits of man's 'nature' is clearly stated, amidst scores of authors, by as authoritative an exponent of mature Humanism as Angelo Poliziano. He wrote, for instance, in the introductory letter to his translation of Epictetus' *Enchiridion* (A. P., *Opera* [Basileae, 1553], p. 393): "Legerat enim apud Platonem in eo dialogo, qui Alcibiades primus aut de natura hominis inscribitur, eum proprie vereque hominem esse, cuius omnis in rationali animo substantia existeret." It is the right use of the rational faculties that makes man free: "Arrianus . . . e . . . eius libris, quasi florem quendam, qui hunc Platonicum, hoc est, verum hominem in libertatem vendicaret, excerpsit, atque in volumen redegit." This exercise is the essence of our nature: the philosopher strives "ad excitandum rationalem animum . . . ut is . . . propriis actionibus secundum naturam utatur." Thus in such a moralistic approach, virtue and freedom are conceived as a state of harmony between the individual and the world, even while man keeps his independence from material, physical nature in order to take his proper place in the cosmos.

On the general question of the Renaissance views on love, cf. I. Tonelli, *L'amore nella poesia e nel pensiero del Rinascimento* (Florence, 1933); on love treatises cf. J. C. Nelson, *Renaissance Theory of Love. The context of G. Bruno's 'Eroici Furori'* (New York, 1958), esp. Chaps. I, II, and the Appendix.

     [2] L. B. Alberti, *Opera inedita et pauca separatim impressa,* ed. G. Mancini (Florence, 1890), p. 1.

     [3] "L'animo mai serva. Serve l'animo quando e' sia cupido, avaro, misero . . . imperoché i vizii signoreggiano . . . l'animo, né mai lasciano aspirarlo con alcuna libertà e leggiadra volontà a degnamente acquistare lode e fama." Cf. L. B. Alberti, *Opere volgari*, I, ed. Grayson, p. 148.

     [4] E. Wind, *Pagan Mysteries in the Renaissance* (New Haven, 1958), esp. Chap. IX and, for the following, Chap. III.

The motto of the Platonic Academy consisted of the identification of the Three Graces as Beauty, Love, and Pleasure. Pulchritudo, Amor, Voluptas as the Three Graces appear again on Pico's medallion with the Graces on one side, the inscription on the other. Pico borrowed the motto from Ficino, although he later diverged from him on this point of mythological interpretation.

For a detailed analysis of the interrelations between literature and social customs from twelfth-century Provence to fifteenth-century Italy, against the background of all European literature and society and with special reference to Italian love treatises (Chap. III), cf. the still useful Thomas F. Crane, *Italian Social Customs of the Sixteenth Century and their Influence on the Literature of Europe* (New Haven, Yale University Press and London, Oxford University Press, 1920).

Many a student of the Renaissance is inclined to lay stress on the influence of Ficino's Platonism and to see it penetrate almost everywhere, but one would do well not to forget that it took several decades to become more than a local, Florentine school, whereas the prevalent Latin humanistic tradition availed itself of pagan and Christian sources as well in deprecating the illness and madness of love. Thus Il Platina (1421–1481) had written a *Dialogus contra amores,* Petrus Haedus *De amoris generibus* or *Anteroticorum libri* (Treviso, 1492), Battista Fregoso his vernacular *Anteros* (Milan, 1496), and Giovan Francesco Pico a *De Venere et Cupidine expellendis carmen* (1512). Nor must we forget that the Florentine Neoplatonism relied chiefly on a doctrine of masculine asceticism strongly tinted with a distrust for the reality of womanhood. As outstanding documents of the Neoplatonic apologia for love ought to be remembered Lorenzo the Magnificent's *Comento* and Girolamo Benivieni's *Canzone d'amore* with Pico's commentary, besides, of course, Ficino's own commentary on the *Symposium.*

For a clear and detailed analysis of Bembo's position against the background of the humanistic tradition see C. Dionisotti's Introduction to his edition of P. Bembo's *Prose e Rime* (Turin, 1960), 9–56.

⁵ The *De Voluptate* is dated 1433, but on the dates of the three versions cf. M. de Panizza, "Le tre redazioni del *De Voluptate* del Valla," *Giornale Storico della Letteratura Italiana,* CXXI (1943), 1–22; id., "Le tre versioni del *De Voluptate* del Valla," *Rinascimento,* VI (1955), 349–364. The text is available in MS Ottob. Lat. 2075 of the Vatican Library and in Vallae *Opera* (Basileae, 1543). Professor Panizza's critical edition is forthcoming. Because of the present unavailability of a critical and easily accessible edition, my page numbers in the text refer to the excellent Italian translation in L. Valla, *Scritti filosofici e religiosi,* ed. and trans. G. Radetti (Florence, 1953). Incidentally, I shall go on using the traditionally established title, although Professor Panizza now proposes to adopt the one of the final draft (*De Vero Bono*).

⁶ Radetti's ed., op. cit., pp. xv-xvii.

⁷ "(Non lasciatevi) irretire dalle astuzie degli uomini che introdussero una certa onestà immaginaria; ma amate e seguite piuttosto la legge di natura" (Radetti trans., p. 43).

[8] There is another passage in Valla that curiously reminds us of Spinoza's *Deus sive Natura:* "Est igitur praecipue in corpore pulchritudo quam scite Ovidius Dei munus appellat, id est naturae" (Radetti trans., p. 47; cf. *Ars Amatoria,* III, 103). Of course one cannot disregard the reference to a context of pagan religion.

[9] P. 139. Naturally, the opinion of the Epicurean and that of the author do not necessarily coincide at all points. For instance, the relative praise of chastity in the *De Professione Religiosorum* does not correspond to the condemnation of virginity in *De Voluptate* I. But regardless of what his intimate feelings on these matters ultimately were, Valla had shrewdly and effectively cast his challenge to his contemporaries without compromising himself too overtly. I should add that the *De Voluptate* must be interpreted in the light of relevant passages and clarifications contained in the *Apologia ad Eugenium Papam.*

[10] The *Hypnerotomachia* is traditionally dated 1467 and attributed to the monk from Treviso, Francesco Colonna. It was printed by Aldo Manuzio in 1499. The authorship has been challenged by A. Khomentovskaia, "Felice Feliciano da Verona," in *Bibliofilia,* XXVII (1935), 154–73, 200–211, XXVIII (1936), 20–47, 92–101, with attribution to Feliciano, but Colonna's claim has now been newly and expertly vindicated by Maria Teresa Casella: see M. T. Casella and G. Pozzi, *Francesco Colonna. Biografia e Opere,* Collana Medioevo e Umanesimo (Padua, 1959, 2 vols.). Cf. *The Dream of Poliphilo,* related and interpreted by L. Fierz-David, trans. M. Hottinger (New York, 1950).

[11] Rossi, *Il Quattrocento,* "Storia Letteraria d'Italia" (Milan, 1933[1]), p. 199.

For a general statement of the problems of Renaissance 'naturalism' see, in English, J. H. Randall, Jr., *The Making of the Modern Mind* (Cambridge, Mass., 1940[2]), Books I and II.

[12] J. Huizinga, "In commemoration of Erasmus" (1936), first published in *Parerga,* ed. W. Kaegi (Amsterdam and Basel, 1939), translated in J. H., *Men and Ideas,* p. 318. Elsewhere Huizinga refers to Erasmus, Rabelais, and More for their common idea of the natural goodness of man, a sufficient guide to him if assisted by faith and piety (and, I should add, education or 'culture'), without special rules and laws: cf. Huizinga, *Erasmus of Rotterdam; with a Selection from the Letters of Erasmus* (London, 1952), p. 107.

[13] Letter of January 30, 1523, to Johannes Botzheim, in Erasmus, *Opus Epistolarum,* ed. P. S. Allen (Oxford, 1906–58, 12 vols.), I, 19, No. 1.

[14] *Men and Ideas,* p. 319.

[15] The scope of this capital episode is widened into the second multiple quarrel (Canto XXVII, oct. 39–126). Discord here celebrates her second triumph among Marfisa, Ruggiero, Rodomonte, and

Mandricardo, to whom are now added Sacripante versus Rodomonte and Gradasso versus Mandricardo. Between the lines the reader cannot help but sense an implicit parody of unchecked individualism, the underlying principle of the Breton cycle as well as of the political and social life contemporary to the Renaissance poet. The cohesion of the knights under the collective ideals of loyalty to king, country, and religion is constantly threatened by their individualistic claims under the sign of Pride (cf. Pride's prosopopoeia in oct. 100–101). At any rate, Ariosto can laugh at any aspect of chivalry, but never at love.

[16] Canto XLV, octaves 100–101. Earlier in the poem (II, octave 65) Bradamante, after a brief moment of hesitation, disregarded the desperate call for help from her own fief in danger, and went on searching for her beloved Ruggiero. In Canto XXXII she awaits Ruggiero for one month and twenty days of inaction in her castle, mindless of the battle of Paris, where her duty calls her. Similarly, when Rinaldo is sent to England by Charlemagne for reinforcements, he obeys but halfheartedly: the delicate image of Angelica looms too large in his mind (Canto II). And in XXVII (esp. octaves 11–15) he leaves the camp in search of Angelica; which gives Satan an opportunity to escogitate the ruinous attack on the Christian troops. Love frequently contrasts with the knightly duties, and frequently wins. The 'Breton' element fights with the 'Carolingian,' and normally has the upper hand, because of "Natura d'ogni cosa più possente" (XXV, 37).

[17] See the end of Canto X. And Ariosto comments as follows: "Raro è però che di ragione il morso / Libidinosa furia addietro volga, / Quando il piacere ha in pronto." But the poet makes light of this betrayal: "Di Bradamante più non gli sovviene / . . . E se gli ne sovvien pur come prima, / Pazzo è se questa ancor non prezza e stima" (XI, 1–2). Accordingly, Zerbino forgives Odorico, his former friend, for attempting to rape his fiancée Isabella (XIII, 20–29), because he recognizes the irresistibility of love's stimuli: " 'l fuoco arde la paglia facilmente." In kidnaping Doralice from the party that escorts her to her betrothed Rodomonte, Mandricardo breaks the rights and duties of chivalry. But this is not a world ruled by any steady, objective laws. The only rules are the subjective ones of sentiment, that is, the state of mind of the moment seen from within, from the relative point of view of the character involved. We are first surprised and momentarily shocked at Mandricardo's initiative to force Doralice to submit to him. Then we 'understand' him and are brought to acquiesce (along with Doralice herself, far from an unhappy victim).

In Ginevra's case Rinaldo shows his (and the author's) ethical liberalism—or naturalistic ethic: "Debitamente muore una crudele, / Non chi dà vita al suo amator fedele" ("It is just and fitting that a cruel woman be put to death, but not one who bestows life on her faithful lover," IV, 63), which was exactly the ethic of Nastagio degli Onesti. And immediately later he states that he is not concerned with the truthfulness of the charge that Ginevra had taken a lover, but with the iniquity of the law which regards love as a crime worthy of punishment by death. That Ariosto meant what his character says is here quite evident: the law must be repealed and the equality of woman's and man's rights recognized. Such a firm stand on moral and social problems is all the more significant in that it is rare in Ariosto's serene world (cf. octave 66).

   [18] The equation of love and madness (incipient or fully developed, as the case may be) is in the very title of the poem, and is repeated in the episode of Orlando's madness: "Ché non è in somma Amor se non insania, / A giudizio de' savi universale." ("The wise universally concur in the judgment that love is, in sum, nothing but madness," XXIV, 1). The meaning of Merlin's fountains as symbols of the basic irrationality of love becomes manifest, if needed, in Ariosto's comments on their effects: O most unjust Love, why do you not match your victims according to their feelings? . . . Angelica hates Rinaldo, he desperately loves her, whereas she once enjoyed his looks as much as he disliked hers. Now she would rather die than have him (II, 1–2).

   [19] The 'conflict' implied in the *Aminta* and in the *Gerusa-lemme* throws light on the whole, dramatic personality of the poet and on his intellectual formation. It is, essentially, the conflict between the 'natural' rights and the 'social' duties of the individual, between the 'freedom' of his instincts and the 'restraint' imposed by his conscience and his reason: the very sort of conflict which has been so effectively 'rediscovered' and reëxamined by modern psychology. It is known that Freud himself and his followers have been wavering between the two horns of a dilemma: whether to recognize the claims of the *id* and grant it freedom of action in its clashes with the ego, or to deny it such rights for the sake of the equilibrium of the psyche. The former alternative responds to the demands of the biological school, the latter to those of the sociological school. In the *Aminta*, in particular, the poet allies himself with his *id*, and dreams of a Golden Age in the triumph of "nature," —a state where the only law is that of obeying our instincts: "S'ei piace, ei lice." This, in fact, and without the qualms of Tasso's tormented conscience, was, in the last analysis, Ariosto's moral: "Al fin mi par che buono / Sempre cercar quel che diletti, sia" ("In conclusion methinks it is always good to seek that which is pleasing," *Orlando Furioso*, XXV, 51).

   More independent from the 'rules,' more self-confident than Tasso was Battista Guarini in his immensely successful *Pastor Fido*. This important play has often been regarded as poetry of evasion, but the idyllic setting was rather a way to disguise dangerous references (generally, the critique of a society founded on the repression of nature) under the fiction of a mere pastime, a delightful game. The dissolution and overturn of courtly love is carried forth by the Satyr (end of Act I): Let us be virile in our love, the woman with a heart of stone will not be bent with tears; such women bear the responsibility for mankind's moral decline, since they have made of Love a cruel god of suffering and despair. Further on physical love is declared to be the just complement (*giusto* and *debito*) of the harmony of the souls, and without much regard for conventions and sacraments (happy the time when loving meant being married, "ed era un nome sol marito e vago"!); and the *legge di natura,* "Ama, se piace" is distinguished from the *legge degli uomini e del cielo,* "Ama, se lice." Cf. B. Guarini, *Il Pastor Fido e il Compendio della Poesia Tragicomica,* ed. G. Brognoligo (Bari, 1914), pp. 42–43, 164–165, 141 respectively. The *Faithful Shepherd* was translated into English at least four times.

²⁰ "Die ungeheuere Macht des Negativen," in *Vorrede zur Phänomenologie des Geistes* (1807). Of course this expression occurs in Hegel in a metaphysical (specifically logical) context, but it reflects a far-reaching attitude pregnant with ethical and aesthetic applications. Further on we read: "The Spirit is this same Power [of facing the Negative] only because it dares to look the Negative in the face and linger by its side. This lingering is the magic force that turns the Negative into Being." Cf. G. W. F. Hegel, *Sämtliche Werke,* ed. H. Glockner, II (Stuttgart, 1927), p. 34.

For the Letters of the Portuguese nun see Marcelle Fauchier-Delavigne, *Visite à la religieuse portugaise. Suivi des Lettres de la Religieuse Mariana Alcoforado* (Paris-Geneva, 1961); Guilleragues, *Lettres portugaises, Valentin et autres oeuvres,* Introduction, notes, glossaire et tables, d'après de nouveaux documents, eds. F. Deloffre and J. Rougeot (Paris, 1962), and, for a particularly interesting study, Leo Spitzer, "Les 'Lettres Portugaises' " (1954), now in *Romanische Literaturstudien* (Tübingen, 1959), 210–247.

²¹ A measure of *Hero and Leander's* running counter to the moral sense of its contemporaries is shown by the continuation by the pedantic Chapman (1598), who made the death of the lovers the well-deserved punishment for their sinful passion, whereas the sense of sin, defiantly introduced by the racy Marlowe, was totally absent in Musaeus' original poem—which Chapman, the Greek scholar, well knew.

²² G. Gendarme de Bévotte, *La Légende de Don Juan* (Paris, 1911, 2 vols.); G. Marañón, *Don Juan* (Buenos Aires, 1940). E. M. Butler, *The Myth of the Magus* (New York, 1948–1952); *Ritual Magic* (Cambridge, England, 1949); *The Fortunes of Faust* (Cambridge, England, 1952); and Ch. Dédéyan, *Le Thème de Faust dans la littérature européenne* [from the Renaissance to the present], (Paris, 1954–1961, 4 vols.).

As to the, for our purpose, equally interesting legend of Tannhäuser, see, in particular, the question of its origins and relationships with Italy and France, in G. Paris, *Légendes du Moyen Age* (Paris, 1903), pp. 67–109, 113–145. The relative parallelism between the *Paradis de la Reine Sibylle* and the Tannhäuser legend had first occurred to Alfred von Reumont. Also cf. Walter Pabst, *Venus und die missverstandene Dido. Literarische Ursprünge des Sibyllen- und des Venusberges* (Hamburg, 1955).

[23] Rousseau's *raison* is difficult to define, but it is different from the *raison* of the *philosophes*. At times *raison* and *nature* can become almost interchangeable, as implied in the following statement from the beginning of Book 5 of the *Émile*, where, speaking of the 'natural' inequality and consequent duality of moral standards between the sexes, Rousseau contends: "Cette inégalité n'est point une institution humaine, ou du moins elle n'est pas l'ouvrage du préjugé, mais de la raison."

Acute and original observations concerning the ethical and psychological aspects of the *Nouvelle Héloïse* can be found in D. de Rougemont, *L'Amour et l'Occident*, IV, 14. De Rougemont speaks of a return to the Provençal *leys de cortezia,* to Petrarch's *acedia,* to his final rejection of the 'religion of love,' and especially deals with the lovers' sublimation of their passion so as to 'enjoy' its tension without spell-breaking, guilty relief by physical rapports.

Cf. Ch. W. Hendel, *Jean-Jacques Rousseau, Moralist* (London and New York, 1934, 2 vols.).

[24] J.-J. Rousseau, *La Nouvelle Héloïse,* ed. D. Mornet, Les Grands Ecrivains de la France (Paris, Hachette, 1925, 4 vols.). Cf. Mornet's fn. 2 in II, 106. Page references will be made to this edition.

[25] *Dei Sepolcri* (1806), vv. 177–179: "Amore in Grecia nudo e nudo in Roma / D'un velo candidissimo adornando, / Rendea nel grembo a Venere Celeste." ("Love, who had gone naked in Greece and Rome, he adorned with a most candid veil and restored to the Heavenly Venus' lap.")

[26] Cf. also, on this subject, Mornet's long fn. on pp. 154–155 of ed. cit., and, for analogous attitudes in the troubadours, cf. our Chap. II, fns. 7 and 12.

[27] This is made even more tangible, rather than being contradicted, by Rousseau's professed distrust for the mysticism of the quietists: cf. the note where Rousseau endorses Julie's condemnation of the *Song of Songs,* and let us remember that he probably had in mind Madame Guyon's *Le Cantique des Cantiques de Salomon interprété selon le sens mystique et la vraie représentation des états intérieurs* (1708): "Comment voir les raports [sic] de l'objet mistique [sic], si l'on ne voit aussi l'objet sensuel, et comment une honnête femme ose-t-elle imaginer avec assurance des objets qu'elle n'oserait regarder?" And Rousseau claims in the note that the *Song of Songs* should be struck

from the Scriptures, even though he implicitly accepts its mystic value (Part 6, Letter 8, p. 270).

Cf. P. M. Masson, *La formation religieuse de Rousseau,* Part 1 of *La Religion de J. J. Rousseau* (Paris, 1916, 3 vols.).

[28] J.-J. Rousseau, *Correspondance générale,* ed. Dufour (Paris, 1933), XIX, 243–244.

In his learned academic course on Rousseau's novel, Charles Dédéyan (*La Nouvelle Héloïse. Etude d'ensemble* [Paris, 1955]) has underlined what he considers a harmonious alliance of the sensual and the spiritual, rather than the dichotomy and ambiguous tension which my analysis tends to indicate: "Par là, c'est reprendre la tradition de Dante et de Pétrarque, c'est sentir à travers le sensuel, en dépit du sensuel, à cause du sensuel, l'appel du spirituel et c'est justifier dans l'amour romantique l'union de la passion et de la vertu." "Au delà du corps désirable . . . l'union des coeurs" (p. 146). At any rate, even if we felt more inclined to adopt this approach, the quite appropriate reference to Dante and Petrarch duly points up the non-naturalistic context of Rousseau's orientation. A propos of Lauretta, the repented courtesan who refuses Milord Bomston's hand, Dédéyan endorses Pierre Trahard's following remark (*Les Maîtres de la sensibilité française au XVIIIe siècle (1715–1789),* 4 vols. [Paris, 1931–1933], Vol. III: "J.-J. Rousseau"): "Avant l'auteur de *Crime et Châtiment,* avant celui de *Résurrection,* Jean-Jacques introduit dans la *Nouvelle Héloïse* cette conception de l'honneur, parce qu'il en éprouve la vérité dans sa propre conscience, où la faute suscite le rachat, et la passion le sacrifice."

[29] "E Richautz la pregava qu'ella li degues far plaser d'amor, e clamava li merce; e la domna li respondet qu'ella volia volontier far li plaser d'aitan que li fos onor, e dis a Richautz que s'el li volgues lo ben qu'el dizia, qu'el non deuria voler qu'ella l'en disses plus ni plus li fezes con ella li fazia ni dizia." Cf. R. T. Hill and T. G. Bergin, *Anthology of Provençal Troubadours* (New Haven, 1941), p. 114. The troubadour's works are now available in Rigaut de Barbezieux, *Le Canzoni,* Testi e Commento a c. di M. Braccini. Accademia Toscana di Scienze e Lettere "La Colombaria" (Florence, 1960), and Rigaut de Berbezilh, *Liriche,* ed. A. Varvaro (Bari, Adriatica ed., 1960).

[30] "E se ella per tems passat non li avia fach plazer, qu'ella li volia far ara" (ibid.).

[31] In a somewhat stilnovistic vein Rousseau rediscovers the principle whereby love is the warrant of true nobility: "L'amour en lui-même est-il un crime? N'est-il pas le plus pur ainsi que le plus doux penchant de la nature? . . . Ne dédaigne-t-il pas les âmes basses et rampantes? N'anime-t-il pas les âmes grandes et fortes? N'ennoblit-il pas tous leurs sentiments?" etc. (Part 5, Letter 13, Vol. IV, p. 171). And cf.

the arguments of Julie to persuade Claire, a noblewoman, to marry her former lover Saint-Preux, a *rôturier*.

[32] Cf. *Émile*, ed. F. and P. Richard (Paris, 1958), pp. 402ff.

[33] True enough, the better part of the Romantic movement consisted of a reaction against the Enlightenment. As part of this reaction, the Encyclopaedists' views on nature were uncompromisingly rebuked by Ugo Foscolo, who dealt with the political, social, and moral myth of the 'state of nature' as follows: "[I propugnatori della perfezione] illudono sè stessi e gli altri, dicendo che la natura ci ha creato innocenti, liberi e benefattori scambievoli; e che la società guasta noi tutti, facendone nemici reciproci e servi; che però, a tornare migliori, fa d'uopo il ravvicinarsi allo stato più naturale. Ma di grazia, e qual è lo stato dell'uomo che non sia naturale?" ("These perfection-hunters delude themselves and the others by claiming that nature has created us innocent, free, and mutually beneficent, whereas society spoils us all, turning us into mutual enemies and slaves; and that, therefore, for the purpose of our improvement it is imperative that we return to a more natural state. But I beg of you, which is the state of man that is not natural?" Cf. *Della Servitù dell'Italia* in *Edizione Nazionale delle Opere di U. F.* (Florence, 1933), VIII, 197.

[34] D. S. Mirsky, *A History of Russian Literature* (New York, 1927), p. 337.

[35] G. Leopardi, *Zibaldone*, ed. F. Flora (Milan, 1937–1938, 2 vols.). Page numbers as given for this work in the text are those of the autograph. Cf. Bruno Biral, "Il significato di 'Natura' nel pensiero di Leopardi," *Il Ponte*, XV (1959), 1264–1280.

[36] This is the interesting, though not entirely convincing, conclusion of L. G. Crocker's *An Age of Crisis. Man and World in Eighteenth Century French Thought* (Baltimore, 1959). For a discussion of his views on de Sade's naturalism see my review in *Studi Francesi*, 12 (1960), 504–506.

[37] The invasion of Western literatures by the 'evil' forces of 'the flesh' from the time of de Sade through Romanticism and Decadentism is brilliantly analyzed in Mario Praz, *La Carne, le Morte e il Diavolo nella Letteratura Romantica* (Milan-Rome, 1930), trans. as *The Romantic Agony* by A. Davidson (London, 1933).

[38] The pre-Romantic revaluation of passion in its most irregular and even violent manifestations first appears, in Italy, with Alfieri. Cf., for instance, the following passage: "Ma egli, vedendo in me un eroe così sconciamente avvilito e minor di sè stesso; ancorché ben intendesse per prova i nomi e la sostanza di fortezza e virtù, non volle con tutto ciò crudelmente ed inopportunamente opporre ai delirj miei la di lui severa e gelata ragione; bensì seppe egli scemarmi, e non poco, il dolore, col

dividerlo meco. Oh rara, oh celeste dote davvero; chi sappia ragionare ad un tempo, e sentire!" ("He perceived in me an unseemly humiliated and lessened hero, but, although he well knew by experience both the language and the practice of fortitude and virtue, he did not choose to counter my deliriousness with the cruelly unseasonable counsel of severe and cold reason. On the contrary, he succeeded in allaying my grief by sharing it with me. O rare and truly celestial gift, when one can reason and yet feel at the same time!") Vittorio Alfieri, *Opere*, I: *Vita scritta da esso* (Asti, 1951), pp. 237–238. (This is the author's Sienese friend Gori, consoling him for the forced separation from the countess of Albany in 1783). This typically shows the positiveness of the negative in the recognition of certain rights of nature to stand up against reason, since reason is at times ineffective and out of place. The feeling for these moments when the heart must count above and before reason is called *sentimento* (*sentire*), and is regarded as a symptom of true 'humanity.'

[39] For the conception of the tragic omnipotence of love as echoed in Romantic literature in the form of the myth of Love-Death, cf., for instance, Mérimée's *La Vénus d'Ille* (1837). See P. Mérimée, *Romans et Nouvelles*, ed. Henri Martineau, Bibliothèque de la Pléiade (Paris, 1951), pp. 409–436.

[40] Th. Mann, "Nietzsches Philosophie," in *Neue Studien* (Stockholm, 1948), pp. 103f.

[41] Mann dramatized the intuition of music as expression of forces irrational and destructive as early as in his *Tristan* of 1903. His musical theories were chiefly based on Schönberg's, as is well known.

[42] Eliseo Vivas, *D. H. Lawrence: the Failure and the Triumph of Art* (Evanston, Ill., 1960).

[43] B. Croce, *La Letteratura Italiana per Saggi storicamente disposti*, ed. M. Sansone (Bari, 1960), Vol. IV, Introduction, p. xvi. The translation is mine.

 Appendix

The Question of Naturalism in Late Medieval and Early Renaissance Art

In art history, lively ideological and terminological polemics have long been centered on the question of realism-naturalism, considered by some a late medieval phenomenon and by others an early-Renaissance development, always a favorite ground for argumentative juggling, never completely illegitimate in its applications, never definitely convincing.

In Italian literary scholarship the term 'naturalism' has long been applied to the Renaissance as a label for a stream that emerged in the *Decameron* and then ran through the fifteenth and sixteenth centuries in reaction to medieval emphasis on the supernatural. More specifically G. Gentile, with particular concern for the philosophical development of the period, distinguished the fundamental naturalism of the Cinquecento from the Humanism of the Quattrocento. With his distinction in mind, a student of the figurative arts could be tempted to assume that the naturalism in Italian painting really begins with Leonardo. Indeed, such modern concepts and their terminology are, though distinct, somehow related to the history of art criticism.

As Johan Huizinga reminded us, Boccaccio already "had extolled Giotto as he who had brought the art of natural painting to life once more after it had lain buried for many centuries."[1] This Giotto had achieved by closely following and successfully imitating nature, the mother of all things, instead of yielding to the ways of his predecessors, "who had intended to please the eyes of the ignorant rather than the intellect of the wise" (*Dec.* VI, 5; Vol. II, pp. 149 5–150 6). This passage (to which one could add *Amorosa Visione* IV, 16–18 for a parallel praise of Giotto) was acknowledged by Huizinga as antedating Vasari's famous (and for the Dutch historian, overrated) praise of Giotto as the originator of the artistic "Renaissance."[2] The same historian found in Burckhardt the confirmation of Boccaccio's and Vasari's judgment on the Renaissance as beginning with Giotto's realism, and related this judgment to the views of Leonardo, Erasmus, Dürer.

Yet, a recent school of thought has methodically used the term naturalism to distinguish from and within the Renaissance a late medieval stream. This terminological shift can be traced back to Woelfflin's *The Classical Art*,[3] which set forth a thesis later to be developed and refined by Georg Weise, who furthermore extended it from the fine arts to literature, while Huizinga presented a successful, original version of the same thesis.[4]

Woelfflin had argued that the true Renaissance, a new type of art which evolved in Italy out of the humanistic revival of ancient forms and from there spread triumphantly throughout Europe, is the Classicism of the sixteenth century. The Italian art of the fifteenth century was, even in its originality, not essentially different from the Flemish, German, and French patterns. It was characterized by a close study of nature, inherited from certain Romanesque and late Gothic strains which emphasized realistic detail and individual peculiarities, whereas the sixteenth-century Classicism was founded on an idealistic preoccupation with general type, abstract, orderly composition, and form.

As Weise claimed in further elaborating this viewpoint, an error of generalization lies in the opposition of Gothic and naturalism.[5] Actually, the latter is, in the fourteenth and fifteenth centuries, nothing but a dialectical development of Gothic, to be found alongside and sometimes hand in hand with the *Gothique Flamboyant* or Late Gothic (*Spätgotik*). Weise even sees a relationship between the realism ("grössere Lebensnähe," "Wirklichkeit") of Nicolò Pisano, Cimabue, and Giotto, and French and German Late Gothic. The *Gotico Internazionale* as found in Italian painting until the early Quattrocento, is for him a "nachträgliche Gotisierung" of the chivalric-*courtois* High Gothic ("ritterlich-höfische Hochgotik") that had been made of refined idealistic spiritualization ("Idealität und Verfeinerung," "Spiritualisierung").

Weise proceeds to define the rapport between Gothic and naturalism as follows: "Just as in the countries north of the Alps, so in Italy too one must understand the coming of the new naturalism above all as the overcoming of the Gothic formal system and as the rejection, out of satiety, of the Gothic idealism with its lyrical sensitivity and linear euphony." ("Der doppelte Begriff . . . ," p. 505). So far, so good. But this antithesis is seen *within* the Gothic movement: transcendental, spiritualistic idealism and naturalism are conceived as the two faces of Late Gothic. Ghiberti and Fra Angelico represent transcendent grace ("Holdseligkeit"), expressed in the eurhythmic line ("Schönlinigkeit"); Donatello and Masaccio, on the other hand, emphasize reality and violent strife ("Wirklichkeitsbejahung," "gewaltsames Ringen"). The associations, one can see, are somewhat summary, but, in their way, evident. In brief, Gothic is not a unilateral movement, but a synthesis of "Transzendentalität" on the one hand and "Naturbejahung" on the other.[6] What happened in the Quattrocento is simply that the latter dissolved the former and finally prevailed.

Earlier and to a greater extent than the Italians, the Flemish artists had developed a narrative realism, the "realism of detail" typical of Late Gothic: so had the van Eyck brothers, Rogier van der Weyden, Claus Sluter at Dijon. It is these achievements which led Michelet (and Burckhardt) to define the Renaissance as "découverte du monde et de l'homme."

True enough, Italy shows a marked advantage in spacial clarity and organic truthfulness to life in the representation of the human body ("räumliche Klarheit," "organische Lebenswahrheit"), yet the North compensates this handicap by a fuller elaboration of the natural environment ("reichere Ausgestaltung des szenischen Beiwerks und der landschaftlichen Umgebung"), a portrait-like physiognomic treatment, a heightened feeling for the autonomy of pictorial values ("höhere Wahrheit im malerischen als selbständiger Wert").

The Renaissance as a new immanent attitude toward life developed and ripened spontaneously and contemporaneously throughout the West, as a natural outgrowth of medieval forms and attitudes. A break with the Middle Ages did come, at last, and it came about in Italy, but only with the classicism of the first third of the sixteenth century—Woelfflin's "neue Idealität."

Now that we have before us the general outline of this rather successful thesis, we may want to pause and ponder some of its apparent weaknesses. Indeed, for the less patient it might perhaps suffice to raise the objection that what makes the art of the Renaissance understandable in its unifying peculiarities (if there be any) is not so much the realism, the naturalism, the introduction of visual and "tactile" space, taken per se and in isolation, but rather a new pervasive attitude, a true *Weltanschauung* at best, on its highest level of consciousness, even though it may never appear systematically expressed in its entirety. An even more impatient student may take Weise's thesis as a shining example of the danger of schematizing the intuitive evaluation of one particular aspect of a civilization and expanding it so as to make it a comprehensive category whereby to judge and assess the nature of a whole period. Taken by itself the 'naturalism' of the Quattrocento seems to be as much an evolution of medieval forms as it is an original opening of the way which was to lead without any break to Cinquecento classicism.

Rather than its *prima facie* theory, the research of Woelfflin's followers has offered a valuable contribution to the establishment of a truth of which most students are now convinced, and of which Burckhardt himself seems to have become aware toward the end of his life: namely the principle whereby, as it pleased Horace to put it, *'natura non facit saltus,'* and for our question, the Renaissance could not have been what it was without the Middle Ages.[7] Yet, once we have reached this conclusion, doubtless a sensible one but disarmingly self-evident, we must not go so far as to forget that at least one factor is an argument for a historic break: the consciousness of the very people of the Renaissance, for most of whom the return to the ancients was a real fact—a fact which, in their minds, had started to occur no earlier than with Petrarch, not with John of Salisbury or any part of what is now called pre-Humanism or medieval Humanism. For them Masaccio's frescoes had meant the revelation of a new way of seeing and doing things, and the authors and artists of the Middle Ages, with a few exceptions, were to be barred *de iure* and were *de facto* obliterated from their consciousness as "barbarians" (as Ermolao Barbaro called them in his famous letter to Pico). This new, revolutionary attitude took place in the minds of the Italians of the fifteenth century, and in the following it gained the rest of Europe; whereas nothing of this kind occurred in the sixteenth century in the way of a discriminative evaluation of the preceding century in Italy.

We have ceased to postulate the absolute novelty of most traits of the Renaissance. However, we must recognize that at that time all the inherited elements of the figurative arts of the fifteenth century, Gothic and classic, Christian and pagan, transcendent and immanent, idealistic and realistic, started to operate as part of a different and new, unitary *forma mentis,* characterized by a spiritual, coherent faith in the autonomous value of our earthly existence.

Naturalism and realism in the early Renaissance have deeply engaged historians and critics from the time when Vasari formulated his thesis whereby the new art, replacing the "Byzantine" art of the past, was characterized by a return to nature, hence to the ancients, the true masters in the imitation of nature. Far from seeing any break between the preceding century and his own, Vasari held that the history of Renaissance art was essentially a progress toward nature, a march of naturalism, up to his own day. After John Ruskin's discovery of the Italian naïve "primitives," with special sympathy for Botticelli, and before the modern critics developed a keen appreciation of the intellectual and formal values in early Renaissance painting, Bernard Berenson, in his masterly way, went beyond Ruskin's romantic naturalism toward a 'scientific' naturalism or realism which it may not be amiss to compare with Vasari's basic viewpoint. Berenson's "tactile values" pointed, although in a rather personal and narrow pattern, toward the intellectual, scientific discovery of the tangible environment through the plastic rendition of volume and spatial perspective. Berenson's views had to be revised and integrated by the rehabilitation of the great perspectivists he had neglected, namely, Paolo Uccello and Piero della Francesca.[8] But this process of comprehension of the true historical role and aesthetic achievement of the Italian Quattrocento, coupled with the study of its general cultural environment, from social to literary and philosophical relationships, has revealed the true characteristics of that 'naturalism' which, under closer scrutiny, turns out to be all impregnated with idealism to the borders of metaphysics, whereas (in contrast to Woelfflin's thesis) at least in this limited sense the Cinquecento appears more 'naturalistic,' 'imitative' than the preceding age.

The conscious 'scientific' strain in Quattrocento art is not to be underrated, and it sharply distinguishes the Italian from the Northern artist. In the anatomy as in the motion of the bodies, in the perspective ordering as in the harmony of planned composition, there lay a will to conquer nature not by reproduction, but by the discovery of its essential inner laws. It is only in this way that the particular, highly intellectual naturalism of the early Italian Renaissance can be truly understood—and nothing of the sort was taking place on such a scale in the North of Europe. There is such a difference between this brand of 'realism' and the Northern 'naturalism' that the most militant and conscious of the Italian theorist-artists, though learning a lot from them, could well, in their hearts, feel superior to the Northern artists.[9] Besides, there is at least one other aspect of the question whereby one can more legitimately speak of naturalism in the Cinquecento than in the Quattrocento. After Leonardo, man really becomes, pictorially speaking, a portion of space, almost an emanation of his environment, ceasing to be separated from it by the sharp outlines of the Quattrocento styles of drawing, now replaced by the new *sfumato*. In the 'humanistic' art, on the other hand, man is the center of the painting as he is theoretically the center of the world of experiences, even inasmuch as the environment is nothing but his sphere of action, a projection of his will and personality, and most of the time a man-made environment, filled with architecture more than with landscapes. In this sense again, from the point of view of the humanists' Renaissance, the "reichere Ausgestaltung des szenischen Beiwerks und der landschaftlichen Umgebung" was entirely out of place. Whether we find it so much to our taste, thinking of future developments, is another matter. The question here is that the 'Humanism' of Quattrocento art is the prerequisite for Cinquecento idealistic classicism, which replaced in the North, for better or for worse, the former taste for scenery, forming a human parenthesis between the landscape painters à la van Eyck and the new late- and post-Renaissance landscapes. The practice of portraying ancient heroes in contemporaneous garb and physiognomies is not legitimately to be construed as opposed to later classicistic habits: the process toward that fully coherent end could be but gradual.

On the other hand, the excessive concern with schematic periodization had led to unconvincing syllogisms such as that of Cossio, who on the pattern of a distinction between expressive art (Middle Ages) and formal art (classic Antiquity, Renaissance), saw in the Michelangelo of the *Last Judgment* the last of the medieval Gothics. Likewise Weise (less paradoxically) pointed out the Late Gothic overtone of Quattrocento mystic naturalism in Ghiberti, Beato Angelico, and Botticelli. Somewhat similarly, though in a mood of extreme, chauvinistic indictments Louis Courajod had charged "l'Italianisme" with determining the decadence of the genius of French art, by destroying its genuine realism. For him the authentic realism was that of France and the Flanders, and this was the true Renaissance, starting as early as the fourteenth century ("Renaissance Septentrionale").[10]

Weise is convincing, I dare say, where he analyzes the origin of certain expressive forms in Quattrocento art, such as the dynamic expressionistic linearism of Ghiberti, Donatello (Paduan bas-reliefs), Pollaiuolo, Andrea del Castagno, the mystic spiritualism of Beato Angelico, the sensual spiritualism of Botticelli, even the flat, sharply cut surfaces of Paolo Uccello. Incidentally, a better use could have been made for this purpose of Jacopo della Quercia's unique style. But in these as in all other cases, above all the extraordinary variety and contrast of techniques and attitudes, Italian Quattrocento art shows an *organic* quality that seems to unify it and identify it at first glance, almost as a sign of the national genius.

I have discussed (Chapter III) the importance of 'organic' structure in the world and style of the *Decameron*. I do not hesitate, now, to draw a close analogy between this characteristic and the organic aspects of Italian Renaissance art, starting at least as early as the early Quattrocento. As Arnold Hauser pertinently put it, "For the new conception of art, the work forms an indivisible unity; the spectator wants to be able to take in the whole range of the stage with a single glance, just as he grasps the whole space of a painting organized on the principles of central perspective, with a single glance." Consequently, the genuine naturalism of the Renaissance is not 'new' in itself, but in its conscious, programmatic character: "Not naturalism in itself, but merely the scientific, methodical, totalitarian character of naturalism was new." "The remarkable thing about the Renaissance was, to put it briefly, not the fact that the artist became an observer of nature, but that the work of art became a 'study of nature.'"[11]

The spiritual center of the pictorial, sculptural organism is always Man, the man of the humanists; and not the individualized, everyday man of the Flemish artists, single and particular, a fragment of the world, but the Individuum-Microcosm, who resumes in himself all his destiny and the universe itself. To separate this protagonist of Quattrocento art from the idealized type of the Cinquecento as Woelfflin had started to do, instead of seeing it as nothing but the true and natural genesis of the latter, seems to me the result of an arbitrary, metaphysical abstraction.

The whole process was shaped in its recognizable, unique peculiarities by the study of the ancients, the "Wiederbelebung des klassischen Altertums." The late Trecento "Detailrealismus" is unacceptable as a sufficient reason for Renaissance naturalism, and Woelfflin's basic distinction can be thrown off balance by the simple above mentioned consideration that in a sense the Quattrocento shows more 'idealism' than the Cinquecento: a human figure by Masaccio or Piero della Francesca is almost the equivalent (if I am allowed to overdo an analogy) of a full-fledged treatise of metaphysics, soberly and bluntly stated, whereas a typical figure of the Cinquecento (with the exception of Leonardo, Raphael, and Michelangelo) tends to be a refined manual of aesthetics. The formalism of the latter derives from the perpetuation of the stylistic tendencies of the former (organic composition, essential order, balance in the objects and their motions). The judgment "indiscriminate, unselective rendition of the singular and picturesque" ("wahllose Wiedergabe des Einmaligen und Charakteristischen," in "Der doppelte Begriff . . . ," p. 515), undoubtedly applies with more fairness to the North than to Italy. If the works of the artists of the period were not self-explanatory, any reader of Quattrocento theoretical literature on art knows how little the motto "truth to life at any price" ("Lebenswahrheit um jeden Preis") could apply to the country of Masaccio and Alberti. Of men, that is, who wanted nature, but a nature into which they had put *their* order!

The "klassisch-normative Tendenz" that identifies the "Idealität" of the Renaissance is the consequence of the mental attitudes and tastes of an Alberti or a della Francesca, far from being the opposite of the mentality of their time. Part of the misunderstanding comes from the narrow and unilateral definition of naturalism-realism as "a striving toward the immediate representation of the natural objects in their individual form."[12] Hence Huizinga's conclusion, to the effect that "the Italian Quattrocento must also be conceived as still fundamentally medieval" (as he had demonstrated the Burgundian fifteenth century to be), precisely on account of its realism.

Weise and Huizinga extended the pattern of their interpretation to other cultural domains than painting and sculpture, especially to the general literature of the fifteenth century. Weise in particular has studied the implications of the Woelfflinian theory as applied to Italian literature.[13] But this presents problems of a nature more delicate than ever. One can fairly easily go along with the interpretation of the Italian chivalric genre (especially in the case of the *Orlando Innamorato*) in the light of Late Gothic taste and inspiration. One can even accept the judgment that the artistically valid creative literature was then more intimately bound to the medieval past than the scholarly and theoretical statements of the humanists, but the usefulness and meaningfulness of a concept such as "Gothic" does not become immediately apparent from Weise's analysis. And the alliance of naturalism and Late Gothic is all but meaningless in the literary field, for, regardless of what we can there do with Gothic, literary naturalism has a complex and varied story through the medieval and modern age.[14] To the general outline of this story I hope to have made a contribution.

Notes for APPENDIX

[1] J. Huizinga, *Wege der Kulturgeschichte,* trans. W. Kaegi (Munich, 1930), pp. 94–95; English version in *Men and Ideas,* trans. J. S. Holmes and H. van Marle (New York, Meridian Books, 1959), p. 247.

[2] G. Vasari, *Le Vite . . . ,* "Proemio," ed. Karl Frey, (Munich, 1911), I, 175–217. "The imitation of nature was the basic principle of art" throughout the Renaissance. Huizinga, *Men and Ideas,* p. 247; Vasari, pp. 168–169.

[3] Heinrich Woelfflin, *Die klassische Kunst. Eine Einführung in die italienische Renaissance* (Munich, 1899).

A similar dichotomy is found in C. Neumann, "Byzantinische Kultur und Renaissancekultur," *Historische Zeitschrift,* XCI (1903), 215–232, but with an inverted valuation: the classical element (rather seen as Byzantine) was negative; it stifled the genuine originality of the medieval spirit by breeding an "urge toward the great, monumental airs and the noble gestures of the ancients, and was removed from any reality of content by formal virtuosity."

[4] Cf., especially, *Der Herbst des Mittelalters* (Munich, 1928), and, more particularly, *Wege der Kulturgeschichte,* essays translated in *Men and Ideas,* "The Problem of the Renaissance" and "Renaissance and realism." Louis Courajod (*Leçons professées à l'Ecole du Louvre* [Paris, 1888], esp. Second Part, "The True Origins of the Renaissance") had maintained that "the Gothic style regenerated itself quite independently by turning toward an absolute naturalism," and from this sprang the Renaissance. "Neither the classical example nor Italy had any causal significance in that process." A 'test' of Courajod's ideas was to be found in Fierens Gevaert, *La Renaissance Septentrionale* (1905), through the analysis of the work of Broederlam, Claus Sluter, the van Eycks ("The Problem of the Renaissance," p. 265). As to the concept of realism, Huizinga finds that "in most cases it seems interchangeable with naturalism, though in common parlance specific distinctions are made between the two." ("Renaissance and Realism," p. 289). He eventually denies the validity of the concept of realism for the understanding of the Renais-

sance, and relates it rather to the spirit and forms of medieval art, which, during the Renaissance, were superseded by the heroic, idealized representation of general 'essences,' in the dialectical tension of chaos-harmony (Rabelais, Ariosto, Michelangelo).

⁵ Cf., especially, for the detailed analysis which follows in the text, "Der doppelte Begriff . . ." "in the following bibliography relative to our subject. Quotes with simple page numbers refer to this article.

G. Weise, "Der doppelte Begriff der Renaissance," *Deutsche Vierteljahrsschrift für Literaturwissenschaft und Geistesgeschichte,* XI, 4 (1933), 501–529. Id., "Italien und das heroische Lebensgefühl der Renaissance," *Germanisch-Romanische Monatshefte,* XXII (1934), 333–343. Id., "Der Realismus des 15. Jahrhunderts und seine geistigen Voraussetzungen und Parallelen," *Die Welt als Geschichte,* VIII (1942), 135ff. and 300ff. (I have been unable to see this essay). Id., "Il termine di tardo-gotico nell'arte settentrionale," *Paragone,* 31 (1952), 24–34. Id., "Die spätgotische Stilströmung in der Kunst der italienischen Renaissance," *Bibliothèque d'Humanisme et Renaissance,* XIV (1952), 99–116. Id., *Renaissance und Antike* (Tübingen, 1953). Id., "Der Humanismus und das Prinzip der klassischen Geisteshaltung," *Bibliothèque d'Humanisme et Renaissance,* XVI (1954), 153–171 and 284–297. Id., *L'Italia e il mondo gotico* (Florence, 1956), trans. of *Die geistige Welt der Gotik und ihre Bedeutung für Italien* (Halle a. S., 1939).

In *Renaissance und Antike* and in "Der Humanismus und das Prinzip . . ." one finds the following modification of the general thesis: the proclaimed 'naturalism' within Renaissance art is shifted toward the end of the fifteenth and into the sixteenth century in opposition to the humanism of the Quattrocento.

⁶ "Das gotische Formensystem war der Ausdruck jener verklärenden und vergeistigenden Idealität gewesen, in der sich Transzendentalität und Naturbejahung, nach der ersten Annäherung an die Wirklichkeit in der Zeit der Frühgotik und nach dem Rückschlag einer abermaligen Spiritualisierung im Lauf des 13. Jahrhunderts, in neuer, für die ganze zweite Hälfte des Mittelalters massgebender Synthese verbunden hatten." Weise, article cited, p. 507.

More logically, if not more appropriately, could the naturalism of medieval art and literature have been traced back to the rebirth of creativity in the eleventh century, with its outburst of naïve and spontaneous faith in life and its earthly values. The time, briefly, of courtly love, refined but, at the same time, sensual. Its parallel style in architecture is the Romanesque, which is all classically earthly and has not yet experienced the upward thrust, the eagerness of ascetic evasion of the succeeding Gothic. The Church, in whose hands the monopoly of intellectual activity had until then remained, soon reclaimed the territory usurped by the independently minded champions of *courtoisie*. Then one witnessed the re-interpretation of lyric modes in the Marian allegorical lyrics; religious symbolism, not without logic but with a certain abuse of power, took possession of Chrétien's unfinished *Perceval*, and by the pen of Robert de Boron the Grail became the Eucharist to be acquired through chastity, until in the following *Queste du Graal* we come by the indictment of womanhood—conclusion and death of the finest flower of romance lyricism, courtly love, at the same time that the Albigensian Crusade crushed the autonomous Southern civilization forever. Italy entered the scene of the romance literatures at the moment when this transformation was being consummated, and acquired the two phases, the courtly and the mystic, juxtaposed in a sometimes ambiguous fusion (as in the potentially ironic finale of Guinizelli's canzone *A cor gentil*). The woman-angel is at once a lover and a carrier of Grace. Dante, the literary ally (if this does not sound irreverent) of Simon of Monfort, the extoller of the "scourges" of the Albigensians, Folc of Marseille and St. Dominic, lifts his lady to the threshold of the Empyrean by choosing her as his guide toward that exalted place. But, just as the feudal aristocracy, the social basis of Gothic art, had played such a comparatively inconspicuous role in Italy, so the Italian 'Gothic' love lyric lacked the social roots on which it rested elsewhere, and therefore remained curiously abstract. Concurrently, as neither the naturalistic nor the mystic phase of *courtoisie* could have deep roots in Italy, neither could the powerful new realism and naturalism of the Quattrocento painters find inspiration in a Gothic movement which had been notoriously weak in their country. Its profound genesis, then, must lie elsewhere, in a realistic substratum only temporarily and superficially covered by 'Gothic' conventions and akin superstructures.

[7] Burckhardt's disciple C. Neumann (*J. Burckhardt* [Munich, 1927], and "Der unbekannte J. Burckhardt. Burckhardt und das Mittelalter," *Deutsche Vierteljahrsschrift für Literaturwissenschaft und Geistesgeschichte*, IX [1931], 201-239) claims that the master later retracted his thesis in his teaching, disapproving of the radical application being made of it, and leaned back to an acknowledgment of medieval culture as the terrain where our civilization must find its truest and most precious source.

[8] Leonardo Olschki, *Geschichte der neusprachlichen wissenschaftlichen Literatur* (Heidelberg, 1919), went as far as judging the theoretician even greater than the painter in Piero della Francesca.

[9] One can realize the humanistic, non-naturalistic character of Italian Quattrocento art by comparing it with the definitely naturalistic qua realistic Dutch painting-like miniature of the late fourteenth-fifteenth century, with its keen rendering of the grotesque and 'ugly,' the unprecedented and elsewhere unequaled individuality of physiognomies, the

spontaneous composition, the everyday sincerity, the depth of expression and feeling. Even in nearby Flanders the fashionable conventionality and polished mannerisms dominant in France operate as an effective check on Dutch influences. There prevail the intellectual stylistic technicisms dictated by French courtly tastes, the opposite of naturalism. The chivalrous idealism and splendid superficiality of Burgundian illumination contrasts significantly with the contemporaneous naturalistic, 'bourgeois' realism of the Dutch schools.

[10] "So ist es viel zutreffender, auch das italienische Quattrocento gerade um seines Realismus willen als im Grunde noch mittelalterlich aufzufassen." Huizinga, *Wege der Kulturgeschichte,* p. 157 (cited and subscribed to by Weise, p. 527, fn. 2). For Courajod, cf. my fn. 4.

[11] A. Hauser, *The Social History of Art* (New York, 1951), pp. 274 and 267. The "stage" in the first quotation is that of the theater, according to Scaliger's criticisms of medieval theatrical practices which involved the viewing of the stage by sections, not as a whole, and the obliteration from consciousness of scenes and characters not presently active.

Indeed, the peculiarity of the Quattrocento lies in stylistic or formal elements which go far beyond any affinity with Northern art in terms of naturalism understood as *Detailrealismus:* mainly, 'classicism,' 'ideal style,' homogeneity (care of the whole composition for a total impression). This last trait is especially important in view of the basically "juxtaposed" structure of Gothic art (Hauser, pp. 272–273), corresponding to the 'fragmented' and 'centrifugal' medieval style of which I spoke in Chap. III, p. 56 and fn. 29. Cf. Hauser's fn. 17, p. 490, for the reference to Dagobert Frey's important *Gotik und Renaissance als Grundlagen der modernen Weltanschauung* (Augsburg, 1929): "D. Frey, who characterizes the difference between the medieval and the Renaissance conception of art by the distinction between the successive and the simultaneous interpretation of the pictorial space, obviously relies on Erwin Panofsky's differentiation of an 'aggregate' and a 'systematic' space (*Die Perspektive als 'symbolische Form,'* 1927). Panofsky's thesis again assumes Wickhoff's theory of the 'continuous' and the 'distinguishing' mode of representation, etc."

For a recent, authoritative assessment of the historical problems of Quattrocento art in the light of its medieval and classical heritage, cf. E. Panofsky, *Renaissance and Renascences in Western Art,* The Gottesman Lectures, Uppsala University, Vol. VII; also published as *Figura,* Studies edited by the Institute of Art History, University of Uppsala, Vol. X (Stockholm, 1960).

For the medieval background of naturalistic art see Max Dvořák,

"Idealismus und Naturalismus in der gotischen Skulptur und Malerei," *Historische Zeitschrift,* CXIX (1919), 1–62, 185–246.

[12] Huizinga, quoted in Weise's art. cit., p. 527.

[13] "Elementi tardogotici nella letteratura italiana del Quattrocento," *Rivista di Letterature Moderne e Comparate,* X, 2 (1957), 101–130, and second part ibid., X, 3–4 (1957), 184–199. For a competent review of this essay cf. G. Ponte in *Rassegna della Letteratura Italiana,* LXV, 3 (1961), 590–592.

[14] In fact, in the articles quoted in the preceding footnote naturalism and realism cease to be associated with Gothic and even become opposed to it, as the true elements of Humanism-Renaissance (cf., e.g., p. 117). But some uncertainty remains in this respect. The early Cinquecento is reconnected to the early Quattrocento, and the Quattrocento itself is, in my opinion, too sharply divided in halves. As a particular consequence, the continuity from Pulci to Boiardo is stressed beyond what seems logically admissible.

For eventual rapports between literary styles and the arts, cf. H. Hatzfeld, "Geist und Stil der flamboyanten Literatur in Frankreich," *Homenatge a A. Rubió i Lluch* in *Estudis Universitaris Catalans,* XXII (Barcelone, 1936), 137–193. Hatzfeld identifies the following motifs: "Intérieurfreude, Liebe zum Détail und zur Anekdote, Hang zur Konversation, Masslosigkeit, Sterbeangst, Depression" (p. 183), and draws parallels with Baroque and Romantic. Also, by the same author, *Literature through Art* (New York, 1952), Chaps. I and II ("The Romanesque and Gothic Epoch," "The Flamboyant and Renaissance Epochs"): a useful and perceptive synthesis, focused on French literature and art.

 Index

INDEX

This index comprises authors and critics, major characters, titles of major literary works, important names appearing in bibliographical titles, and a few place names of especial significance. Writers and artists are sometimes listed under the first name when this is the better-known part.